U. S. CENSUS of 1850
for
BARBOUR COUNTY, ALABAMA

Compiled by:
Helen S. Foley

Southern Historical Press, Inc.
Greenville, South Carolina

This volume was reproduced
from a personal copy located in
the Publishers private library

Please direct all correspondence and book orders to:
SOUTHERN HISTORICAL PRESS, Inc.
PO Box 1267
Greenville, SC 29602-1267

ISBN #978-1-63914-309-2
Printed in the United States of America

Foreword

Barbour County, Alabama, was formed in 1832 from parts of Henry and Pike Counties and the Cession of 1812. It was named for James Barbour of Virginia.

This census was copied from a microfilm and parts of it were very dim and almost illegible. The heads of the households are arranged alphabetically, the value of their property, age, sex and birthplace are given. Any member of a group with a different surname will be found in the household and also in the alphabetical listing.

Abbreviations of foreign countries:

Can.	Canada	Ire.	Ireland
Den.	Denmark	Pol.	Poland
Eng.	England	Pru.	Prussia
Fr.	France	Rus.	Russia
Ger.	Germany	Scot.	Scotland
Hol.	Holland	Switz.	Switzerland

SEVENTH CENSUS OF THE UNITED STATES

1850 CENSUS BARBOUR COUNTY, ALABAMA

110 Farmer ($250)
ABNEY, Nathaniel 29 m SC
Martha 19 f "
Elizabeth 11/12 f Ala

1722 Farmer ($2500)
ABNEY, William 47 m SC
Elizabeth 42 f "
Sampson P. 20 m Fla
Ann 17 f "
Rosanna 14 f SC
Mary 11 f Ala
Sarah 6 f "

248 Farmer ($250)
ADAMS, Allen 58 m NC
Mary 58 f "
Margaret 30 f "
Julia 18 f Ga
Allen (Farmer) 20 m "

ADAMS, David F. (See Jas. Mabry)

29 Farmer ($300)
ADAMS, Elwin(?) B. 31 m NC
Martha 27 f Ga
Elizabeth 8 f "
Alfred 6 m "
Nancy 4 f "
Eliphar 3 f Ala
Georgia A. 11/12 f "

1866 Farmer ($1,000)
ADAMS, Harmon H. 39 m Ga
Martha 39 f "
Thomas 12 m "
Florida 10 f Fla
Mary 8 f "
Catherine 5 f Ala
Louisianna 3 f "
Missouri 2 f "
Sarah 6/12 f "
HILL, Wm. (Farmer) 32 m SC

1315 Merchant ($2,000)
ADAMS, H. P. 30 m Mass
Elizabeth 32 f SC
(Married within the year).

2125 Farmer
ADAMS, John Q. 26 m Ga
Chloe 21 f "
Jefferson 3 m Ala

1681 Farmer ($250)
(Cont.)

1681 Farmer ($250)
ADAMS, Lewis 33 m NC
Alley J. 27 f Ga
Mary 8 f "
Fabian 6 m "
John 4 m "
Margaret 2 f "

ADAMS, Mary
Thomas
(See Chas. G. Brantley)

1193 Farmer
ADAMS, Munro 28 m Ga
Frances 25 f SC
William 5 m Ala
John Z.(?) 3 m "
James 1 m "

243 Farmer ($400)
ADAMS, Richard S. 45 m Ga
Nancy 42 f "
James 7 m Ala
William 4 m "
Susan 2 f "

2142 Farmer ($800)
ADAMS, Thompson T. 42 m Ga
Mary 36 f "
Sarah 13 f "
John 11 m Ala
Thomas 9 m "
William 7 m "
Mary 5 f "
Susan 2 f "

24 Minister (M. E.)
ADAMS, William B. 39 m SC
Margaret 42 f NC
Sophy 15 f Ga

2147 Farmer
ADCOCK, William 22 m Ga
Nancy 22 f "
Mary 1 f Ala

1628 Farmer ($200)
ADKINS, John R. 34 m Ga
Ally 27 f "
Rebecca 10 f "
Milton 8 m "
Mary 6 f "
Robert 4 m Ala
William 2 m "

1627 Farmer
ADKINS, Robert 60 m Ga
Mary 57 f "
Rebecca 35 f "
Nancy 25 f "

246 Blacksmith
ADKINS, William 48 m Va
Catherine 30 f SC
WEEKS, Martha 9 f Ga
CAMERON, Elizabeth 6 f "

1192 Farmer
ALBRITTON, Lanier 46 m Ga
Martha 53 f "
Martha 19 f "
Pleasant 17 m "
William 13 m "
Mary 13 f "
John 10 m "

ALBRITTON, William
(See Ferney Westbrook).

41 Farmer ($6000)
Alexander, Ezekel 47 m Ga
David (Farmer) 24 m Ala
Jonas D. " 22 m Ala
Minerva E. 20 f "
Emeline 18 f "
Asa 16 m "
Moses 14 m "
Mary F. 12 f "

Alexander, Francis M.
(See Jesse B. Coleman).

2286
Alexander, Sarah 50 f SC
Clementine 20 f "

1241 Farmer ($200)
Allen, Benjamin 56 m Ga
Anna 46 f NC
George F. (Farmer) 20 m Ala
Amanda 15 f Ga
Esther 12 f Ala
Lidia 10 f "
Jane 6 f "

1788 Laborer
ALLEN, Dixon 25 m Ga
Mary 21 f "
James 5 m "
Eliza 2 f "

1262 Merchant
ALLEN, G. L. 40 m Scot
(Cont.)

(# 1262 ALLEN cont.)
Janet 38 f Scot
Margaret 14 f "
Catherine 6 f Ala
Mary 2 f "
George 1 m "
Mary 60 f Scot

ALLEN, Hansford
(See Young H. Rhodes).

148 Farmer ($250)
ALLEN, William 27 m Ga
Penelope 18 f "
Susan 2 f Ala
William 1/12 m "

2103 Carpenter ($700)
ALLEY, John 30 m Pa
Rebecca 27 f "
STRIPLIN, Francis M. 7 m Ala

1632 Farmer
ALLISON, Reuben 43 m Ga
Louisianna 32 f "
Alfred 13 m "
William 11 m Ala

ALSOBROOK, Thomas
(See James M. Pruitt).

1776 Farmer
ALLSTON, James W. 32 m Ala
Elizabeth 30 f Ga
John 10 m "
Mary 7 f "
Daniel 6 m "
Sarah 4 f "
James 2 m "

ALSTON, John J.
Elizabeth
(See Martin Boliver).

270 Wheelwright
ALSTON, Theophilus 26 m Ga
Adeline 27 f SC
Thomas 5 m Ala
Amanda 2 f "

93 Farmer
AMMONS, Josiah 34 m NC
Elizabeth 32 f SC
Howell 12 m Ga
Rebecca 10 f "
James 5 m "
Stephen 3 m Ala
Reuben 1 m "

944 Tailor ($1,000)
ANDERSON, C. B. 25 m NC
Alice 38 f Ga
Thomas 4 m Ala
Charles 2 m "
ROUSE, Ann 13 f "
Mary 15 f "
WILLIAMS, William 10 m "

ANDERSON, Fanny
William
John (See Daniel O'Bryan).
Mary

490 Farmer
ANDERSON, Henry 32 m Ga
Rebecca 32 f SC
Joel 13 m Ga
Ann 11 f Ala
John 8 m "
Henry 5 m "
Narcissa 4 f "
Celia 3 f "
Moore 1/12 m "

1321 Farmer
ANDERSON, Samuel 33 m SC
Elizabeth 27 f Ga
STEWART, Elizabeth 45 f SC
Charles (Farmer) 19 m Ga
James " 17 m "
Sarah 15 f "
Eli 12 m "

1750 Ditcher
ANDERSON, Thos. H. 55 m Ire

1889 Farmer
ANDERSON, Wiley 24 m Ga
Frances 23 f "
William 3 m "
Jordan 1 m "
BISHOP, Martha J. 15 f "

800 Farmer ($5,000)
ANDREWS, C. J. M. 29 m Ga
Catherine 27 f Fla
Louisa 9 f Ala
Vasalona 2 f "
HARRALL, William 18 m Ga
(Laborer)
PORTUS, John 17 m Fla
(Laborer)

1239
ANDREWS, Rhoda 62 f Ga

667 Overseer
ANDREWS, William 22 m Ala
Nancy 19 f "
Jane 6/12 f "
GRUBBS, Marthena 20 f "

1238 Physician ($3120)
ANDREWS, William A. 31 m Ga
Martha 26 f "
Laura 5 f Ala
Medora 3 f "

2240 Farmer ($3000).
ANGLIN, Franklin 46 m Ga
Nancy 26 f "
Sarah 16 f "
Thomas 11 m Ala
William 9 m "
James 6 m "
Mary 4 f "
Thomas 2 m "

2285 Laborer
ANGLIN, Owen 21 m Ala
Mary 20 f NC
Sarah 3/12 f Ala

2284 Farmer ($2000)
ANGLIN, William 52 m Ga
Lovey 47 f "
Harvey 18 m Ala
Malinda 16 f "
Roxanna 12 f "
Sarah 10 f "
MADDOX, Matilda 45 f Ga
((Idiot).

Appling, Sarah
(See Robt. T. Tate).

1906 Occup. - none
APPLING, Thomas 75 m Ga
Nancy 56 f "
Jane 15 f Ala
Jasper (Farmer) 18 m "

1092 Farmer ($3,000)
APPLING, Thomas K. 25 m Ga
Sarah 18 f Fla
Sarah 2/12 f Ala

1905 Farmer
APPLING, William 30 m Ala
Elizabeth 25 f SC
Thomas 3 m Ala
Elizabeth 8/12 f "

1322 Farmer ($1,000)
ARCHER, Williamson 46 m SC
Mary 28 f Ga
Judson 14 m "
Roger 8 m Ala
Manley 5 m "
Cullen 2 m "

ARMSTRONG, Labun
(See D. B. Bridges).

1453 Farmer
ARMSTRONG, Larkin 43 m Ga
Robert (Farmer) 19 m "
John " 15 m "
Eliza 12 f Ala
Elizabeth 10 f "
Nancy 8 f "
James 6 m "

ARNOLD, Frances
(See John Roquemore).

ARNOLD, James A.
(See John F. Comer).

699 Farmer ($400)
ARRINGTON, Elisha 38 m Ga
Mary J. 30 f "
Nancy 14 f "
William 13 m "
Mary 9 f Ala
Eliza 6 f "
John 4 m "
Susan 1 f "

705 Farmer ($2,000).
ARRINGTON, William 72 m NC
Elizabeth 60 f "
Francis (Student) 22 m Ga
Aems(?) (Farmer) 17 m "

2223 Farmer
ASHLEY, James 42 m NC
Sarah 38 f "
Elizabeth 15 f Ga
William 13 m "
Mary 11 f Ala
Eliza 8 f "
John 5 m "

396
ATKINSON, Daniel J. 22 m Ala
Clarley 23 f "
John 3 m "
Mary 1 f "
LUDLAM, Elizabeth 10 f "

491 Farmer ($200)
ATKINSON, Joseph 39 m NC
Milbra 36 f "
Sarah 13 f "
Edna 11 f Ala
Pinckney 9 m "
Mary 5 f "
Solomon 3 m "
BASS, Andrew 22 m NC

610 Farmer
ATKINSON, William J. 20 m Ala
Sarah A. 22 f SC
(Married within the year).

385-398 & 395-399 Farmer
ATKINSON, William N. 44 m NC
Rebecca 40 f Ga
Elizabeth 14 f Ala
CARROLL, Rebecca 18 f "
KIRKLAND, James 8 m "
LUDLUM, Wiley 6 m "
LUDLUM, Edw. (Farmer) 22 m "
Sarah 16 f "
Elizabeth 1/12 f "

ATWELL, Alexander
Rosanna
(See Sarah Crane).

1688 Farmer
ATWELL, George W. 24 m NC
Sarah 20 f "
(Married within the year).

1008 Farmer ($150)
ATWELL, James 50 m NC
Mary 46 f "
Sarah 22 f Ga
John 17 m "
Martha 15 f "
Molsey 12 f "
FRASIER, James 18 m "
(Farmer)

209 Farmer
ATWELL, Zeph 24 m Ga
Elizabeth 19 f "
Thomas R. 9/12 m Ala

1084 Farmer
AVANT, William J. 46 m SC
Elizabeth 45 f "
Pinckney (Farmer) 23 m "
Levina 21 f "
Catherine 18 f "
(Cont.)

(# 1084 AVANT cont.)
William 16 m Ga
Asbury 12 m "
Andrew 10 m "

AVERETT, Early
(See Early Everett).

1522 Farmer
AVERETT, Matthew J. 20 m Ga
Sarah 20 f "
(Married within the year).

1515 Farmer
AVERETT, Matthew 65 m Ga
Keziah 60 f "
Washington(Occp. none) 21 m "
Martha 25 f Ala

1523 Farmer ($3500)
AVERETT, William 45 m Ga
Susan 35 f "
Marion (Student) 18 m "
Amenias " 15 m Ala
Jasper 12 m "

178 Farmer ($300)
AYRE, Samuel 39 m SC
Nancy 37 f "
Rebecca 11 f Ala
David 10 m "
Jason 8 m "
Nancy 7 f "
John T. 2 m "
Robert 1 m "

1005 Farmer ($400)
BABBITT, Thomas 58 m SC
Ann 38 f Ga
Lucy 17 f Ala
Caroline 15 f "
Mary 13 f "
Sophronia 10 f "
William 8 m "
Nancy 6 f "
Amanda 5 f "
Jerome 3 m "
Marion 1 m "

866 Farmer ($1,500)
BAILEY, Hosea 42 m Ga
Ann 60 f "
Bryant (Farmer) 17 m "
William " 15 m "

1738 Farmer ($200)
BAILEY, James 42 m Ga
(Cont.)

(# 1738 BAILEY cont.)
Martha 39 f Ga
William (Farmer) 21 m "
Elizabeth 17 f "
Nancy 15 f "
James 11 m "
Sarah 4 f Ala
Martha 3/12 f "

1430 Carpenter ($300)
BAILEY, John 49 m Ga
Margaret 45 f "
JORDAN, Nancy 40 f "

BAIRD, Benjamin A.
(See Grave A. Pease).

1328 Lawyer ($2600)
BAKER, Alpheus, Jr. 25 m SC

764 ($500)
BAKER, Elizabeth 54 f Ga
Thos. (Student) 16 m "
James M. (Farmer) 20 m "
Elizabeth 18 f Fla
(Jas. M. & Eliz. married within the year).

759 Farmer ($1300)
BAKER, Franklin E. 28 m Ala
Elizabeth 28 f Ga
Salina 8 f "
Susan 6 f Ala
Oliver P. 4 m Ga
Robert F. 1 m Ala
JOHNSTON, Turner 21 m Ga
(Laborer).

721 Tailor
BAKER, H. W. 32 m Mass
Eliza 30 f SC
Martha 7 f Ala
Charles 5 m "
Mary 1 f "

86 Farmer ($700)
BAKER, James J. 32 m SC
Nancy 19 f Ala

684 Farmer ($400)
BAKER, Lauchlin 43 m SC
Ellen 37 f "
Nathaniel (Farmer) 19 m "
William " 17 m "
James " 15 m "
Alexander 13 m "
Warren 7 m "
(Cont.)

(# 684 BAKER cont.)
Pickens 4 m SC
Margaret 12 f "
Mary A. 10 f "
Sarah A. 9 f "

215 ($400)
BAKER, Lydia 40 f SC
William (Farmer) 20 m "
Eneos " 22 m "
Lydia 17 f Ga
Peggy 14 f "
Winney 12 f Ala
James 7 m "

BAKER, Patience
(See W. A. Tharpe).

1805 Farmer ($200)
BAKER, Robert 60 m SC
Jarret (Farmer) 22 m "
Susannah 20 f "
Mary 18 f "

940 Farmer ($1600)
BALL, Edward 24 m SC
Harriet 22 f Ga
Martha L. 3/12 f Ala
Levinia 20 f SC

68 Farmer ($200)
BALLARD, Blake 32 m NC
Maria 32 f "
John J. 13 m Ala
Catherine 12 f "
William 9 m "
Elizabeth 7 f "
Julia 5 f "
Augustus B. 1 m "

1290 Clerk
BANKS, James 33 m Eng

1856 Farmer ($900)
BANKS, Robert P. 39 m SC
Mary 36 f "
Catherine 17 f "
Abner (Farmer) 16 m "
Nathaniel 12 m Ala
William 10 m "
John 6 m "
Susan 2 f "
KELLY, Elizabeth 12 f SC

758 Farmer ($4,500)
BARBER, Jared P. 42 m Ga
(Cont.)

(# 758 BARBER cont).
Mary 35 f NC
Peyton 1 m Ala
SMITH, Milton 19 m Ga
(Merchant).
BARBER, Virgil 32 m Ga
(Occupation - none)
WINN, E. W.(Doctor) 22 m Ga
JOHNSTON, Alexr. P. 25 m SC
(Teacher).

34 Laborer
BAREFIELD, Grady 45 m NC
Winneford M. 33 f Ga
John A. 11 m Ala
George W. 6 m "
Charlotte 5 f "
Catherine 4 f "
Mary 3 f "
James M. G. 7/12 m "

BAREFIELD, James
(See Peter Stewart).

2235
BAREFIELD, Nicey 38 f Ga
Rolla (Laborer) 15 m "
SHEPPARD, Jas. " 20 m "

1870 Farmer
BAREFOOT, George 40 m Ga
Mary 34 f "
Sarah 10 f Ala
John 8 m "
William 6 m "
Thomas 2 m "

1841 Farmer
BAREFOOT, Samuel 28 m NC
Mary 29 f "
Sally 3 f Ala
John 1 m Fla

2119 Farmer ($4100)
BARHAM, William A. 31 m NC
Mary 38 f Ga
Sarah 2 f Ala
Allen 1/12 m "
GRIFFIS, M. M. 23 m Ga
(Overseer)
TURMAN, George J. 22 m "
(Farmer)
William (Student) 18 m "
J. M. " 18 m "

578 Farmer ($300)
(Cont.)

(# 578 cont.)
BARKER, Ellison 25 m SC
Mary 22 f Ala
(Married within the year).

576 Farmer ($1,200)
BARKER, George W 36 m NC
Tempey 36 f Va
William 16 m Ga
John 14 m "
Mary 12 f "
George 9 m Ala
Sarah 7 f "
Reuben 4 m "
Martha 1 f "

1338 Farmer ($1,800)
BARKSDALE, B. R. 35 m Ga
Emily 33 f "
Henry 11 m Ala
Beverly 9 m "
Franklin 7 m "
Mary 5 f "
John 3 m "
Thomas 2 m "
Eliza 1 f "
NEWMAN, John 23 m Ga
(Overseer).

1770 Farmer ($1,500)
BARKSDALE, Joseph C. 37 m Ga
Elizabeth 25 f SC
William 7 m Ala
Marion 6 m "
Americus 4 m "
Henrietta 1 f "

BARNES, Alberton
(See John McBryde).

BARNES, Joseph
(See A. J. Barron).

BARNES, Milton
(See William Wood).

57 Laborer
BARNES, Thomas 25 m Ga
Elizabeth 23 f "
Anderson 3 m Ala
Caroline 5/12 f "

1539 Physician
BARNETT, A. W. 25 m Ga
Celestia 17 f SC
(Married within the year).

571 Carpenter ($1,650)
BARNETT, Thomas J. 38 m Del
(Cont.)

(# 571 BARNETT cont.)
Mary 35 f Ga
Julius 8 m Ala
Mary 3 f "
Sarah 2 f "
MARTIN, Elmira 36 f Ga

760 Overseer ($800)
BARR, John G. 25 m Va

689 Laborer
BARRS, William 25 m SC
Jane 21 f "

1572 Farmer ($2,500)
BARRET, James E. 28 m NC
Lucy 25 f Ga
Martha 2/12 f Ala

2095 Farmer ($600)
BARRON, A. J. 32 m Ga
Sarah 26 f "
Ann 9 f "
William 7 m "
James 5 m Ala
Sarah 3 f "
Elizabeth 1 f "
BARNES, Joseph 11 m Ga

733 Saddler ($200)
BARRON, Benjamin A. 30 m Ga
Mary 25 f Ala
Ann E. 5 f "
Leonidus 2 m "
BROWN, Mark(Laborer) 18 m Ga
NEICE, Henry " 18 m SC

1218 Farmer
BARRON, Henry W. 32 m Ga
Sarah 30 f "
James 10 m "
Balsara 8 f "
Harriet 6 f Ala
Henry 4 m "
Mary 10/12 f "

988 Farmer
BARRON, Herdon(?) 47 m Ga
Elizabeth 50 f NC
Sarah 25 f Ga
William (Farmer) 24 m "
John " 23 m "
Hiram " 22 m "
Thomas " 20 m "
James 14 m "

1784 Farmer ($1,500)
BARROW, J. W. 29 m Ga
(Cont.)

(# 1784 BARROW cont.)
Lucy 24 f Ga
Lucy E. 3 f "
Jacob 1 m "

1785 Farmer
BARROW, William J. 32 m Ga
Ann H. 16 f Ala
(Married within the year).
DAVIS, Richard 11 m Ala

1994 Lawyer
BARRY, George L. 37 m Md
Margaret 27 f "
Charles 14 m Ga
Lavaller 12 m Ala
Veto Tyler 10 m "
Clinton 8 m "
James O. A. 6 m "
William 3 m "

2211 Boatman
BARRY, Thomas 40 m Fr
MEHAN, Thos. (Boatman) 40 m "
MORRIS, Rich'd. " 31 m Va

594 Farmer ($200)
BARRY, W. J. G. 45 m Pa
Letty 33 f SC
Eliza J. 13 f "
Copeland W. 12 m Ga
Eli C. 10 m Ala
Eliza C. 8 f "
Isaac A. C. 6 m "
Mary 4 f "
Seth 3 m "
Esther 2 f "

BART, Sarah A. B.
John W.
(See Sarah Heidt).

647
BARWICH, Louisa 35 f SC
GLOVER, Lucretia 80 f NC

356 Farmer ($800)
BASS, Allen 52 m NC
Frances 46 f "
Willis 15 m Ga
Mary 13 f "
Elizabeth 4 f Ala

BASS, Andrew
(See Joseph Atkinson).

1665 Overseer
BASS, Bryant (cont.) 25 m Ga

(# 1665 BASS cont.)
Shilemath 16 f Ga
(Married within the year).

2033 Farmer ($1,700)
BASS, Buckner 60 m NC
Ann 25 f Ga
Jeptha 21 m "
Cinthia 18 f "
Emily 11 f "
Thomas 10 m "

349 Farmer ($300)
BASS, Hardy 27 m NC
Clarkey Ann 19 f Ga
Sarah 4 f Ala
William J. 1 m "
LONG, Martha A. 14 f Ga

655 Farmer
BASS, Hezekiah 23 m NC
Lucinda 22 f "
John 1 m Ala

519 Farmer ($500)
BASS, John 62 m NC
Isabel 45 f Ga
STONE, John (Farmer) 19 m "

674 Farmer ($125)
BASS, Josiah, Jr. 21 m NC
Ailsey 15 f Ala
(Married within the year).

673 Farmer ($1,000)
BASS, Josiah, Sr. 46 m NC
Mary 37 f "
Harriet 15 f Ga
Lecidey 13 f Ala
Eady 12 f "
Chaney 10 f "
Abel 8 m "
Zachariah 6 m "
Enoch 3 m "
Fanny 4/12 f "
ROBINSON, Nathan 16 m Ga
(Laborer)

BASS, Martin
Meedy
Rebecca
(See Peter Tew).

BASS, Sarah
(See Colin McDonald).

BASS, Sarah
(See Edward McPhail).

675 Farmer
BASS, Willis 42 m NC
Jane 35 f "
Allen 15 m Ala
John 13 m "
Louisa 11 f "
William 9 m "
Lucinda 8 f "
Willis 4 m "
Wiley 1 m "

1767 Farmer
BASSETT, Francis 62 m SC
Elizabeth 45 f "
Elizabeth 14 f "
Francis 11 m Ga

2193 Farmer
BATEMAN, Stephen W. 38 m SC
Elizabeth 27 f Ga
Mary 13 f "
William 11 m Ala
Sarah 8 f "
James 5 m "
John 2 m "

561 Farmer ($2,500)
BATES, George M. 44 m SC
Rosanna M. 34 f "

2172 Farmer ($6,000)
BATES, Wilson M. 34 m SC
Nancy 38 f "
Milledge L. 12 m Ala
Andrew 8 m "
Mary 5 f "

#1295 Farmer ($50,000)
BATTLE, Cullen 65 m NC
Jane 51 f "
Cullen A. (Student) 21 m Ga
Junius K. 12 m Ala
McSWAIN, Colin 18 m "
(Student)

917 Farmer ($11,000)
BATTS, Jesse 32 m Ga
Mary 26 f "
Charles 4 m Ala
Jesse 1/12 m "
JORDAN, Olivia W. 32 f Ga

374 Farmer
BAXLEY, Barnabas 26 m SC
Mary 25 f Ga
Eli B. 4 m Ala
John 3 m "
William H. 4/12 m "

BAXLEY, Barney
(See David Beasley)

372 Farmer ($500)
BAXLEY, James 54 m SC
Rebecca 23 f "
Sarah 22 f "
Rhody 17 f "
Riley 17 m "
Joseph 1/12 m Ala
HARTZOG, Isaac 15 m "
(Laborer)

378 Laborer
BAXLEY, Reddin 21 m SC
Rachel 18 f Ga
(Married within the year).

373 Farmer
BAXLEY, William 29 m SC
Catherine 26 f NC
Lydia 6 f Ala
Elliot 4 m "
Harriet 3 f "
Patsey A. 2 f "
Aaron 2/12 m "
HEATH, Lemuel 3 m "

1114 Farmer ($1,500)
BAXTER, James S. 28 m SC
Sarah 25 f NC
James 4 m Ala
Daniel 2 m "

1190 Farmer ($1,000)
BAXTER, Thomas F. 23 m Ala
Mary 22 f "
Missouri 3 f "
Pleasant 1 m "
Sarah 55 f SC

2059 Farmer ($1,000)
BAZETT, James 75 m NC
Elizabeth 60 f "
Thomas 20 m Ala
Sabriney 18 f "

955 Farmer
BEASLEY, Asa F. 25 m Ala
Sarah 17 f "
(Married within the year).

1057 Farmer
BEASLEY, Daniel 25 m Ala

954 Farmer
BEASLEY, Daniel F. 25 m Ala
Jane 17 f NC
(Married within the year).

1931 Blacksmith
BEASLEY, David 41 m Ga
Martha 38 f "
Larkin 17 m "
John 12 m "
William 10 m "
Wiley 5 m Ala
David 2 m "
Eliza 16 f Ga
Sarah 11 f "
Mary 7 f Ala
BAXLEY, Barney 14 m NC

956 Teacher
BEASLEY, John C. 26 m NC
Barbara 16 f Ala
(Married within the year).

953 Farmer ($ 2,500)
BEASLEY, John G. 52 m NC
Martha 46 f Ga
John C. (Overseer) 22 m Ala
Mary 16 f "

952 Farmer ($1,500)
BEASLEY, J. T. 29 m Ala
Rebecca 22 f "
Narcissa 4 f "
Milton 1 m "

1935 Farmer
BEASLEY, Robert J. 20 m Ga
Celia 22 f NC

2117
BEASLEY, Susan 45 f Ga
James (Farmer) 17 m Ala
Lawson " 15 m "
Thomas 12 m "
Matthew 10 m "
Mary 8 f "
Joseph 6 m "

2100 Farmer
BEASLEY, William 27 m Ala
Matilda 23 f "
James 5 m "
John 3 m "
Samuel 1 m "

1136 Farmer ($1,500)
BEASLEY, William 48 m NC
Elizabeth 36 f Ga
Daniel 17 m Ala
Asa 16 m "
John 14 m "
(Cont.)

(# 1336 BEASLEY Cont.)
William 12 m Ala
James 8 m "
Sarah 6 f "
Mary 7 f "
George 1 m "

1413 Farmer ($4,000)
BEAUCHAMP, Green 47 m Ga
Caroline 35 f "
Joseph (Student) 18 m Ala
Henry 14 m "
Thomas 13 m "
Richard 12 m "
TULLIS, Thos. E. 24 m "
(Physician)
KENNON, Jane 65 f Ga

1488 Farmer ($1,000)
BEAUCHAMP, A. H. 23 m Ala
Sarah 22 f SC
William 4 m Ala
John L. 1 m "

BECK, Letty
(See Columbus Hudspeth).

1597 Laborer
BECK, Stephen 47 m NC
Henrietta 43 f "
Letty 17 f Ga
Robert 15 m "
George 12 m "
Amelia 10 f "
Henry 9 m Ala
Francis 5 m "
Willard T. 2 m "

BECKHAM, Amanda J.
Green C.
(See T. R. Sylvester)

558 Farmer
BECKLEY, William 19 m SC
Sarah 18 f "

BEDLE, Catherine
(See Martha Lamar).

1696 Farmer ($1,700)
BEDSOLE, John 48 m NC
Catherine 41 f "
Janet 17 f Ga
Sarah 15 f "
Mary 13 f "
Nancy 11 f "
Emeline 9 f "
(Cont.)

(# 1696 BEDSOLE cont).

Cherry	7	f	Ga
William	5	m	"
John	3	m	"
Catherine	8/12	f	"

1697 Farmer

BEDSOLE, Stephen	20	m	NC
Harriet	17	f	"

(Married within the year).

562 Laborer ($200)

BELCHER, Matthew	45	m	Ga
Mary	40	f	"
Martha	18	f	"
John	14	m	"
Nancy	12	f	Ala
Emily	10	f	"
Rebecca	8	f	"
Sarah	5	f	"
Samuel	3	m	"

933 Farmer ($1,500)

BELL, John	43	m	SC
Laney	42	f	"
Mary	13	f	Ala
William	11	m	"
John	9	m	"
Kervin	7	m	"
Laney	2	f	"

1261 Butcher ($650)

BELL, Orestes	31	m	NC
Elizabeth	24	f	Va
William	3/12	m	Ala
Catherine	70	f	NC
Joseph (Wheelwright)	42	m	"
Eliza A.	16	f	Ga

716 Wheelwright ($140)

BELL, R. W. W.	26	m	NC
Mary	24	f	Ga
Eliza	4	f	"
Hiram	3	m	"
Ethelia	1	f	Ala
BROWN, James (Laborer)	18	m	Ala
MARSHALL, Elias "	30	m	Ga

BELL, Samuel
(See Robert Pickett).

1958 Farmer

BENEFIELD, Arnold	27	m	Ga
Ann	25	f	SC
Martha	6	f	Ala
John	4	m	"

BENEY, Christian
(See Amaria Day).

1626 Farmer

BENNET, Ezekiel	24	m	Ga
Martha	22	f	Ala

1624 Farmer

BENNET, John H.	32	m	Ga
Jane	24	f	"
Elam	8	m	"
John	6	m	"

875 Farmer ($300)

BENNET, Orren	26	m	Ala
Elizabeth	80	f	NC
Elizabeth	20	f	Ala
MYERS, Wm. (Farmer)	35	m	SC

1625 Farmer ($300)

BENNET, Randel	57	m	Ga
Jemima	51	f	"
Elizabeth	25	f	"
Maria	12	f	"

1006 Farmer ($880)

BENNET, Redman	53	m	NC
Mary	35	f	SC
George W.	18	m	Ala
Elizabeth	16	f	"
Green	13	m	"
Matilda	11	f	"
Amanda	5	f	"
Joanna	3	f	"
Zach. T.	8/12	m	"

2231 Farmer ($1,800)

BENNET, Ryan	41	m	NC
Emily	35	f	Ga
Wesley	14	m	Ala
William	12	m	"
Elizabeth	10	f	"
Martha	8	f	"
Josiah	4	m	"
SAPP, Allen (Laborer)	35	m	Ga

BENNET, Samuel
(See T. J. Roquemore).

810 Farmer ($200)

BENNET, S. A.	38	m	Ga
Matilda	23	f	"
Louisa	10	f	Ala
Risten	8	m	"
Sarah	6	f	"

2086 Farmer

BENNET, Thomas B.	39	m	SC
Elizabeth	29	f	Ga
William	14	m	"
Lucy Ann	12	f	Ala

(Cont.)

(# 2086 BENNET cont.)
Nancy 10 f Ala
James 7 m "
Eliza 6 f "
Philip 4 m "
Martha 2 f "
Elizabeth 1/12 f "

879 Farmer ($1,200)
BENSON, George W. 44 m NC
Susan 42 f SC
Susannah 7 f Ala
Charlotte 4 f "
George 2 m "
GRAHAM, John 60 m SC
HARRELSON, Nancy 92 f SC

BENSON, John F.
(See Thomas Cooper).

902 Poorhouse
BENSON, Rebecca 34 f Va

288 Farmer ($800)
BENTLEY, John 50 m NC
Fanny 34 f "
Rhody 16 f "
William 13 m "
James 10 m Ala
Moses 1/12 m "

1067 Farmer
BENTLEY, John 20 m NC
Catherine 16 f SC
Vicey Ann 2/12 f Ala

343 Farmer
BENTON, George S. 34 m Ga
Catherine 23 f SC
John P. 10 m Ga
Elizabeth 8 f "
Lucy 4 f "
George W. 2 m "

340 Grocer
BENTON, Henry 36 m SC
Luraney 20 f Ala
Harriet 3 f Ga
Moses A. 7/12 m Ala
Henry B. 7/12 m "
Mary 80 f SC

483 Farmer ($175)
BENTON, Isaac 32 m SC
Letty 26 f Ga
Samuel 8 m Ala
(Cont.)

(# 483 cont.)
India 6 f Ala
James M. 4 m "
Susan J. 2 f "
Ira T. 9/12 m "
Sarah 54 f NC

49 Blacksmith
BENTON, John 44 m SC
Eugenia 42 f "
Emily 15 f Ga
Amanda 13 f "
Charlotte 7 f "
John G. 5 m "
Renby T. 2 f "

500 Farmer
BENTON, Samuel 24 m Ala
Marina 28 f SC
Sarah 4 f Ala
Mary 2 f "
Lucinda 1/12 f "

2110 Farmer ($500)
BENTON, Wright 34 m SC
Frances 30 f Ga
Martha 11 f Ala
Benjamin 9 m "
John 7 m "
Sarah 5 f "
Thomas 3 m "
Samuel 1 m "

161 Farmer ($350)
BERRY, John W. 35 m Ga
Palmyra 32 f "
George S. 10 m "
Sarah 8 f Ala
John 6 m "
Mary 3 f "

1620 Farmer
BERRYHILL, John S. 57 m NC
Sarah 45 f Ga
COVINGTON, Elizabeth 27 f "
Emily 5 f "
Mary 3 f Ala
Jeremiah 1 m "
BERRYHILL, Isabella 23 f Ga
Nancy 18 f "
John (Farmer) 15 m "
Jane 13 f "
Henry 10 m "
Thomas 7 m "
Levin 5 m "
Mary 2 f Ala

138 Laborer
BERSANT, Matthew 47 m NC
Serena 36 f Ga
Isena(?) 17 f Ala
Benjamin 15 m "
James 10 m "
William 7 m "
Alexis 5 m "
Amanda 4/12 f "

BESSON, J. A. B.
(See Ranson Godwin).

BESSON, William E.
(See J. G. L. Martin).

2144 Farmer
BETHUNE, John S. 19 m Ga
Nancy 23 f "
Penelope 6/12 f Ala

BETHUNE, Mary
(See Joseph Jones).

1643 Farmer ($2,500)
BETTS, Elisha 62 m Va
Marie 50 f Ga
NIX, Thos.(Overseer) 21 m SC

2254 Farmer ($800)
BEVERLY, B. F. 27 m NC
Elizabeth 27 f NY
(Married within the year).

251 Farmer ($50)
BEVERLY, Daniel 34 m NC
Nancy 20 f Ala
Mary 12 f NC
Ann 10 f "
Christina 7 f "
William 4 m Ala
Martha 5/12 f "

945 Carpenter
BEVIL, Thomas 56 m SC
Milly 42 f "
Sarah 17 f "
Ann 14 f "
Robert 12 m Ala
William 10 m "
Alexander 8 m "
George 6 m "

1595 Farmer ($4,000)
BIGHAM, James 47 m Ga
Isabella 40 f "
PARSONS, Thomas 10 m "

BILLINGS, Harriet
Hollis
(See John Black).

165 Farmer
BINUM, James S. 36 m Ga
Nancy 26 f "
Turner 5 m Ala
Elizabeth 4 f "
Reuben 2 m "
Jefferson 3/12 m "

2198 Farmer
BIRD, Allen 26 m Ga
Catherine 22 f NC
Gilbert 5 m Ala
Mary 3 f "
Thomas 1 m "

452 Farmer ($550)
BIRD, Edward 32 m NC
Louisa 30 f Ga
Charles B. 11 m Ala
Curtis 9 m "
Caroline 7 f "
Newton 6 m "
David 5 m "
Jesse H. 2 m "
LENHORN, Mary 21 f ---
SAULS, David 21 m Ga
(Farmer)

2014 Farmer ($120)
BIRD, Peter 37 m SC
Thursey 30 f Ga
William 10 m Ala
Catherine 7 f "
Martha 4 f "
Joseph 2 m "

1830 Farmer
BIRD, William 38 m Ala
Rebecca 36 f NC
Dinkey 13 f Ala
Michael 11 m "
Daniel 10 m "
John 8 m "
Susan 2 f "

BIRDSONG, Josephine
(See William McLeod).

BIRDSONG, Martha
(See Samuel Harwell).

BIRDSONG, Simanthe
(See A. B. Holleman).

1636 Farmer
BISHOP, Erwin 39 m Ga
Fortune 30 f "
Elizabeth 4 f Ala

916 Farmer ($1,200)
BISHOP, J. B. 35 m SC
Nancy 28 f NC
Martha 5 f Ala
Mary 3 f "
Emma 1 f "
William 1/12 m "

BISHOP, Martha J.
(See Wiley Anderson).

979 ($1,000)
BISHOP, Nancy 56 f SC
William (Overseer) 27 m Ala
Dixon H. (Student) 17 m Ala
McDUFFIE, John 25 m SC
(Teacher)
GLASS, Rebecca 45 f Ga

929 Farmer ($3,000)
BISHOP, Wesley 30 m Ga
Cinthia 22 f Ala
Nancy 1 f "

425 Farmer ($2,650)
BIZZELL, Bennet 75 m NC
Mary 65 f SC
Sophronia 11 f Ala

424 Farmer
BIZZELL, Henry A. 40 m SC
Mary 23 f Ala
Henry 16 m "
James 15 m "
Mary 10 f "
Elizabeth 3 f "
Zachariah 8/12 m "

634 Farmer
BIZZELL, William A. 25 m Ala
Jemima 21 f Ga
Mary J. 2 f Ala
George McD. 1 m "

1280 Druggist
BLACK, Hugh 32 m Scot

1354 Printer ($400)(East Can.)
BLACK, John 28 m Can
Mary 24 f Ga
Caroline 2 f Ala
BILLINGS, Harriet 41 f Ga
(Cont.)

(# 1354 BLACK cont.)
Hollis (Printer) 15 m Ga
TREADWELL, James 18 m Ga
(Printer)
REYNOLDS, William 21 m "
(Printer)

1654
BLACK, Martha 40 f SC
Laura 19 f "
John (Wheelwright) 18 m "
James 14 m Ala
Elizabeth 12 f "
Peter 9 m "
Thomas 7 m "
Dougald 4 m "

1533 Farmer ($1,200)
BLACKSTOCK, Jesse 29 m Ga
Elizabeth 28 f "
Sarah 8 f Ala
Joseph 6 m "
Henry 4 m "
John 3 m "
Nancy 1 f "

1096 Farmer
BLADES, Israel 77 m Md
Elizabeth 75 f NC

370 Farmer ($200)
BLAIR, Michael W. 31 m SC
Martha 19 f Ala

1134 Farmer ($1,200)
BLAIR, William 45 m SC
Elizabeth 38 f "
Nancy 18 f Ala
Thomas (Farmer) 16 m "
Wesley 14 m "
Roxanna 12 f "
William 10 m "
Sidney 8 m "
Elizabeth 6 f "
John H. 4 m "
Derrell 3 m "

761 Farmer ($450)
BLAKE, Daniel N. 30 m Ga
Mary 25 f "
Elizabeth 55 f "
Joseph (Farmer) 16 m "
(Daniel & Mary married within the year).

1171 Farmer ($1,000)
BLAKEY, Asa 40 m Ga

2174 Farmer ($1500)
BLAKEY, B. S. 35 m Ga
Council (idiot) 42 m "
Margaret 40 f "
Alley 37 f "

897 Farmer
BLAKEY, F. S. 48 m Ga
Mary 45 f "
Columbus C. (Farmer) 20 m "
Emily 21 f "
James W. 18 m "
REEVES, Mary 3 f "

1170 Farmer ($2,000)
BLAKEY, Hartwell G. 40 m Ga

930 Farmer
BLAKEY, Jackson 26 m Ga
Mary 17 f NC

Blakey, James
(See William Cowart).

1172 Farmer
BLAKEY, John D. 29 m Ga

1099 Farmer ($1,000)
BLAKEY, S. W. 35 m Ga
Sarah 38 f "
Samantha 7 f Ala
Miralean 5 m "
Leonora 4 f "

BLANCHETT, Lemuel
John
Caroline
Sharp
Jane
(See Alfred Harrison).

1537 Farmer ($1,000)
BLOUNT, Hugh A. 38 m NC
Ann 12 f Fla

Blunt, Sarah M.
(See Levi T. Daniel).

1244 Merchant ($1244)
BLUDWORTH, J. M. 38 m NC

2192
BLUDWORTH, Martha A. 34 f Ga
Pastora 8 f "
WARING, Jane M. 30 f "
KENNON, Emily 32 f "

1466 Overseer
BLUDWORTH, Milton 32 m NC

1922 Clerk
BLUDWORTH, Patrick 29 m Ga

1921 Merchant ($250)
BLUDWORTH, Peyton 31 m Ga

757 Farmer ($500)
BLUDWORTH, Thomas F. 49 m NC
Thursey 46 f "
Jefferson (Farmer) 21 m Ga
Thomas " 16 m "
John 14 m "

968 Farmer
BLUDWORTH, T. W. 24 m Ga
Charlotte 22 f SC
Thomas 1 m Ala
Thursey 2/12 f "

756 Farmer
BLUDWORTH, William H. 22 m Ga
Mary 19 f SC
Sarah 3/12 f Ala

BODEFORD, Drucilla
(See Stephen Gibbens).

735 Farmer ($200)
BODEFORD, Wesley H. 23 m SC
Jane 23 f Ala
Sarah 3 f "
Cornelia 2/12 f "
SMITH, Wm. (Laborer) 23 m Ga

1465 Farmer
BOLIVER, Martin 72 m NC
Elizabeth 49 f Ga
ALSTON, John J. 20 m "
(Farmer, $250)
Elizabeth 11 f "

468 Carpenter
BOLTON, Eli 35 m SC
Elizabeth 22 f Ga
Wesley 10 m "
Philip 8 m Ala

BOND, James
(See J. L. Watson).

120 Overseer ($2,000)
BONDS, Jefferson S. 24 m Ga
Martha A. 20 f "
Mary J. 2 f Ala
(Cont.)

(# 120 BONDS cont.)
WINDHAM, Elisha 50 m Va
(Laborer)
BRADY, Elijah 10 m Ala

1511 Laborer (Mulatto)
BOOTH, Abraham 42 m Ga

1370 Lawyer ($1,000)
BOOTH, John P. 45 m Ga
Martha 33 f "
Leonora 13 f Ala
James 3 m "

BOOTH, Joseph
(See William D. Hailey).

BOOTH, William
(See R. E. DuBose).

#2281 Farmer ($400)
BORDERS, William M. 35 m Ga
Martha 34 f "
Ellender 12 f "
Sarah 10 f "
Hopkins 8 m "
Joseph 6 m "
Georgia 4 f Ala
William 2 m "

1806 Farmer ($250)
BOREN, William 55 m Ga
Louisa 25 f "
Elizabeth 9 f "
Emmet 6 m "
Curron 2 m "
RAY, Archibald 6 m "

629 Farmer
BOSTICK, Henry R. 25 m Ga
Elizabeth 22 f "
Thomas 4 m Ala
Duncan 2 m "
James 6/12 m "

1847 Farmer
BOSTICK, Joshua J. 30 m Ga
Sarah 27 f "
Mary 13 f Ala
Joshua 10 m "
Martha 8 f "
Francis 6 m "
Robert 4 m "
Thomas 2 m "
Mercy 1 f "

BOSWELL, William H.
Elizabeth
(See John J. Lowman).

2054 Farmer ($500)
BOTTOMS, James 32 m Ga
Nancy 23 f Ala
Jefferson 3 m "
James 6/12 m "

BOTTOMS, John
(See Elvey Lewis).

BOTTOMS, Mary A.
(See M. R. Sims).

2058 Farmer ($2,500)
BOULWARE, F. P. 26 m SC
Mary 24 f "
Reuben 4 m "
Rebecca 6/12 f Ala
REED, William 24 m SC
(Farmer)

2242 Farmer ($250)
BOUNDS, Jesse 38 m Ga
Nancy 36 f SC
Priscilla 13 f Ala
William 10 m "
James 8 m "
Nancy 6 f "
Jesse 4 m "
Mary 2 f "

1071 Farmer ($400)
BOUNDS, William 45 m NC
Martha 37 f Ga
Elizabeth 17 f Ala
Stephen (Farmer) 16 m "
William 14 m "
Amanda 12 f "
Julia 10 f "
Lucinda 8 f "
Rebecca 6 f "
Osborn 4 m "
John 2 m "
Jane 46 f NC

934 Farmer ($400)
BOWDEN, James 48 m NC
Elizabeth 45 f "
Henry (Farmer) 22 m "
James 19 m "
Francis 14 m Ala
Sarah 6 f "

1196 Farmer
BOWDEN, Jesse B. 32 m NC
Ann 32 f Ga
Elizabeth 13 f Ala
William 8 m "
Nicholas 5 m "
Elliphar 3 f "
Hartwell 1 m "

925 Farmer
BOWDEN, William B. 25 m NC
Eliza 20 f "
Eady 2 f Ala

BOWDEN, Elijah
(See William T. Upshaw).

822 Overseer
BOWEN, Levi 45 m NC
Mary 42 f "
Martha 17 f Ga
John 12 m "
Jane 10 f "
Ann 8 f Ala
Susan 5 f "
Josephine 3 f "
Georgiann 6/12 f "

BOWERS, Joseph
(See William Truet).

701 Farmer ($150)
BOYD, F. M. 27 m SC
Mary 28 f NC
Joseph 6 m Ga
James 4 m Ala
Elizabeth 1 f "

2259 Laborer
BOYKIN, Elias 40 m SC
Hester 35 f "
Henry 7 m Ala
Sarah 5 f "
David 3 m "
Thomas 1 m "

1563 Farmer ($4,000)
BOYKIN, Francis 24 m Ga
Louisianna 19 f "
CASON, James R. 27 m "
(Overseer)

BOYLESTON, Caroline
(See Elliot Thomas).

603 Farmer ($1,000)
BOYLESTON, Joseph C. 49 m SC
(Cont).

(# 603 BOYLESTON cont.)
Leonora C. 30 f SC
Julia Anna 15 f "
Margaret 13 f "
Elliot T. 10 m Ala
McDuffie H. 8 m "
Joseph 5 m "
Jane 18 f SC
Caroline 7 f Ala
John L. 2 m "

830 Farmer ($200)
BRADBERRY, Bryan 30 m Ga
Maria 38 f "
Minerva 12 f "
Thomas 10 m "
Joseph 8 m "
William 4 m Ala
Allen 2 m "

829 Machinist ($1,200)
BRADBERRY, James H. 36 m Ga
Jane 32 f SC
William 14 m Ga
Martha 13 f "
Joseph 11 m "
Saramanda 9 f "
Cornelia 7 f Ala
Harriet 5 f "
Virginia 2 f "
William (Overseer) 23 m Ga

1365 Overseer
BRADLEY, Abden 52 m Ga

2296 Overseer
BRADLEY, Henry 32 m Ga
Sarah 26 f "
Joshua 7 m "
Thomas 4 m Ala
Susan 2 f "
James 4/12 m "

2274 Farmer ($800)
BRADLEY, Robert 41 m SC
Elizabeth 41 f "
Hobbs (Farmer) 22 m Ala
Ezekiel " 20 m "
Selatheil " 17 m "
Henry 14 m "
George 12 m "
John 8 m "
Abraham 6 m "
James 4 m "
Martha 2 f "

885 Farmer ($400)
BRADLEY, S. C. 51 m Ga
Delilah 50 f "
Yelverton (Farmer) 26 m "
Martha 18 f Fla
Louisa 12 f Ala

BRADY, Elijah
William
(See Hanson B. Stephens).

BRADY, Elijah
(See William Johnston).

BRADY, Elijah
(See Jefferson S. Bonds).

909 Farmer
BRANCH, Charles J. 38 m NC
Nancy 27 f "
Winneford 5 f Ala
Nancy 4 f "
John 2 m "
Henry 1 m "
Viney 7 f "

1507 Occupation - none
BRANDON, Henry P. 44 m Conn

809 Farmer
BRANTLEY, B. H. 39 m NC
Moly 25 f Ga
Sarah 6 f "
John 5 m "
Buena Vista 1 f Ala
WILLIAMS, George 21 m Ga
HAWKINS, Pinckney 18 m "

2124 Farmer ($500)
BRANTLEY, Charles G. 38 m Ga
Elvira 27 f "
Ellifair 8 f Ala
Ann 6 f "
George 5 m "
John 6/12 m "
ADAMS, Mary 56 f NC
Thos. (Farmer, $500) 24 m Ga

2071 Farmer
BRANTLEY, W. G. 27 m Ga

2070 Farmer ($1,000)
BRANTLEY, William 40 m NC
Eliza 27 f Ga
John 7 m "
James 5 m "
William 3 m "
(Cont.)

(# 2070 BRANTLEY cont.)
Henry 1 m Ga
WORRELL, Eliza 60 f "
Julia 25 f "
Ann 22 f "
Charlotte 18 f "

143 Farmer
BRASSELL, Henry 21 m Ala
Darling 18 f "

BRASWELL, Green 23 m Ala
(See N. N. Walterman).

BRASWELL, Jeptha
(See James Orr).

230 Laborer
BRASWELL, Kenneth 38 m Ala
Nancy 35 f SC
Robert 11 m Ala
William 10 m "
Sarah 8 f "
Martha 7 f "
Catherine 4 f "

BRASWELL, Letty
(See William A. Horne).

Braswell, Martha
Eliza R.
(See James McAdams).

695 Overseer
BRASWELL, Rigden 30 m SC
Artemisia 26 f Ga
John 5 m Ala
Churchill 3 m "
George 6/12 m "
Temperance 20 f "

598 Farmer ($300)
BREWER, Lanier 50 m SC
Celia A. 42 f "
Henry O. (Farmer) 18 m "
Eliza 12 f Ala
Leonora 10 f "
Lorenzo 5 m "

946 Farmer
BRIDGES, D. B. 33 m Tenn
Elizabeth 27 f Ga
William 8 m "
Nathaniel 6 m "
Elizabeth 4 f "
Thomas 1 m Ala
ARMSTRONG, Labun 60 m ---
(Occupation - none).

BRIDGES, Mary
(See Wesley Williams).

BRIGHT, Evelina
Levi D.
(See Nath. Roach).

BRITT, John H.
(See George W. Rice)

2205 Farmer ($4,000)
BRITT, Matthew 52 m Va
Elizabeth 26 f Ga
Catherine 9 f Ala
Matthew 8 m "
Asa 6 m "
Sarah 4 f "
John 1 m "

623 Farmer ($250)
BROACH, William 30 m SC
EIDSON, Rhoda 60 f "
BROACH, Rachel A. 25 f "
EIDSON, Francis 16 m Ala
(Farmer).

1421 Farmer ($150)
BROCK, James 38 m SC
Martha 22 f NC
William 5 m SC
Temperance 3 f Ala
Mary 1 f "
CARROLL, George W. 19 m SC
STONAKER, Eliza 39 f Ga

105 Farmer ($2,200)
BROOKS, Esau 42 m Ga
Martha 41 f "
Alpheus 15 m "
Elizabeth 12 f "
Lawrence D. 10 m Ala
Andrew J. 9 m "
Cicero 7 m "
Jane 5 f "
Louisa 3 f "
Sarah 2 f "

BROOKS, James
(See William H. Finch).

1418 Farmer
BROOKS, Middleton 37 m Ga
Mary 40 f SC
Martha 17 f Ala
Elizabeth 15 f "
Mary 14 f "
Thomas 12 m "
(Cont.)

(# 1418 BROOKS cont.)
Hannah 11 f Ala
Franklin 10 m "
James 8 m "
Sarah 6 f "
Nancy 5 f "
James 2 m "

2253
BROOKS, Nancy 60 f Ga
Lucretia 16 f "

1398 Farmer (15,000)
BROWDER, Isham C. 45 m NC
Mary 25 f Ala
Hartwell 6 m "
Ann 7 f "
Milton 4 m "
Isham 1 m "
ROSE, Hugh F. 15 m Ga
(Farmer).

1748 Farmer ($16,000)
BROWDER, Milton A. 48 m NC
Mary 36 f "
Macon 10 m Ala
HUNT, William 27 m Tenn
(Farmer)

252 Farmer
BROWN, Aaron 52 m NC
Ann 48 f SC
Harriet 16 f Ga
Eveline 14 f "
Abner 6 m "

996 Farmer ($1,500)
BROWN, C. L. 26 m Ga
Mary 25 f SC
Mary E. 4 f Ala
Ann 1/12 f "

1487 Farmer ($500)
BROWN, C. L. 25 m Ga
Magdaline 22 f SC
Mary E. 3 f Ala
Judson 1/12 m "

1288 ($200)
BROWN, Dolly 54 f SC
Harvey (Shoemaker) 20 m "
Elizabeth 16 f Ala

BROWN, Elizabeth J.
Mary
(See J. Myers).

442 Miller
BROWN, Fielding 44 m SC
Mary 48 f "
Samantha 13 f Ala
Amanda 7 f "

BROWN, George H.
(See William T. Simpson).

51 Farmer
BROWN, Isaac S. 60 m SC
Lucinda 40 f Ga
Louisa J. 18 f "
Caroline 17 f "
William T.(Farmer) 16 m "
Reuben 14 m "
Absolom 12 m "
Mary A. 10 f "
Martha A. 6 f "

BROWN, James
(See R. W. W. Bell).

2229 Farmer ($300)
BROWN, Jesse 52 m Ga
Elizabeth 45 f "
John (Farmer) 20 m "
Sarah 17 f "
Wenlock " 16 m "
Ellender 14 f "
Elizabeth 13 f "
James 11 m "
William 10 m "
Jane 9 f Ala
Thomas 7 m "
Samuel 5 m "
Richard 2 m "

517 Farmer
BROWN, John 56 m NC
Elizabeth 37 f SC
Jesse D. 11 m Ala
Rebecca 8 f "
William T. 5 m "
John C. 2 m "
Joseph R. 1/12 m "

1647 Farmer
BROWN, John P. 41 m Ga
Julia 41 f "
Maria 18 f Fla
Thomas (Farmer) 16 m "
Lidia 14 f "
Dorcas 12 f "
Amanda 11 f "
James 9 m Ga
(Cont.)

(# 1647 BROWN cont.)
Jesse 8 m Ga
Joseph 6 m "
Henry 5 m "
Sarah 2 f Ala
John 1 m "
HAWKINS, Robert 23 m "
(Farmer).

1540 Farmer ($16,000)
BROWN, John W. 51 m Ga
Martha 41 f "
James 10 m Ala
Louisa 8 f "
Martha C. 3 f "

98 Farmer ($100)
BROWN, Jonathan 65 m SC
Eliza 50 f NC
Andrew 12 m Ga
Louisa 10 f Ala
John 7 m "
Green 3 m "
KEILS, Martha 17 f Ga
Joseph (Farmer) 15 m "

BROWN, L.
Jane
William
(See J. B. Myers).

852 Carpenter
BROWN, Lorenzo D. 35 m SC
Elizabeth 19 f Ga
Mary 1/12 f Ala

BROWN, Mark
(See Benjamin A. Barron).

BROWN, Mary
(See Martha Snipes).

1602 Carpenter
BROWN, Nathan L. 45 m Tenn
Elizabeth 28 f Ala
Bartley 10 m "
James 8 m "
Nathan 7 m "
Elizabeth 5 f "
Mary 2 f "

1485 Minister M.P. ($1,200)
BROWN, Reuben E. 56 m SC
Elizabeth 54 f "
John H. (Farmer) 17 m Ga
Celesta 15 f "
TAYLOR, Mary 7 f "

1486 Music Teacher
BROWN, Reuben E., Jr. 23 m Ga
Hester 20 f SC
Martha 1 f Ala

1737 Farmer
BROWN, Samuel J. 26 m SC
Letty 20 f Ga
Nancy 2 f Ala

204 Farmer ($ 300)
BROWNING, Archibald 39 m SC
Sarah 40 f "
HOOKER, James D. 23 m Ala

346 Farmer ($200)
BROWNING, Jesse 49 m SC
Jane 53 f "
Cornilius 18 m "
Jesse 12 m Ala

205 Farmer ($200)
BROWNING, Johnson W. 28 m SC
Rethena 27 f Ala

BRUCE, Eliza A.
(See Randolph Lignoski).

401 Farmer ($400)
BRUMBELS, Abraham 35 m NC
Harriet 14 f Ala
Elbert 3 m "
McCALL, Martha 16 f "
BRUMBELS, Aaron 5 m "
Sarah 1 f "

1461 Overseer
BRUNDAGE, Elam S. 37 m Ga
Sarah A. 28 f "
Daniel C. 8/12 m Ala

1449 Farmer ($600)
BRUNSON, Charles J. 23 m Ga
Mary 16 f "
John 2 m Ala

1802 Farmer ($3600)
BRUNSON, M. A. 43 m SC
Catherine 24 f "
Alice 6/12 f Ala

1543 Farmer
BRYAN, Frederick 23 m Ga
Surrintha 18 f "
(Married within the year).

1555 Overseer
BRYAN, Joseph F. 38 m Ga
(Cont.)

(#1555 BRYAN cont.)
Emily 34 f Ga
Virginia 15 f "
Henry 12 m "
Tabitha 10 f "
Robert 8 m "
Narcissa 6 f "
Sarah 5 f "
Emily 2 f Ala

55 Farmer ($2,000)
BRYAN, Moses 66 m Ga
Fanny 64 f NC

BRYAN, Richard
(See Nathan Minshew).

821 Farmer ($300)
BRYAN, Robert 64 m Ga
Tabitha 65 f SC
MIMS, Eliza 17 f Ga
Benjamin 15 m "

1542 Farmer ($2,000)
BRYAN, Theophilus 51 m NC
Levina 30 f Ga
Theophilus (Farmer) 18 m "
Margaret 16 f "
John 13 m "
Mary 12 f "
Joseph 2 m Ala

BRYANT, Annis
(See William Holland)

BRYANT, Fortunatus
Elizabeth
Henry
(See Isaac Campbell).

122 Farmer ($1,000)
BRYANT, George 30 m Ga
Mary M. 24 f "
Amanda M. 6 f Ala
Eliza A. 4 f "
Benjamin L. 2 m "
William 5/12 m "
BRYANT, Susan 53 f SC
Faithey 18 f Ga
Susan 15 f "
Green L. 13 m Ala

1367 Farmer
BRYANT, H. L. 30 m NC
Mary 26 f Ga
Jane 12 f "
William 8 m Ala
(Cont.)

(# 1367 cont.)

Ann	6	f	Ala
Miranda	4	f	"
John	1	m	"

1721 Farmer ($300)

BRYANT, John	50	m	SC
Susan	32	f	NC
Sarah	19	f	Ga
Elizabeth	15	f	"
Peter	12	m	Ala
Frances	10	f	"
Mary	8	f	"
Rosanna	4	f	"
Susanna	4	f	"
John	2	m	"

1376 Farmer ($1,200)

BRYANT, John C.	36	m	Ga
Janet	34	f	"
William	11	m	Ala
John	10	m	"
Sarah	9	f	"
Francis	7	m	"
David	5	m	"
Mary	2/12	f	"

BRYANT, Mary
(See Charles Sutton).

1197 Farmer ($400)

BRYANT, Needham	31	m	Ga
Elizabeth	31	f	"
William	5	m	Ala
Sarah	4	f	"
John	2	m	"
Mary	1	f	"

1377 Farmer

BRYANT, William M.	34	m	Ga
Epsey	26	f	"
William	9	m	Ala
James	7	m	"
Epsey	5	f	"
Richard	3	m	"
Montgomery	2	m	"

1123 Farmer

BUCKHALTS, Needham J.	36	m	Ga
Mary A.	25	f	SC
James	4	m	Ga
William	2	m	"

1429 Lawyer ($3500)

BUFORD, Jefferson	43	m	SC
James (Student)	23	m	Tenn

(Cont.)

(# 1429 BUFORD cont.)

Mary	30	f	NC
Tip (?)	9	m	Ala
Jefferson	7	m	"
Mary	6	f	"
Sarah	4	f	"
Jane	2	f	"

765 Farmer ($400)

BULLARD, Henry	32	m	SC
Emily	35	f	Ga
James	12	m	"
Elizabeth	10	f	Ala
Jeremiah	8	m	Ga
Martha	6	f	"
Cain (Farmer)	18	m	"

1175 Farmer ($500)

BULLARD, Henry	31	m	NC
Emily	32	f	Ga
James	10	m	"
Elizabeth	8	f	Ala
Jeremiah	6	m	Ga
Martha	4	f	"
Frances	2	f	Ala
BULLARD, N. L. C. (Farmer)	17	m	Ga

1270 Brickmason ($300)

BULLARD, James	39	m	NC
Frances	39	f	Va

2199 Farmer

BULLARD, James	40	m	SC
Mary	36	f	"
John	11	m	Ala
Thomas	9	m	"
Jane	7	f	"
Mary	5	f	"
Joseph	3	m	"
Nathan	1	m	"

1220 Farmer

BULLARD, Jeptha	31	m	Ga
Ada	29	f	"
Sarah	7	f	"
Thomas	4	m	"
Elizabeth	3	f	"
John	2	m	Ala

1316 Lawyer

BULLOCK, E. C.	27	m	SC
Mary	23	f	SC
Eliza	3	f	Ala
Edward	1	m	"

BULLOCK, Isabella
(See Ezekiel Wise).

96 Farmer
BULLOCK, John 49 m Ga
Mary A. 18 f Ala
Susan 16 f "
John W. 12 m "
Ransom 10 m "
Sarah 8 f "
Haney 13 f "

BULLOCK, Polly
William
(See William Smith).

9 Farmer
BUNTING, Jeremiah 21 m Ga
Margaret 27 f SC
William 3 m Ga
Mary A. E. 1 f "

229 Farmer
BUNTING, Jeremiah 22 m Ga
Margaret 25 f SC
William 3 m Ga
Mary 1 f "

1727 Farmer ($300)
BURGESS, Dempsey 52 m NC
Roxanna 58 f "
Martha 22 f Ga
Nancy 20 f "
John (Farmer) 17 m "

664 Farmer (500)
BURGESS, Dempsey 52 m NC
Roxanna 60 f SC
Martha 22 f Ga
Nancy 21 f "
John (Farmer) 17 m "

1011 Farmer
BURLESON, Aaron 65 m Ga

589 Blacksmith
BURLESON, Aaron D. 37 m Ga
Elizabeth 32 f NC
Nancy 16 f Ala
Jane 11 f "
Lawson G. 9 m "
James M. 2 m "

1174 Farmer ($600)
BURLESON, S. W. 42 m Ga
Molsey 36 f NC
(Cont.)

(# 1174 BURLESON cont.)
Larkin (Farmer) 18 m Ala
Eliza 12 f "
Martha E. 10 f "
James 8 m "
Cinthia 7 f "
Green 3 m "
Calvin 1 m "

1012 Farmer ($1,000)
BURLESON, Seaborn J. 37 m Ga
Malinda 37 f "
Elizabeth 15 f "
Franklin 13 m "
Aaron 12 m "
Solomon 10 m "
Henry 8 m Ala
Lucinda 6 f "
Simon 5 m "
Deborah 2 f "

1014 Farmer ($400)
BURLESON, Simeon 40 m Ga
Molsey 37 f "
Larkin 20 m Ala
Eliza 14 f "
Martha 12 f "
Ann 10 f "
Marion 8 m "
Green 6 m "
Calvin 2 m "

1536 Farmer ($1,200)
BURNET, Alexander 48 m Ga
Martha 52 f SC
James (Farmer) 20 m Ga
Martha 12 f Ga
RILEY, Mary A. 16 f "
Martin 10 m "

BURNETT, John
(See Josiah Little).

59 Farmer ($200)
BURNHAM, Benjamin 30 m Ga
Ann 32 f NC
Elvey A. 10 f Ala
Washington 8 m "
Marion 3 m "
Greenberry J. 1 m "
FRANKLIN, David 12 m Ga

71 Farmer
BURNHAM, Bryant 40 m NC
Arpey (?) 44 f "
(Cont.)

(# 71 BURNHAM cont.)

Josiah	16	m	NC
Zilpha	12	f	Ala
Polly J.	10	f	"
Martha	8	f	"
Blake	6	m	"
Charlotte	4	f	"

67 Farmer ($200)

BURNHAM, Edward	62	m	Va
Melinda	55	f	NC
James	18	m	"
Charlotte	20	f	"

65 Farmer

BURNHAM, John	25	m	NC
Elizabeth	20	f	SC
Francis M.	9	m	Ala
Martha	1	f	"

68 Blacksmith ($200)

BURNHAM, William	32	m	NC
Sarah	21	f	Ala

1289 Cigar Manufacturer

BURNLEY, J. B.	40	m	Ga

1928 Laborer

BURTON, Jesse	24	m	NC
Mary	25	f	Ga
Catherine	2	f	Ala

581 Farmer ($1,500)

BUSH, Charles D.	21	m	Ala
Salina	20	f	SC
Frances J.	2	f	Ala

295 Farmer ($600)

BUSH, Council	33	m	Ga
Rebecca	25	f	Ala
Louis	7	m	"
William	5	m	"
Ryan	3	m	"
Dixon H.	1	m	"

730 Farmer ($400)

BUSH, David A.	30	m	Ga
Julia	28	f	"
Epsey	6	f	Ala
Americus B.	3	m	"
David	1	m	"

964 Farmer ($600)

BUSH, Greenberry	27	m	Ala
Nancy	22	f	Ga
Sarah	1	f	Ala
WILLIAMS, Braddock (Farmer)	16	m	"

1179 Farmer

BUSH, John	34	m	Ga
Mary	25	f	NC
Bryant	11	m	Ala
Epsey	9	f	"
Elizabeth	8	f	"
Amanda	6	f	"
Sarah	4	f	"
William	2/12	m	"
Calvin	3	m	"

35 Overseer ($300)

BUSH, Joseph A.	28	m	Ga
Mary A.	25	f	SC
Martha	6	f	Ga
Magy	4	f	Ala
Mary A.	3	f	"
Josephine H.	1	f	"

BUSH, Mary
(See James Orr).

292 ($1,400)

BUSH, Nancy	35	f	NC
Priscilla	15	f	Ala
Roxanna	13	f	"
Savannah	10	f	"
Johnston	8	m	"
Tyson	7	m	"
Thena	3	f	"

117 Farmer ($600)

BUSH, Nathan	48	m	Ga
Elizabeth	44	f	SC
Pamela	14	f	Ga
Levi	12	m	"
George	10	m	"
Mary	8	f	"
James	6	m	"
Alexander	4	m	"
Dorcas	1	f	Ala
DAVIS, Noah	14	m	"

902 Overseer Poorhouse

BUSH, Richard	46	m	Ga
Penelope	32	f	NC
C. D. Jane	16	f	Ga
Martha A.	11	f	Ala
Council	9	m	"
Greenberry	6	m	"

587 Farmer

BUSH, William	27	m	Ga
Mary	23	f	Ala
Ailsey	3	f	"
Jane	1	f	"

901 Farmer
BUSH, William G. 27 m Ga
Mary 22 f Ala
Ailsey 4 f "
Sarah 1 f "

147 Farmer ($600)
BUSH, William G. 28 m Ala
Mary A. 23 f Ga
William H. 4 m Ala
Amanda 1 f "

950 Farmer ($3500)
BUSH, Zachariah 54 m Ga
Ruth 17 f Ala
Lucinda 10 f "

588 Farmer ($1,000)
BUSH, Zachariah, Jr. 24 m Ala

540 Occp. - none, blind
BUTLER, Robert 53 m SC
Mary 55 f SC

2224 Farmer
BUTLER, Samuel 58 m Ga
Sarah 54 f "
Berry (Farmer, $100) 26 m "
James " 17 m "
Thomas 14 m "
Mary 10 f Ala

865 Farmer ($200)
BUTLER, Samuel 51 m Va
Elizabeth 45 f NC
John 14 m Ala
Francis 12 m "
Ellfair 8 f "
Narcissa 6 f "

BUTLER, Solomon
(See Neill McKeller).

366 Farmer ($ 1,000)
BUTTS, Charles 38 m Ga
Louisa 28 f SC
Nancy A. 14 f Ala
Sarah A. 11 f "
Lydia L. 8 f "
Amanda 6 f "
Philip 3 m "
Thomas 1 m "

BUTT, Elizabeth
(See Mary R. Weyman).

1610 Farmer ($1,600)
BUTT, Francis C. 29 m Ga
(Cont.)

(# 1610 BUTT cont.)
Catherine 24 f Ga
Mortimer 4 m Ala

1759 Physician ($1,000)
BUTT, Jeremiah 38 m Ga
Ann 33 f "
Elizabeth 13 f "
Melman(?) 11 m "
Susan 9 f "
William 7 m Ala
Thomas 5 m "
Mary 1 f "

1530 Merchant
BUTT, Joseph H. 28 m Ga

1525 Merchant ($3,000)
BUTT, M. M. 44 m Ga
Ann 37 f "
Edmund 11 m "
Eugenia 9 f "
James 6 m Ala
Francis 5 m "
William 2 m "

363 Farmer ($200)
BUTTS, Solomon 43 m Ga
Sarah 30 f Ala
Nancy 13 f "
Sarah M. 11 f "
Elizabeth 8 f "
Frances S. 6 f "
Redonia 5 f "
Mary 2/12 f "
Thomas 4 m "
Edward 3 m "
Hardy J. 2 m "

1980
BYNUM, Martha 30 f SC
Daniel 10 m Ala

2111 Farmer ($500)
BYNUM, Smith L. 37 m Ga
Delilah 45 f SC
Samuel 14 m Ala
James 12 m "
Munro 8 m Ala

BYRD, Daniel
Nicey
(See William Spurlock).

20 Farmer ($200)
CABBINESS, Jesse M. 41 m Ga
Sarah 36 f "
(Cont.)

(# 20 CABBINESS cont.)
Elizabeth 15 f Ga
Lucy 13 f Ala
George C. 11 m "

1672 Tanner
CABANESS, John 30 m Ga

1223 Farmer ($3,800)
CADE, James J. 37 m Ga
Susan 33 f "
Dozier 16 m "
James 15 m "
Ann 13 f Ala

CADENHEAD, Ivey P.
(See Ivey P. Cattenhead).

2123 Physician ($2,000)
CALDWELL, Grover 26 m Ga
Mary 21 f "
Marcus 3 m Ala
Thomas 1 m "
LUDEN, John 62 m NC
(Overseer)

786 Farmer ($1,300)
CALDWELL, John J. 35 m Ga
Francina 25 f "
Daniel R. 7 m Ala
Whitfield 3 m "
Lucretia 1/12 f "

707 Farmer
CALHOUN, James 45 m Ga
Nancy 32 f SC
Elizabeth 8 f Ala
Ann 6 f "
Nancy 4 f "
Vincent 2 m "
JORDAN, M. (Farmer) 15 m Ga

2062 Farmer ($1,000)
CALLOWAY, Daniel 51 m Ga
Elizabeth 49 f NC
Sarah 21 f Ga
Mary 20 f "
Lucinda 18 f "
Jane 17 f "
Caroline 15 f "
Emeline 14 f Ala
Benjamin 12 m Ala
William 9 m "

799 Farmer
CALLOWAY, Henry 45 m Ga
(cont.)

(# 799 CALLOWAY cont.)
Priscilla 38 f Ga
Mary 17 f "
Elizabeth 15 f Ala
James 12 m "
William 11 m "
Nancy 9 f "
Sarah 6 f "
Martha 5 f "
Henry 2 m "
Thomas 2/12 m "

1305 Merchant ($450)
CALLOWAY, J. S. 26 m Ga
Melissa A. 21 f "
Mary E. 1 f Ala
Narcissa L. 3/12 f "

1306 Merchant ($1,500)
CALLOWAY, P. M. 38 m Ga
Ellen 34 f "
Julia 13 f "
Mary 11 f Ala
Alef 9 f "
Medora 7 f "
Ella 4 f "

2082 Overseer
CALLOWAY, Robert 25 m Ga

1551 Overseer
CALVIN, Thomas 30 m SC
Nancy 26 f "
John 3 m Ala
Thomas 1/12 m "

2113 Farmer
CAMERON, Archibald M. 29 m Ala
Louisa 28 f "
Sidney Ann 10 f "
James 7 m "
Duncan 5 m "
William 4 m "
John 2 m "
Mary 3/12 f "

CAMERON, Elizabeth
(See William Adkins).

CAMERON, James
(See Sarah Odum).

1440 Drayman ($1,200)
CAMERON, John 26 m NC
Nancy 25 f Ga
John 3 m Ala
(Cont.)

(# 1440 CAMERON cont.)

Nancy	1	f	Ala
William (Drayman)	22	m	SC
Allen (Boatman)	17	m	Ga
Thomas	14	m	"

807 Farmer ($650)

CAMERON, Lochlin	65	m	NC
Christian	60	f	"
Caroline	22	f	"
John (Farmer)	21	m	"

808 ($800)

CAMERON, Nancy	67	f	NC
Christian	63	f	"
Mary	67	f	"

1002 Blacksmith

CAMERON, Willis	53	m	NY
Agnes	38	f	NC
Agnes J.	2	f	Ala

1826 Farmer ($50)

CAMPBELL, Abner	30	m	SC
Mary	34	f	Ga
Savannah	12	f	Ala
Elizabeth	10	f	"
William	8	m	"
Cornelius	4	m	"
Geraldine	14	f	"

1825 Farmer ($250)

CAMPBELL, Abner	72	m	SC
Susan	60	f	"

921 Farmer ($200)

CAMPBELL, Archibald	36	m	NC
Mary	33	f	"
William	4	m	Ala
Lewis	9/12	m	"

CAMPBELL, D. C.	34	m	NC

(See Daniel Gillis).

1829 Blacksmith ($1,200)

CAMPBELL, Daniel	40	m	SC
Cornelia	36	f	Ga
Mary	15	f	Ala
Cithy	11	f	"
Nancy	7	f	"
Cinthia	5	f	"
Duncan	1	m	"

1828

CAMPBELL, Elizabeth	53	f	SC
Joab (Farmer)	18	m	Ala

1330 Farmer
(Cont.)

(# 1330 CAMPBELL cont.)

CAMPBELL, Isaac	30	m	SC
Margaret	35	f	"
BRYANT, Fortunatus (Farmer)	17	m	"
Elizabeth	15	f	"
Henry	10	m	Ala
SINGLETON, Reuben (Farmer	31	m	SC

637 Farmer ($250)

CAMPBELL, J. E.	20	m	Ala
Mary	18	f	"

(Married within the year).

1826 Farmer ($300)

CAMPBELL, Jacob	32	m	SC
Martha	22	f	Ala
Britton	4	m	"
Jacob	3	m	"
Robert	6/12	m	"

617

CAMPBELL, John	63	m	NC
Nancy	10	f	Ga
Polly	8	f	"
Martin	6	m	Ala
Jesse	4	m	"
Frances	2	f	"
Lucinda	37	f	Ga

552

CAMPBELL, Nancy	27	f	Ga
Lucy	9	f	Ala
Joel	7	m	"
Anderson	5	m	"
WILKINS, Jemima	35	f	Ga

1842 Farmer

CAMPBELL, Robert	25	m	SC
Ann	23	f	Ga
Mary	4	f	Ala
George	2	m	"
Robert	2/12	m	"
SMITH, Mary	20	f	"

CAMPBELL, Sarah
Alexander
(See William Cox).

CAMPBELL, W. C.
(See George W. Carriker).

1827 Farmer

CAMPBELL, W. W.	32	m	SC
Charlotte	20	f	Ala
Ann	1	f	"

2079 Farmer
CANADY, Jesse 25 m NC
Mary 15 f Ga
Thomas 3 m Ala
Sarah 1 f "

2078 Farmer ($2,500)
Canady, Joseph 65 m NC
Silva 38 f "
John (Farmer) 20 m "
Sheppard 13 m "
Samuel 7 m Ala
Gilbert 3 m "
Catherine 80 f NC

2144 Occupation - none
CANNON, S. R. 57 m SC
Penelope M. 46 f Ga
(Married within the year).
Eliza 13 f Ga
John 11 m Ala
James A.P.J. 8 m "
BETHUNE, John S. 19 m Ala
Nancy 23 f "
Penelope 6/12 f "

CANNON, Thomas J.
(See David Hall).

509 Farmer ($500)
CAPEL, James 52 m NC
Mary 35 f "
Melinda 16 f Ga
Mary 14 f "
Frances 12 f "
James 9 m Ala
Catherine 4 f "
Margaret 2 f "
Alexander 1 m "

1528 Farmer
CARENTON, Richard 42 m Ga
Hester 35 f NC
Martha 4 f Ga
Dinky 8 m "

1527 Farmer ($500)
CARENTON, Wilson 34 m Ga
Mary 26 f "
Ichabod 6 m Ala
Elizabeth 4 f "
Mary 1 f "

CAREW, Franklin
(See John P. Glover)

1739 Printer
(cont.)

(# 1739 CARGILL cont.)
CARGILL, Austin 58 m Mass
Orlando M. 25 m Ky
Austin C. 20 m "
(Cabinet Maker)
Amelia B. 42 f SC
Maria A. 16 f Ky
Amelia J. 14 f La
JORDAN, J. W. 35 m NC
(Painter - $200)

1401 Tanner ($1,000)
CARGILL, Thomas 48 m Ga
Louisa 41 f "
Elizabeth 20 f Ala
Julia 18 f "
John (Student) 15 m "
Thomas 12 m "
Caledonia 9 f "
William 7 m "
Benjamin 3 m "

1520 Farmer ($800)
CARINGTON, Risen 68 m Ga
Rhody 65 f NC
Keziah 21 f Ga
Nancy 19 f "
Doctor (Farmer) 18 m "
Elizabeth 12 f "
Harris 4 m Ala

849 Overseer
CARLISLE, S. J. 34 m Ga
Elizabeth 32 f "
Mary 11 f Ala
Louisa 9 f "
Martha 6 f "
Sarah 1 f "

CARLISLE, Sophia
(See John McBryde).

776 Physician ($1,500)
CARMICHAEL, Arch'd. 33 m SC
Elizabeth 22 f Ga
Abraham 6 m "
George 4 m Ala
Eliza Ann 1 f "
McDUFFIE, Geo. 25 m SC
(Physician)
HARRIS, Thomas 28 m NC
(Merchant - $350)
CARMICHAEL, Malcolm 22 m SC
(Student)
SHANKS, John 24 m "
(Student)
STEWART, Peter 50 m Scot
(Teacher)

778 Blacksmith
CARMICHAEL, H. W. 40 m SC
Flora 36 f NC
Nathaniel 17 m "
John 14 m Ala
Duncan 11 m "
William 4 m "

1008 Farmer ($600)
CARR, James S. 21 m Ala
James (Farmer) 51 m SC
Elizabeth 63 f "
Eliza 23 f Ga

CARR, Mary
(See Tildey Glover).

CARR, Solomon
(See Jesse Ham).

2146 Farmer
CARR, Thomas 35 m Ga
Caroline 34 f "
Thomas 17 m Ala
Frances 14 f "
Louisa 7 f "
James 1 m "
SEAY, Laura 17 f Ga

448 Farmer ($150)
CARR, Tryon 25 m SC
Lucy Ann 15 f "
(Married within the year).
KETCHUM, Wm. W. 6 m Ala
James K. 4 m "
Gilbert M. 2 m "

1745 Painter
CARREN, Michael 38 m Ire
Sarah 28 f Ga
Mary 10 f Ala
Amanda 6 f "
Martha 5 f "
Catherine 4 f "
Ada 9/12 f "
NEWMAN, Clarissa 25 f Ga
Angeline 18 f "

112 Farmer ($10,000)
CARRIKER, George W. 39 m NC
CAMPBELL, W. C. 45 m Ga
(Carpenter)

803
CARRINGTON, James 36 m Ga
Lucy 22 f "
(Cont.)

(# 803 CARRINGTON cont.)
Joseph 4 m Ala
Jane 2/12 f "

CARROLL, George W.
(See James Brock).

725 Farmer ($300)
CARROLL, Henry 24 m NC
Jane 2 f Ala
John W. 1 m "

CARROLL, John
Benjamin
(See Daniel McCall).

276 Farmer ($250)
CARROLL, John 35 m SC
Elizabeth 30 f "
William 14 m Ala
Sarah 12 f "
John 10 m "
Mary 8 f "
Stephen 6 m "
Robert 2 m "

CARROLL, Martha
(See Christina Walker).

CARROLL, Rebecca
(See Wm. N. Atkinson).

135 Farmer
CARROLL, Robert 31 m SC
Elizabeth 22 f "
Rufus 4 m Ala
Irvin 2 m "
Sarah 1 f "
Daniel 13 m SC

447 Farmer
CARROLL, Thomas 50 m NC
Sarah 38 f "
Catherine 13 f "
Elijah 11 m "
Joseph 9 m Ala
James 7 m "
Sarah 6 f "
Frederick 7 m "
Nancy 3 f "
Lucinda 8/12 f "

405 Laborer
CARROLL, Thomas 32 m SC
Nathan 1 m Ala

467 Farmer
(Cont.)

467 Farmer
CARTER, Benjamin 23 m SC
Priscilla J. 24 f "
Joanna T. 3 f Ala
James B. 2 m "
Elizabeth 5/12 f "

625 Farmer ($100)
CARTER, E. D. 39 m SC
Catherine 22 f "
Caroline 5 f Ala
Clementine 2 f "
John W. 1 m "
RAMSEY, Marg. 18 m NC

446 Farmer
CARTER, John 55 m SC
Elizabeth 50 f "
Nancy 25 f "
Sally 17 f "
Moses 19 m "
Esther 12 f "
Gerlaine 11 f Ga

CARTER, Robert
(See Esther Phillips).

CARTER, Salina
(See Henry Goumillion).

CARTER, Samuel
(See George Conner).

2060 Blacksmith
CARTER, William 42 m Ga
Elizabeth 28 f "
Elizabeth 18 f "
Sarah 16 f "
Mary 7 f Ala
William 5 m "

CARTER, William
(See John S. Dobbins).

CARTWRIGHT, Mary
(See Edward Cox).

CASEY, Alfred
(See Harriet Cox).

2271 Farmer
CASEY, Hampton 26 m NC
Epsey 28 f "
Sarah 6 f Ala
Thomas 5 m "
James 2 m "
William 4/12 m "

2272 Farmer
CASEY, James 60 m NC
Nancy 23 f "
Mary 7 f Ala
James 3 m "

529 Farmer ($400)
CASEY, James 25 m NC
Mary 22 f --
Nancy 9/12 f Ala

1835 Farmer ($400)
CASEY, Lemuel 38 m NC
Nancy 34 f Ala
Henry 14 m "
Sarah 12 f "
Mary 10 f "
Edward 8 m "
Julia 6 f "
Nancy 4 f "

CASEY, Louisa
(See James Young).

271 Farmer
CASON, James 44 m NC
Sarah 30 f Ga
James 11 m Ala
Sarah 1 f "

CASON, James R.
(See Francis Boykin).

CASSIDY, Crissey
(See Robt. Worthington).

1277 Lawyer ($2000)
CATO, L. L. 28 m Ga
Martha 20 f "
Sterling G. 33 m "
1276
CATO, Martha 65 f Va

1493 Farmer ($2,500)
CATON, John D. 60 m NC
Euphemia 54 f Ga
Charles (Farmer) 18 m "
Samuel " 15 m "
Allen 13 m "
Tobias 11 m Ala
ROSE, Caroline 16 f Ga
Dorcas 12 f "
KEEN, Lucinda A. 10 f "

1053 Farmer
CATTENHEAD, Ivey P. 29 m Ga
Sarah 30 f SC
(Cont.)

(# 1053 CATTENHEAD cont.)
Powell 4 m Ala
John 2 m "
William 5/12 m "

1394 Trader
CATTERVILLE A. 43 m Fr
Julie (Insane) 36 f "
Ernest 13 m Ala

CAUGHMAN, Isaias
(See Joel Hammeter).

235 Farmer ($800)
CAUSEY, Cullen 50 m NC
Dorothy 45 f "
William (Farmer) 21 m "
Calvin " 18 m "

236 Farmer
CAUSEY, George W. 26 m NC
Martha 18 f Ga
Georgianna 4/12 f Ala

121 Farmer ($150)
CAUSEY, L. C. 23 m NC
Hilda 19 f Ga

1024 Farmer ($200)
CAUSEY, Randerson 25 m NC
Nancy 60 f "
James L. (Farmer) 20 m "
Joseph W. " 18 m "

2013 Farmer
CAWTHON, Joseph 19 m Ala
Elizabeth 18 f Fla

557 Farmer ($2,500)
CAWTHON, William W. 43 m Ga
Charity 39 f "
Josiah 19 m Ala
Simon 13 m "
William W. 12 m "
Sidney 6 m "
Martha 4 f "
Sarah 1 f "

1508 Overseer
CAYTON, George M. T. 24 m Ga

489 Farmer
CHAMBERS, Daniel 90 m NC
Jane 70 f "

1950 Farmer
CHAMBERS, David 47 m SC
Elizabeth 40 f "
(Cont.)

(# 1950 CHAMBERS cont.)
Mary 20 f SC
Joseph 18 m "
Darinda 15 f Ala
Hulda 12 f "

652 Farmer ($1,000)
CHAMBERS, Isaac 38 m SC
Melinda 28 f "
Martha 14 f Ala
Clarinda 12 f "
Louisa 10 f "
Amanda 8 f "
William 6 m "
James 4 m "
Isaac 1 m "

972 Farmer
CHAMBERS, L. D. 43 m SC
Mary 26 f "
(L.D. & Mary married within the year).
Elizabeth 16 f SC
Maria 11 f "
Ezekiel 8 m "
Martha 4 f Ala
Marshall 3 m "
Adeline 1 f "

1102 Ditcher
CHANDLEY, Thomas E. 48 m Ire

CHANEY, James O.
(See Robt. T. Hightower)

287 Farmer ($800)
CHANEY, John 50 m NC
Milbra 53 f "
Savime(?) Milbra 3 f Ala

409 Miller ($100)
CHEESBRO, James 51 m Ct*
Anna 40 f SC
Mary 17 f "
Irena 16 f Ga
Gordon 14 m "
Elizabeth 13 f "
John 11 m "
Prentiss 6 m "

2036 Farmer ($600)
CHESNUT, Mitchell 44 m NC
Sarah 34 f Ga
Georgia 13 f "
(Cont).

* Ct. Connecticut?

(# 2036 CHESNUT cont).

Delphia 10 f Ala
James 4 m "
Catherine 6 f "
John 3 m "
Mitchell 6/12 m "

414 Farmer
CHILDS, Elijah 33 m NC
Nancy 33 f "
Penelope 11 f "
Ellen 9 f "
Mary J. 7 f "
Lilly Ann 5 f Ala
Lydia 2 f "

1839 Farmer
CHILDS, Holden 28 m NC
Sarah 23 f Ga
Elizabeth 8/12 f Ala

410 Farmer ($400)
CHILDS, John 50 m NC
Eliza 41 f "
James (Farmer) 19 m "
Harriett 17 f "
Elijah 14 m "
Sarah 11 f "
Eliza 8 f "
Benjamin 6 m "
Andrew J. 3 m Ala
Philip 1 m "
CARR, John W. 1 m "
David 5/12 m "

1840 Farmer
CHILDS, Philip 35 m NC
Elizabeth 30 f "
Judy 25 f "
Sarah 25 f "
Sarah 77 f "

951 Overseer
CHITWOOD, James 40 m Ga
Frances 26 f "
Lewis 8 m "
Octavus 4 m Ala
Frances 1 f "

2101 Farmer ($2,000)
CHRISTIAN, Lewis 23 m SC
Cinthia 20 f Ga
Emily 2 f "
Sarah 2/12 f Ala

15 Farmer
(Cont.)

(# 15 CLARK cont.)

CLARK, Daniel 45 m SC
Eliza 39 f "
Samuel (Farmer) 20 m Ga
Daniel " 17 m "
Charlotty 16 f "
James 12 m "
Sarah 10 f "
Stephen 8 m "
Andrew 5 m "
Caroline 2 f "

CLARK, George
(See A. B. Starke).

958 Farmer ($2,000)
CLARK, James 58 m SC
Harriet 55 f "
Mary 34 f "
Elizabeth 16 f Ga
Martha 14 f "
DANFORTH, Mary E. 10 f "
Angela 8 f "
WISE, Arch'd. 43 m SC
(Occp. - none)
MAYS, M. G.(?) 18 m Ala
(Laborer)

1661 Farmer ($200)
CLARK, John G. 40 m SC
Lucinda 35 f Ga
William 17 m "
Hilliard 14 m "
Mary 12 f "
Sarah 10 f Ala
Martha J. 6 f "
Caroline 8 f "
Lucinda (?)20 f "

708 Merchant
CLARK, John W. 25 m SC
Emeline 19 f Ala
(John W. & Emeline married within the year).
Whit (Merchant) 24 m SC
DANFORTH, Francis 15 m Ga
(Clerk)

CLARK, William
(See William Fleming).

1346 Machinist ($1,000)
CLARKE, Henry 50 m Conn
Sophia 40 f "
Henry W. (Boatman) 22 m Ohio
Georgia 9 f Ala

145 Farmer ($1,000)
CLARKE, John 46 m Ga
Elizabeth 36 f SC
William (Farmer) 16 m Ala
Warren 12 m "
Elizabeth 11 f "
Amanda 9 f "
John J. 7 m "
Linson G. 2 m "
Mary C. 1 f "

155 Farmer
CLARKE, John F. 34 m Ga
Nancy 26 f NC
Missouri 12 f Ga
Stephen 9 m Ala
Mary 7 f "
Charles 5 m "
John F. 1 m "

146 Farmer ($300)
CLARKE, Thomas J. 42 m Ga
Eliza 41 f NC
Thomas (Farmer) 17 m Ala
William 15 m "
Nancy 13 f Ga
John H. 11 m "
Eliza 8 f Ala
James 6 m "
Augustus 2 m "

264 Farmer
CLARKE, William J. 51 m SC
Mary 45 f "
Dreurry (Farmer) 24 m Ga
Matthew " 21 m "
Jane 18 f "
Ann 15 f "
James 13 m "
Daniel 9 m Ala
Margaret 7 f "
John 2 m "

712 Lawyer ($1,000)
CLAYTON, Henry D. 23 m Ga
Victoria 18 f SC
(Married within the year).

1226 Teacher
CLEGHORNE, W. C. P. 46 m Scot
Drady 31 f SC
Richard 2 m Ala
William 6/12 m "

922 Farmer ($800)
CLEMENTS, James 50 m SC
(Cont.)

(# 922 CLEMENTS cont.)
Nancy 39 f Ga
George (Farmer) 19 m Ala
Mary 15 f "
John 12 m "
James 10 m "
Benjamin 7 m "
Zachariah 4 m "
Sarah 2 f "

1724 Farmer ($400)
CLEMENTS, Jesse 25 m Ga
Lupina 21 f Ala
Francis 2 m "
James 1 m "

2130 Farmer ($500)
COBB, James A. 33 m Ga
Elizabeth 17 f "
Winfield 1 m Ala

831 Farmer
COBB, Joseph 51 m Ga
Elizabeth 41 f "
Franklin (Farmer) 22 m Ala
Jeremiah 16 m "
Jacob 16 m "
Thomas 10 m "
Ann M. 4 f "
Henrietta 2 f "
JOSEY, J. J. 22 m NC
(Farmer)

1757 Farmer ($1,300)
COBB, McCURIN 37 m Ga
Harriet 33 f "
Joshua (Farmer) 18 m "
John 17 m "
Mary 16 f "
Susannah 14 f "
Walton 13 m "
Jesse 11 m "
Nancy 10 f "
Francis 9 m "
Carey 4 m "
Harriet 5/12 f Ala

2131 Farmer ($350)
COBB, William 27 m Ga
Molsey 20 f SC
Bethena 4 f Ala
Jacob 1 m "
WEAVER, David 19 m Ga
(Farmer)
WHITTINGTON, Jacob 12 m Ala

266 Lawyer ($2,000)
COCHRAN, John 37 m Tenn
Mary 27 f Ga
Alfred W. 2 m "

801 ($1,000)
CODEY, Mary 50 f Ga
Michael (Farmer) 23 m "
Sophronia 16 f "
Benjamin 12 m "
Milman 9 m "
STINSON, Sarah 80 f SC

802 Farmer
CODY, Green 28 m Ga
Millia 23 f "
James 4 m "
Southward 3 m Ala
Sarah 2 f "

1644 Farmer ($1,200)
COKER, Isaac N. 34 m SC
Elizabeth 40 f "
Thomas M. (Farmer) 16 m "
Emma 14 f "
Elizabeth 12 f "
Seaborn 10 m "
Adrianna 8 f Ala
Mary 6 f "
George 4 m "
Louisianna 2 f "

263 Farmer
COKER, John M. 45 m SC
Nancy 25 f "
William 17 m "

1278 Merchant
COLBY, John 38 m Ire
Charlotte 25 f Ga
Mary 5 f "
Ann 2 f "
Susan 1 f "
MORGAN, Jas. C. 27 m "
(Clerk)
DUTTON, M. (Tailor) 27 m Eng

38 Overseer
COLE, James 37 m Ga
Rebecca 24 f "
SIMPSON, Mary H. 19 f "
MORRIS, W. F. 26 m Va
(Millwright)

2226 Farmer
COLE, John S. 35 m Ga
Mary 28 f "

839 Farmer
COLE, J. S. 52 m NC
Nancy 48 f "
Zilpha 24 f "
Elizabeth 22 f "
Catherine 20 f "
Caroline 19 f Ala
David 16 m "
Mary 14 f "
Nancy 8 f "
Josiah 6 m "
Martha 5 f "

COLE, Mary
(See Joel Sims).

COLE, Sarah
(See Thomas S. Locke).

713 Carpenter
COLEMAN, Jesse B. 38 m Ga
Nancy 26 f "
Eugenia 5 f Ala
Albert 3 m "
Ann 1 f "
VENTRESS, Nancy 60 f Ga
ALEXANDER, Francis M. 23 m "
(Carpenter)

769 ($3,000)
COLEMAN, Keziah 50 f SC
William T. (Farmer) 23 m Ga
Benjamin F. 10 m Ala
PRUETT, R. A. 18 m Ga
Virginia 2 f "
ROBERTS, James 24 m "
(Overseer)

1575 Farmer ($1,700)
COLEMAN, Thomas R. 35 m Ga
Mary 28 f "
Richard R. 11 m Ala
Sarah 8 f "
Mary 5 f "

893 Overseer
COLEMAN, William J. 38 m Ga
Mary 24 f SC
Sarah 9 f Ala
Elizabeth 7 f "
William 5 m "
James 3 m "
Jesse 1 m "

COLLINS, Hartwell
(See Seth Mabry).

1959 Farmer
COLLINS, John 26 m Ga
Elizabeth 24 f "
John 7 m Ala
William 5 m "
James 2 m "
Mary 6/12 f "

932 Farmer
COLLINS, Munford 25 m Ala
Mary 21 f Ga
(Above two married within the year).
William (Farmer) 19 m Ala

666 Farmer ($7000)
COLLINS, Wilson 64 m NC
Adeline 9 f Ala

844 Farmer ($4000)
COMER, John F. 40 m Ga
Catherine 26 f "
Hugh N. 7 m "
John W. 5 m "
St. George L. 3 m Ala
Bragg 1 m "
ARNOLD, James A. 27 m SC
(Teacher)

1964 Laborer
CONDRY, James 35 m SC
Ailsey 38 f Ga
Susan 16 f Ala
John 14 m "
Elizabeth 12 f "
Catherine 7 f "
Daniel 5 m "
John 3 m "
William 6/12 m "

1069 Farmer ($2,000)
CONDRY, John 45 m SC
Elizabeth 33 f "
Dennis (Farmer) 17 m Ala
Mary 15 f "
John 12 m "
George 1 m "
WOOD, Wm. (Farmer) 35 m Ga
CONDRY, Elizabeth 7 f Ala

787 Farmer ($700)
CONNELLY, J. Z.(L?) 48 m SC
Rachel 40 f "
James (Farmer) 20 m "
Martha 16 f "
William 14 m "
(Cont.)

(# 787 CONNELLY cont.)
Amanda 13 f SC
Emily 11 f "
McPherson 10 m "
David 8 m "
Capers 6 m "
Polk 4 m Ala
Jane 2 f "
Caroline 6/12 f "

1556 Farmer
CONNER, George 55 m SC
Louisa 35 f Ga
Henrietta 16 f SC
Francis 14 m "
William 9 m Ala
Louisa 6 f "
Sophronia 4 f "
George 1 m "
CARTER, Samuel 70 m Va
(Farmer)

1567 Physician ($3,000)
CONNER, George D. 30 m SC

1557 Tailor
CONNER, James G. 32 m SC
Frederika 16 f Pa
(Married within the year).

369 Farmer
COOK, Alexr. H. 32 m SC
Eliza 20 f Ala
Martha 3 f "
William M. 2 m "
Jesse 1 m "

COOK, Amanda
William
(See Ferdinand Lee).

1216 Farmer
COOK, Hiram 27 m Ga
Sarah 24 f "
Peter 6 m "
Mary 2 f Ala
Sarah 4/12 f "

2225 Farmer ($300)
COOK, John 55 m Ga
Elizabeth 50 f "
Jasper 21 m "
Mary 17 f "
William 13 m "

1460 Farmer
COOK, John 76 m NC
(Cont.)

(# 1460 COOK cont.)
Mary 75 f Ga

2115 Farmer
COOK, Joseph 30 m Ga
Elizabeth 25 f SC
John 6 m Ala
Mary 4 f "
Joseph 2 m "

2169 Overseer
COOK, William 28 m Ga
Mary 22 f "
Elizabeth 4 f Ala
Amanda 3 f "
Mary 2 f "

COOLEY, Sarah
(See Peter Haigler)

1063 Farmer ($780)
COOPER, A. D. 49 m Ga
Elizabeth 49 f NC
Emeline 20 f Ala
Thomas 16 m "
Sarah 14 f "
John 12 m "
Jason 10 m "
Archibald 5 m "

1496 Farmer ($300)
COOPER, Thomas 43 m NC
Elizabeth 31 f SC
Mary 9 f Ala
Sarah 8 f "
Missouri 6 f "
John 3 m "
Elizabeth 1 f "
BENSON, John F. 66 m NC
(Teacher)

1425 Blacksmith
COOPER, Wiley L. 30 m Ala
Elizabeth 26 f "
Thomas 5 m "
Nancy 3 f "
James 1 m "

1984 Laborer
COOPER, William D. 22 m Ala
Matilda 23 f "

1229 Farmer
COPELAND, John N. 38 m SC
Carolina 38 f "
Florida 8 f Ala
(Cont.)

(# 1229 COPELAND cont.)
Preston 4 m Ala
John 2 m "
Caroline 23 f Ga
GARVIN, L. L. 17 f SC

779 Teacher ($800)
CORLEY, J. C. 37 m SC
Virginia 20 f Fla

1183 Blind
CORLEY, Mary 70 f SC
Nancy 45 f "
(Deaf & dumb).

1513 Overseer
COSBY, A. Y.(G.?) 33 m Ga
Jane 16 f "
(Married within the year).

2290 Farmer
COSTEN, Owen 40 m NC
Ellender 38 f "
Martha 14 f "
Joseph 9 m Ala
Effey 7 f "

COTTON, George W.
(See S. S. Walkley).

1381 Grocer ($1,200)
COURIC, Charles M. 32 m Fr
Henrietta 45 f "
Charles 9 m Ala
Alexis 7 m "
Frances 5 f "
Alida 3 f "

1674 Farmer ($100)
COURTNEY, Griffin 48 m SC
Mary 40 f "
William (Farmer) 24 m "
Lucy 22 f "
John " 18 m "
Janet 15 f "
Levi 12 m "
Thomas 10 m "
Elizabeth 8 f "
James 7 m "
Goran 5 m "
Mary 1 f "

COVINGTON, Elizabeth
Emily
Mary
Jeremiah
(See John S. Berryhill).

1812 Insane
COWART, J. E. P. 46 m Ga
Louisa 38 f "
Addison (Farmer) 17 m "
Georgia A. 15 f "
Regina 12 f Fla
John 10 m Ala
John 9/12 m "

911 Farmer ($10,000)
COWART, William 67 m SC
Susan 28 f NC
William 4 m Ala
Michael 2 m "
BLAKEY, James 22 m Ga
(Overseer)

2160 Farmer ($1,000)
COWEN, E. B. 34 m Ala
Catherine 23 f SC
Daniel 6/12 m Ala
ROLLINS, Sarah 40 f Ga
John 7 m "

1153 Farmer
COWEN, James 35 m Mass
Elizabeth 35 f SC
James P. 12 m "
Julietta 5 f Ala
Daniel W. 3 m "
Anna 1/12 f "

1497 Preacher, P. B. * ($750)
COWEN, John G. 44 m SC
Mary 42 f NC
George (Farmer) 20 m Ga
Narcissa 17 f "
Mary 16 f "
Samuel 14 m "
John C. 9 m "
Joshua 6 m Ala
James 3 m "
Franklin 1 m "

1254 Physician ($7000)
COWEN, William L. 43 m Tenn
Ann 38 f Ga
Maldonetta 13 f Ala
Laura 11 f "
James 10 m "
Mary 8 f "
Ann 6 f "
Emily 4 f "
(Cont).

* P. B. - Primitive Baptist

(# 1254 COWEN cont.)
Rosa 2 f Ala
WARE, Edward 22 m Ga
(Preacher).

2234 Judge ($1,500)
COWEN, William R. 38 m Ga

1529 Clerk
COWLES, W. T. 31 m Ga
Caroline 23 f "
(Married within the year).

1880 Farmer
COX, Caleb 50 m Ga
Eliza 48 f "

1832 Farmer
COX, Edward 70 m SC
CARTWRIGHT, Mary 58 f NC
GRUBBS, Stephen 30 m Ala
(Farmer)
Caroline 25 f Ga
John 8 m Ala
Elizabeth 6 f "
Edward 1 m "

597 ($5500)
COX, Emanuel 54 m NC
Sarah 45 f "
Ann 20 f Ala
John (Student) 18 m "
Elizabeth 16 f "
Charles M. 13 m "
William 13 m "
Hamilton 7 m "
James L. 5 m "

COX, Green S.
(See Edwin James).

1887 ($100)
COX, Harriet 28 f NC
Amanda 6 f Ala
CASEY, Alfred 21 m NC
(Farmer).

1881 Farmer
COX, James 22 m Ga
Julia 17 f "
(Above two m. within the year).
Elizabeth 12 f Ala
Alexander 13 m "
John 10 m "

618 Farmer ($400)
COX, Jesse 41 m Ga
(Cont.)

(# 618 COX cont.)

Sarah	41	f	NC
Nancy	15	f	Ala
Mary	12	f	"
Helen	10	f	"
William	6	m	"
John	2	m	"
Charles	8/12	m	"

504 Farmer ($1,600)

COX, Jimsey	39	m	Ga
Rachel	40	f	SC
Rosa A.	15	f	Ala
Nancy	13	f	"
Mary A.	11	f	"
Sarah	9	f	"
Rachel	6	f	"
Julia	2	f	"

1854 Laborer

COX, Joseph	33	m	SC
Letty	30	f	"
Idonia	8	f	Ala
John	6	m	"
Mary	4	f	"
William	2	m	"

1879 Farmer ($300)

COX, Sherman	26	m	Ga
Maria	23	f	NC
Caroline	2	f	Ala
Mary	2/12	f	"

1833 Farmer

COX, William	65	m	SC
Jane	60	f	"
William (Farmer)	22	m	Ala
Vicey	16	f	"
Matilda	20	f	"
Curran	14	m	"
Catherine	14	f	"
John	11	m	"
CAMPBELL, Sarah	26	f	"
Alexander	2	m	"

1517 Farmer ($500)

CRAIG, Loderick	53	m	SC
Rebecca	47	f	Ga
Frances	23	f	"
John (Farmer)	21	m	"
Jane	20	f	"
Lucinda	18	f	"
Rebecca	17	f	"
Mary	15	f	"
William	13	m	"

(Cont.)

(# 1517 CRAIG cont.)

Susan	12	f	Ga
James	10	m	Ala
Henry	8	m	"
Elizabeth	5	f	"
PEDDY, Jeremiah	21	m	Ga

210 Laborer

CRANE, Sarah	50	f	Ga
ATWELL, Alexander	19	m	"
Rosanna	16	f	"

1534 Farmer ($5700)

CRAPS, Benjamin	56	m	SC
Louisa	54	f	"
Emily	11	f	Ala
Mary	12	f	Ga
HUGENON, Sarah	58	f	SC

CRAPS, Jane V.
(See John C. P. Kennyman)

CRAULEY, Patience
(See Henry Hall)

1459 Farmer ($10,000)

CRAWFORD, A. P.	45	m	Va
Cassandra	38	f	Ga
Ella R.	9	f	Ala
Virginia	7	f	"
Alexander	5	m	"
Virgil	1	m	"

173 Farmer ($1,000)

CRAWFORD, Nicholas W.	35	m	NC
Linsey B.	28	f	"
James W.	5	m	Ala
Melissa	4	f	"
Mary	2	f	"
Arthur	4/12	m	"
Pipkin, Jackson (Farmer)	23	m	NC

CRAYON, Mary F. & James
(See Daniel Shehan).

2258 Farmer ($300)

CREECH, Aaron	29	m	NC
Charity	21	f	Ala
Mary	1/12	f	"
CREECH, Jane	65	f	SC

CREECH, David
Wesley & Franklin
(See Levi Glass).

2232 Farmer ($500)
(Cont.)

(# 2232 CREECH cont).

CREECH, William C.	40	m	Ga
Amanda	30	f	"
Josephine	10	f	Ala
Sidney	8	m	"
Henry Clay	7	m	"
Francis	5	m	"
Margaret	3	f	"
Amanda	3/12	f	"

1416 Farmer ($175)

CREEL, John	23	m	SC
Mary	21	f	"

275 Farmer ($1,250)

CREEL, Levi	44	m	SC
Sina	47	f	"
Daniel (Occp. - none)	22	m	"
William F. (Farmer)	20	m	"
James "	16	m	"
George	14	m	"
Mary	12	f	Ala
Preston	10	m	"
Levi	8	m	"
Duncan	6	m	"
Frances	3	f	"

341 Farmer ($400)

CREEL, Thomas	36	m	SC
Louisa	34	f	"
Mary	9	f	Ala
Georgia	7	f	"
William	6	m	"
Thomas	3	m	"
Elizabeth	1	f	"

1967 Farmer ($200)

CREEL, William	35	m	SC
Sarah	34	f	Ga
John	13	m	Ala
Jane	11	f	"
Solomon	7	m	"
Mary	5	f	"
Sarah	2	f	"

590 Farmer ($3,000)

CREWS, Arthur	57	m	Ga
Mary	54	f	SC
CREWS, John E. (Farmer)	30	m	Ga

585 Farmer ($1,500)

CREWS, W. B.	33	m	Ga
Catherine	28	f	NC
Mary	7	f	Ala
Nancy	1	f	"

1811 Farmer

CRIDER, David	30	m	NC
Drucilla	21	f	SC
Mary	6	f	Ala
William	4	m	"
Melissa	1	f	"

CRIMES, Cornelia J.
(See Henry L. Jordan).

1941 Farmer ($500)

CROCKER, Cary	45	m	NC
Rebecca	40	f	"
Dorcas	15	f	Ala
John	12	m	"
Bethel	10	m	"
Martha	8	f	"
Wiley	6	m	"
Ann	2	f	"

1857 Farmer ($300)

CROCKER, Munroe	35	m	Ga
Eliza	33	f	"
John	8	m	Ala
Eliza	8	f	"
Nancy	5	f	"
Mary	2	f	"
LEWIS, Penny	25	f	Ga

353 Laborer

CROCKER, William	22	m	Ala
Catherine	19	f	Ga
James A.	2	m	Ala
John C.	11/12	m	"

1985 Laborer

CROSS, Cullen	36	m	Ga
Lucinda	27	f	"
Mary	10	f	"
Sarah	8	f	"
Susan	5	f	"
Jane	2	f	Ala

58 Farmer

CROW, Madison M.	37	m	SC
Melvina	28	f	Ga
Mary B.(?)	10	f	"
Thomas T.	7	m	Ala
Randolph	6	m	"
Barbary M.	2	f	"

1001 Farmer

CROWLEY, Alfred	29	m	SC
Mary	27	f	"
Eubirnum	10	m	Ala

(Cont.)

(# 1001 CROWLEY cont.)

Martha	7	f	Ala
John	3	m	"
Catherine	1	f	"
RIALLS, Eveline	22	f	Ga
John	2	m	Ala

2222 Laborer

CROWLEY, Washington	24	m	Ga

1284 Farmer ($1,600)

CRUMBLEY, W. R.	30	m	Ga
Mary	30	f	"
William	3	m	Ala

1708 Laborer

CULPEPPER, John	21	m	Ga
Elizabeth	21	f	SC
Martha	1	f	Ga

812 Preacher, M. Baptist ($350)

CUMBIE, Andrew	46	m	SC
Celia	43	f	"
Emeline	22	f	"
James (Farmer)	21	m	"
Lucy	18	f	Ga
Barnebas (Farmer)	16	m	"
Thomas	14	m	"
Judson	12	m	"
Chisley	10	m	"
Samantha	8	f	"
Angeline	6	f	"
John	4	m	Ala
William	5/12	m	"

751 Farmer

CUMBIE, H. D.	21	m	SC

768 Preacher, M. Bapt. ($600)

CUMBIE, John D.	38	m	SC
Ann	39	f	"
Amanda	16	f	Ga
Louisa	15	f	"
John J.	14	m	"
Mary	12	f	"
Andrew	11	m	"
Marthena	9	f	"
Sarah	8	f	"
Lucinda	7	f	"
William	5	m	"
Elvira	4	f	"
Richard	2	m	Ala
Gainey	1/12	m	"

681 Farmer

CUMMINGS, S. J.	25	m	Ga
Mary P.	20	f	NC

1669 Farmer

CUNNING(?), Joseph	17	m	Ga

107 Farmer ($1,200)

CUNNINGHAM, Duncan	50	m	NC
John (Farmer)	19	m	Ala
Margaret	16	f	"
Archibald	13	m	"
Rankin	11	m	"
HUTCHINSON, John (Laborer)	16	m	"

CUNNINGHAM, James
(See John McLeod)

CUNNINGHAM, James
(See Grave A. Pease).

CUNNINGHAM, James B.
Elizabeth
Thomas
James
(See Thomas Fail).

924 Farmer

CUNNINGHAM, Peter	30	m	Ala
Dovey E.	19	f	Fla
Catherine	2/12	f	Ala
JERNIGAN, Fereby M.	16	f	Ga

2016 Farmer ($500)

CURENTON, Seaborn O.	24	m	Ga
Sarah	26	f	"
Susan	4/12	f	Ala

656 Farmer ($1,600)

CURRIE, Daniel	53	m	NC

501 Wheelwright

CURRIE, Daniel W.	55	m	NC
Jemima	39	f	"
John M. (Farmer)	17	m	SC
Gilbert L. "	15	m	"
William H.	10	m	Ala
Phillip R.	3	m	"
Margaret	13	f	SC
Mary E.	8	f	Ala

CUSHMAN, George F.
(See William T. DeWitt).

548 Merchant ($800)

DAFFIN, William R.	43	m	Md.
Mary	32	f	NC

(Cont.)

(# 548 DAFFIN cont.)

Philip	9	m	Fla
Horace E.	7	m	"
Frances	5	f	Ala
Charlotte	3	f	"
Mary	1	f	"
FINLEY, Benjamin	14	m	NC

1283 Farmer ($8,000)

DALE, Robert O.	47	m	Ga
Catherine	48	f	"
Jane	74	f	NC
MOSELY, Angeline P.	6	f	Ala

1101 Carpenter

DALTON, Tristam	40	m	Me
Ann	33	f	Ga
Jeremiah	9	m	Ala
George	5	m	"
Thomas	4/12	m	"
SIMMONS, Augustus	13	m	"

1949 Farmer ($100)

DANFORD, Abraham	68	m	SC
Sarah	65	f	"
Martha	27	f	Ala
Edward (Farmer)	17	m	"

DANFORD, Eli M.
(See George Herring).

450 Farmer

DANFORD, Joseph	36	m	NC
Jane	28	f	"
James F.	9	m	Ala
Abraham	7	m	"
Polly	6	f	"
John	4	m	"
Alexr.	6/12	m	"

516 Blacksmith ($325)

DANFORD, Thomas	40	m	NC
Louisa	30	f	Ga
John M.	14	m	Ala
Alexander	11	m	"
Thomas J.	9	m	"
Elizabeth	5	f	"
Zach. T.	2	m	"

499 Laborer

DANFORD, William	30	m	NC
Mary	25	f	"
Amanda	8	f	Ala
Patsey	9	f	"
John	5	m	"
James	2	m	"

1228 Merchant ($800)

DANFORTH, David	32	m	Ga
Frances	26	f	NY
Grace	1	f	Ala
WILLIAMS, Ella	11	f	---
DANFORTH, Oliver (Merchant)	62	m	Mass

DANFORTH, Francis
(See John W. Clark).

2209 Post (Port?) master
(Property: $3,000)

DANFORTH, JOSHUA H. *	33	m	Ga *
Sarah A.	26	f	SC
Rachel M.	9	f	Ala
William S.	7	m	"
Wesley D.	4	m	"
Henry	2	m	"
SAYRE, P. Tucker (Lawyer)	26	m	Va
HILL, John M. (Overseer)	25	m	SC

1077 ($125)

DANIEL, Ann J.	40	f	SC
James	14	m	Ala
Wayne	5	m	"
Malinda	3	f	"

1592 ($4,100)

DANIEL, Eliza C.	48	f	Ga
Samuel (Student)	18	m	"
Juliet	15	f	"
Sarah	13	f	Ala
HILL, Hulda	18	f	Ga
REES, Marietta	14	f	"

1992 Laborer

DANIEL, F. A.	24	m	Ga
Elizabeth	21	f	Ala
Jane	4	f	"
Thomas	2	m	"

DANIEL, James
(See E. B. Young)

1565 Farmer

DANIEL, James H.	22	m	Ga

460 Laborer

DANIEL, John	33	m	NC
Jane	6	f	Ala

(Cont.)

* Married Sarah Ann Snipes (b. 8 Feb. 1823, dau. of W. H. & Mariah Snipes, Barbour Co., Ala.)

(# 460 DANIEL cont.)

Lydia A.	4	f	Ala
Martha M.	3	f	"

DANIEL, John L.
(See Henry L. Jordan).

2137 Farmer ($ 3,600)

DANIEL, Levi T.	33	m	Ga
Ellen	23	f	"
James	4	m	Ala
Martha	2	f	"
Sarah	4/12	f	"
BLUNT, Sarah M.	55	f	NC

1087 Farmer

DANIEL, Moses	31	m	Ga
Louisa	27	f	Ala
Mary	9	f	"
Littleton	7	m	"
Sarah	4	f	"
Amanda	6/12	f	"

1452 Carpenter ($2,000)

DANIEL, Zodoc J.	40	m	NC
Ann	38	f	"
Missouri	16	f	Ga
Virginia	4	f	Ala
Zodoc	2	m	"

633 Occp. not given. ($1,000)

DANNER, Thomas M.	40	m	Ga
Mary	40	f	SC
Mary A.	15	f	Ala
Elizabeth	13	f	"
Thomas	12	m	"
Abraham	11	m	"
Jane	10	f	"
John	8	m	"
Sarah	7	f	"
Virginia	5	f	"
Martha	4	f	"
William H.	3	m	"
James D.	1	m	"

484 Farmer ($900)

DANSBY, Isham	40	m	SC
Abigail	27	f	"
Mary	10	f	Ala
Martha	8	f	"
Lawrence	6	m	"
Thomas P.	4	m	"

416 Farmer ($1,000)

DANSBY, John	45	m	SC

(Cont.)

(# 416 DANSBY cont.)

Sarah	33	f	Ga
Hiram (Farmer)	18	m	Ala
Martha	16	f	"
Elizabeth	14	f	"
Daniel	12	m	"
Vinsey	10	f	"
John	11	m	"
George	9	m	"
Catherine	7	f	"
Hasten	6	m	"
Harmon	4	m	"

457

DARE(?), Rachel	50	f	SC
Nicey	14	f	Ala

2034 Farmer

DAVEY, Marshall C.	30	m	Ga
Jane	25	f	"
Wellborn	10	m	"
Reuby Ann	6	f	"
Marshall	4	m	"
Mercer	2	m	"

902 Poorhouse

DAVIS, Atwell	80	m	Va

1075 Farmer

DAVIS, Benjamin A.	27	m	SC
Mary	23	f	Ga
Calvin	3	m	Ala
James	2	m	"

DAVIS, David
(See Samuel Marshall)

736 Farmer ($300)

DAVIS, Elisha	47	m	Ga
Serena	35	f	"
John (Farmer)	16	m	Ala
Mason	13	m	"
Pleasant	11	m	"
Elizabeth	9	f	"
Nash	4	m	"
Orran	2	m	"
Sarah	1	f	"

1783 Farmer ($2,000)

DAVIS, Gardner H.	45	m	Ga
Mary	36	f	"
Hiram	15	m	Ala
Epenetus	13	m	"
James	11	m	"
Henry	9	m	"
William	6	m	"

(Cont.)

(# 1783 DAVIS cont.)

Sarah	4	f	Ala
Zachariah	2	m	"

2181 Laborer - convict

DAVIS, Henry B.	43	m	SC
Elizabeth	28	f	Ala
George	4	m	"
Frances	3	f	"
Rosaline	1	f	"

525 Wheelwright

DAVIS, James	30	m	Ga
Martha	25	f	"
Sarah	8	f	"
Mary	6	f	"
James	4	m	"
Robert	2/12	m	Ala

2150 Farmer ($1,100)

DAVIS, John	49	m	NC
Mary	42	f	Ga
Thomas (Farmer)	18	m	"
John "	15	m	"
Martha	12	f	"
Wright	9	m	"
Darling	7	m	Ala
Jarnigan	5	m	"
James	1	m	"
William (Farmer)	21	m	Ga

887 Farmer ($1,000)

DAVIS, John F.	52	m	Ga
Catherine	46	f	SC
David	21	m	Ga
Wesley (Farmer)	19	m	Ala
Eliza	17	f	"
John F.	14	m	"
Zachariah	9	m	"
Berrien	7	m	"
Joseph	2	m	"

1960 Farmer

DAVIS, Jonathan	46	m	Ga
Mary	38	f	"
John (Farmer)	16	m	"
Wade	14	m	"
Sarah	12	f	"
Elizabeth	10	f	Ala
Mary	8	f	"
Thomas	6	m	"
James	3	m	"

2098 Farmer ($200)

DAVIS, Leroy J.	25	m	SC

(Cont.)

(# 2098 DAVIS cont.)

Jane	21	f	SC
Mary	8	f	"
Thomas	6	m	"
John	5	m	"
Caroline	3	f	Ala
Leroy	1	m	"

46 (Property: $400)

DAVIS, Margaret	50	f	SC
Gayles A. (Farmer)	16	m	Ala
Calvin J.	13	m	"
Henry M.	10	m	"
Capers	8	m	"
Jane	6	f	"
Elizabeth	4	f	"

DAVIS, Martha
Eliza
(See William Green).

DAVIS, Mary
(See Thomas Smart).

DAVIS, Nancy
Mary A. E.
Lucy
(See James Grantham).

DAVIS, Noah
(See Nathan Bush).

Davis, Richard
(See William J. Barrow).

1645 Laborer

DAVIS, Starling	25	m	Ga
Frances	20	f	"
Reuben	6	m	Ala
Allen	2	m	"

45 Farmer ($400)

DAVIS, Western K.	26	m	SC
Sarah	27	f	Ga
Melinda	9	f	Ala
Sarah A.	1	f	"

1142 Farmer

DAVIS, William	60	m	Ga
Rebecca	47	f	"
John (Idiot)	26	m	"
Elizabeth	20	f	"
William (Farmer)	18	m	"
Abner (Idiot)	14	m	Ala
Vincent	12	m	"
Richmond (Idiot)	8	m	"
Rebecca	7	f	"

989 Farmer

DAVIS, William	60	m	Ga
Rebecca	47	f	"
John (Farmer)	24	m	"
Elizabeth	22	f	"
William "	18	m	"
Abner "	14	m	Ala
Vincent	10	m	"
Richmond	8	m	"
Rebecca	6	f	"

DAVIS, William E.
Mildred
(See Aaron T. Spence).

1117 Farmer ($3,000)

DAWKINS, A. T.	44	m	Ga
Mary	32	f	Ala
A. J.	11	m	Ga
Sarah	16	f	"
MOORE, William B.	13	m	Ala
Americus	8	m	"
James	6	m	"
Mary	3	f	"

2265 Farmer ($65)

DAWSON, John	56	m	SC
Keziah	44	f	Ga
Henry (Farmer)	17	m	"
Sarah	15	f	"
Joseph	14	m	"
Mary E.	12	f	"
Martha	10	f	"
Thomas	8	m	Ala
Susan	6	f	"
John	5	m	"
Louisa	3	f	"
James	1	m	"

1059 Farmer ($200)

DAWSON, Joseph	35	m	SC
Eady	19	f	NC
Martha	12	f	Ala
Mary E.	7	f	Ga
Thursy	6	f	Ala
William	2	m	"
John	10/12	m	"

719 Farmer ($50)

DAY, Amaria	45	m	NC
Elizabeth	52	f	"
BENEY, Christian	88	f	"

DAY, James
(See Martin McGilberry)

1709 Farmer ($300)

DAY, Reddin	68	m	Va
Jane	54	f	NC
Thomas (Farmer)	20	m	Ala
Mary	18	f	"

1710 Farmer

DAY, William	24	m	Ala
Sarah	23	f	"
Frances	5	f	"
Emeline	3	f	"

1778 (Occp. not given)

DEAN, James	54	m	NC
Mary	50	f	"
Elizabeth	19	f	"
William	13	m	Ga
James	11	m	"
John	8	m	Ala
Emeline	5	f	"
Sarah	3	f	"

1503 Farmer

DEAN, Robert	42	m	NC
Piety	50	f	"
Emeline	16	f	"
Murdock	14	m	Ga
Joseph	12	m	"
John (Idiot)	9	m	"

1903 Farmer

DEES, Edward	29	m	Ga
Martha	25	f	NC
Frances	4	f	Ga
Mary	3	f	"
Nancy	1	f	"

393 Farmer

DELLEM(?), Benjamin	40	m	NY
Nancy	25	f	SC
Mary	4	f	"
Piety	1	f	Ga

960 Laborer

DELOACH, John G.	39	m	SC
Minerva	24	f	Ala
Sarah	8	f	"

1570 Farmer ($500)

DELOACH, Samuel	49	m	SC
Catherine	29	f	NC

1221 Farmer ($1,900)

DENNARD, J. E.	57	m	Ga
Janet S.	30	f	"
Natilla	17	f	"

DENNIS, Joseph F.
(See Alexander McRae).

1791
DENSON, Augustus R. 38 m NC
Elizabeth 31 f Ga
Mary 10 f Ala
John B. 8 m "
Julia 6 f "
William 4 m "
Augustus 3/12 m "

1578 Farmer ($1,500)
DENSON, Jethro 72 m NC
Rebecca 64 f "

1793 Carpenter ($400)
DENSON, Matthew 45 m NC
Bethia 40 f "
William (Farmer) 19 m Miss
Samuel 13 m Ala
Joseph 11 m "
Amanda 9 f "
Lidia 7 f "
Robert 5 m "
Frances 3 f "
Seaborn 1 m "

2039 Farmer ($6,000)
DENT, John H. 35 m RI
Mary E. 32 f SC
Emma 12 f Ala
Harry(?) 10 m "
Elizabeth 8 f "
Herbert 5 m "
Anna 3 f "
Charles 1 m "

1030 Farmer ($500)
DESHAZO, Benj. F. 28 m SC
Laura 24 f Ga
James L. 2 m Ala
DESHAZO, Gracey 63 f SC
William (Farmer) 17 m "
Thomas 13 m Ala
Andrew 7 m "

1742
DESHAZO, Eliza 36 f Ga
Richard 14 m Ala
Louisa 12 f "
John 9 m "

1979
DESHAZO, Sarah 39 f Ga
Thomas (Laborer) 20 m Ala
James " 16 m "
Elizabeth 10 f "

1978 Farmer ($1,000)
DESHAZO, Wilson 46 m SC
Dilley 41 f Ga
Paul (Farmer) 19 m Ala
Moses " 16 m "
Hugh 12 m "
Louisa 10 f "
Annis 6/12 f "

DeWITT, Ann
(See John A. Mosely).

279 Farmer ($12,000)
DeWITT, William T. 42 m SC
Elizabeth 45 f "
William (Student) 16 m "
John 13 m "
Elizabeth 6 f Ala
CUSHMAN, George F. 35 m RI
(Episcopal) Minister

856 Farmer
DICKENS, Ephriam 60 m NC
Missouri 38 f Ga
Elizabeth 8 f "
Benjamin 6 m "
Thomas 4 m "
Louisa 2 f "
Virginia 1/12 f Ala

1350 Blacksmith ($200)
DICKERSON, A. H. 33 m Va
Louisa 27 f Ga
Arthur 11 m "
Alfred 6 m "

DICKSON, Ann
(See William Wilkins).

723 Miller ($1,100)
DILL, Robert 44 m NH
Thomas (Student) 20 m Ala
William 12 m "
Delilah 10 f "
Adelia 6 f "
Jackson 2 m "
MOCK, David 35 m Va
(Millwright)
Mann, Thomas 22 m SC
(Millwright)

1951 Farmer
DILLISHAW, Jacob 57 m SC
Mary 47 f "
Susan 17 f "
Emily 14 f "
John 12 m Ala
(Cont.)

(# 1951 DILLISHAW cont.)
Elvira 9 f Ala
Hester 6 f "

2116 Prim. Bapt. Preacher ($1,200)
DIXON, J. J. 45 m Ga
Mary 42 f "

630 Farmer
DIXON, William 56 m Ga
Nancy 40 f "
Eliza 19 f Ala
Susan 18 f "
George 15 m "
Mary 12 f "
Martin 11 m "
Allen 9 m "
Marion 7 m "
William 4 m "
Sarah 1 f "

1512 Teacher ($2,500)
DOBBINS, John S. 37 m Ga
Evelina 37 f "
Sarah 10 f "
Roberta 8 f "
Moses 5 m Ala
Anderson 3 m "
Robert 1 m "
CARTER, Wm. (Student) 18 m Ga
PATTERSON, William T. 13 m "

1726 Laborer
DODD, Benjamin 30 m Ga
Martha 35 f "
PEARSON, Green 17 m "

1091 Merchant
DONEY, M. D. 31 m Ga

927 Farmer ($400)
DORMAN, William 49 m SC
Penelope 36 f Ga
William (Farmer) 17 m Ala
Eliza 19 f "
John L.(Z.?) 15 m "
Jerusha 12 f "
Thomas 9 m "
James 7 m "
Alpheus 4 m "
Sarah 2 f "

DOSTER, Simeon J.
(See James M. Pruitt)

42 Teacher
DOUGLASS, J. B. 33 m Ga
(Cont.)

(# 42 DOUGLASS cont.)
Mary 24 f Ga
Robert E. F. 9 m "
William B. 7 m Ala
Sarah C. 4 f Ga
SPENCE, Louisa M. 26 f "

1731 Farmer
DOVE, James H. 26 m Va
Nancy 29 f NC
James 2 m Ala
William 3/12 m "

1339
DOWDY, Martha 54 f Ga
Enoch (Laborer) 21 m "
Hiram " 18 m "
Seaborn 14 m "

1022 Farmer ($800)
DOWLING, Elias 63 m SC
Mary 62 f NC
Keziah 22 f SC

915 Farmer ($400)
DOWLING, Elias 29 m SC
Lucilla 24 f NC
Frances 1 f Ala
FLOURNOY, James 5 m "
Leander 3 m "

1020 Farmer ($1,680)
DOWLING, Hansford 32 m SC
Martha 24 f Ga
Walter 2 m Ala
Zaccheus 9/12 m "
WINSLETT, Madison 19 m "
WEAVER, F. J. 20 f Ga

1761
DRIGGERS, Ann 50 f SC
James 27 m "
(Blk.smith, $700)
Meredith (Farmer) 25 m "
Charles " 22 m "
Isham " 19 m "
Harriet 28 f "

1445 Laborer ($200)
DRIGGERS, Caleb 36 m SC
Elizabeth 32 f "
Edith 12 f Ala
Rebecca 9 f "
LaFayette 6 m "
DeKalb 4 m "
Roseline 6/12 f "

2195 Laborer
DRIGGERS, John 23 m SC

1058 Farmer ($300)
DRIGGERS, Samuel 32 m SC
Elizabeth 32 f "
John 9 m Ala
Charles (Farmer) 21 m SC

935 Brickmason ($150)
DRIGGERS, Samuel 26 m SC
Eliza 20 f "
Mary 6 f Ga

977 Laborer
DRIGGERS, Stephen 40 m SC
Nancy 28 f "
Christopher 10 m Ala
Oliver 6 m "
Emily 8 f "
Tabitha 4 f "

1386 Laborer
DRIGGERS, Windsor 55 m SC
Sarah 50 f Ga
Ebaline 22 f Ala
Georgia 18 f "
Washington 12 m "

169 Farmer
DRISKELL, Elgit 37 m NC
Elizabeth 33 f Ga
Arvagina 13 f Ala
Martha 11 f "
Elizabeth 7 f "
Moses 6 m "
Cinthia 4 f "
Sarah 2 f "

2200 Farmer ($250)
DuBOSE, D. D. 30 m SC
Mary 28 f "
Elizabeth 7 f Ala
Sarah 5 f "
Robert 4 m "
James 2 m "
Ann 4/12 f "

1550 Farmer ($8,000)
DuBOSE, E. E. 47 m SC
Caroline 35 f "
Chester (Student) 18 m "
Eugenia 15 f "
Julia 13 f "
Louisa 11 f Ala
Ella 9 f "
Edwin 7 m "
Laura 5 f "
William 4 m "
(Cont.)

(# 1550 DuBOSE cont.)
Endora 2 f Ala
Caroline 4/12 f "
TYE, Sarah 16 f SC
PERSON, Sarah 13 f Ga
OWENS, Jane 12 f "

231 Farmer
DuBOSE, Isaiah 19 m SC
Edney 20 f Ga
Malichi 5/12 m Ala

367 Farmer ($200)
DuBOSE, James 49 m SC
Mary 36 f "
Nancy 12 f Ala
Sarah 11 f "
Jane 10 f "
Jeptha 7 m "
Arabella 6 f "
Ailsey 4 f "
Robert 8/12 m "

DuBOSE, Jasper
(See V. H. Tate)

404 Farmer ($600)
DuBOSE, R. E. 37 m SC
Ailsey 25 f "
Sarah 6 f Ala
BOOTH, Wm. (Laborer) 17 m ---

232 ($100)
DuBOSE, Sarah 48 f SC
Joel (Farmer) 17 m "
Mary 13 f Ala
Josephine 6 f "

1816 Farmer ($2,500)
DuBOSE, Seaborn J. 48 m Ga
Zilpha 40 f SC
Sophronia 16 f "
Drucilla 15 f "
John P. 13 m "
Julius 11 m "
Caroline 7 f Ala
Lidia 3 f "
George 5 m "
Jane 1 f "

555 Gunsmith
DUDLEY, Oliver 59 m Conn
Jane 50 f Ga
Sarah E. 22 f "
Sidney 11 m "
Mary C. 9 f "

1747 Farmer
DUFFEL, John D. 36 m Ga
Margaret 27 f "
Augustus 10 m "
Jamesann 4 f "
Margaret 1 f "

908 Farmer ($1,400)
DUKE, David 45 m Ga
Malda 41 f "
Rhody 24 f "
Louisa 18 f "
Amanda 15 f "
Martha 13 f Ala
Lillis 5 f "

2000 Farmer ($350)
DUKES, Garret J. 30 m Ga
Elizabeth 25 f "
Archibald 7 m "
Zilpha 5 f "
Harriet 4 f "
Elias 3 m Ala
Susan 2 f "
James 1/12 m "

DUKES, Sarah
(See Grief Palmore).

153 Farmer
DUKES, William 38 m Ga
Margaret 32 f SC
Elizabeth 15 f Ga
Alista 13 f "
George 10 m Ala
Martha 8 f "
James 5 m "
Sarah 3 f "
Nancy 1 f "

DUNAWAY, Rhoda
(See Greenberry Hinote).

1916 Laborer
DUNFORD, Daniel 32 m Ga
Dolly 25 f "
Mary 7 f Ala
Elizabeth 7 f "
Jane 5 f "
Eliza 3 f "
Sarah 1 f "

1997 Farmer ($350)
DUNFORD, Thomas J. 30 m SC
Sarah 24 f Ga
Elizabeth 9 f Ala
(Cont.)

(# 1997 DUNFORD cont.)
John 7 m Ala
James 5 m "
Rosanna 1 f "

1477 Physician ($800)
DUNN, E. A. 53 m Ga
Nancy 38 f "
Louisa 12 f Ala

1074 Farmer
DUNN, Levi 32 m Ga
Sabrina 10 f "
Levina 8 f "
Jane 5 f "
John 2 m Ala

DUTTON, M.
(See John Colby)

2216 Farmer
DYE, William 34 m SC
Affey 33 f Ga
Frances 12 f "
John 10 m "
Tabitha 7 f "
Lethe 4 f Ala
James 1 m "

99 Farmer
DYE, William 29 m SC
Alpha 30 f Ga
Frances 9 f "
John 7 m "
Tabitha 6 f "
Letha 4 f Ala
James G. 1 m "

2202 Laborer
DYKES, David 24 m Ga
Mary 19 f "
James 2 m Ala

11 Farmer ($400)
DYKES, J. 31 m Ga
Elizabeth 23 f "
Archibald 9 m "
Zilpha 8 f "
Harriet 6 f "
Elias 3 m Ala
Susan 1 f "

2201 Farmer
DYKES, Shade 28 m Ga
Eliza 25 f Ala
William 4 m "
Mary 2 f "
Sarah 4/12 f "

1675 Farmer
EASTERLING, David S. 25 m SC
Celia 16 f "
(Married within the year).

569 Minister, M. B.
EATON, George H. 36 m Mass
Louisa A. 21 f SC
Harriet 3/12 f Ga

1155 Farmer ($600)
ECHOLS, Clark 33 m Ga
Hester 33 f "
Elijah 12 m "
Laney A. 8 f Ala
Mary 6 f "
Amanda 4 f "
JONES, Orren (Farmer) 31 m Ga

1650 Farmer ($300)
EDGE, Jesse L. 43 m Ga
Eliza 29 f "
Obediah (Farmer) 20 m Ala
James " 15 m "
Phoebe 14 f "
George 12 m Ga
John 9 m Ala
William 7 m "
Jane 4 f "
Jesse 1 m "

530 Farmer ($250)
EDGE, Jesse L. 43 m Ga
Eliza 35 f "
Obediah (Farmer) 20 m Ala
James " 16 m "
Phoebe 14 f "
George 12 m "
John 11 m "
William 8 m "
Jane 4 f "
Jesse 1 m "

495 Farmer ($700)
EDGE, William 50 m Ga
Cassia 52 f "
Lewis (Farmer) 18 m Ala
Eli 18 m "
Jane 12 f "
HENDERSON, David 20 m "
(Farmer)
Leroy (Occp. - none) 26 m Ga

EAFORD *, Thomas
Gillis
(See Joel D. Warren).

* Efurd

2257 Farmer ($350)
EFORD *, J. A. 28 m SC
Mary 25 f NC
Frances R. 5 f Ala
Eliza 4 f "
Mary 3 f "
Cornelius 6/12 m "

1137
EFORD *, Lucy 79 f SC
FOWLER, Enoch 76 m "
(Farmer)

942 Farmer ($2000)
EFURD, T. C. 50 m SC
Mary 45 f "
William (Farmer) 22 m Ala
Thomas " 18 m "
Mary A. 16 f "
Giles 12 m "
LEWIS, Mary 6 f "

1132 Farmer
EIDSON, James 62 m SC
Rhoda 63 f "
Sarah 24 f Ga
Emeline 22 f "
Nancy 20 f "

1658 Farmer
EIDSON, Orrin 33 m Ga
Sarah 25 f Ala
James 3 m "
Susan 1 f "

EIDSON, Rhoda
Francis
(See William Broach).

1133 Farmer ($500)
EIDSON, Wiley 26 m Ga
Martha 25 f Ala
John 4/12 m "

214 Farmer ($300)
ELKINS, John 32 m SC
Julia 27 f Ga
William (Farmer) 15 m "
ELKINS, Joshua 43 m SC
(Insane).

2292 Laborer
ELLIOT, James 47 m SC
Jane 35 f "
William 14 m Ala
John 12 m "
Thomas 10 m "
James 8 m "
(Cont.)

(# 2292 ELLIOT cont.)

Joseph	6	m	Ala
Samuel	2	m	"
Cullen	6/12	m	"

257 Farmer ($500)

ELLIS, John W.	46	m	NC
Margaret	45	f	"
William (Farmer)	16	m	Ga
Henry H. "	15	m	"
Thomas	12	m	Ala
Julia	9	f	"
Cricket	7	f	"
SANDERS, Penny	80	f	NC

ELLIS, Joseph
(See Edward McPhail).

ELLIS, Thomas
Ann
Mandana (f)
Louisa
(See R. M. McCracken).

1417 Farmer ($700)

EMERSON, B. H.	41	m	Ga
Narcissa	39	f	"
Sarah	15	f	Ala
Martha	14	f	"
James C.	12	m	"
Antionette	11	f	"
Cinthia	9	f	"
Wade	7	m	"
John	6	m	"
Green	4	m	"

1901 Farmer ($100)

EMERSON, William	48	m	Ga
Jane	36	f	"
William (Farmer)	15	m	"
John	9	m	Ala
Martha	6	f	"
Mary	4	f	"
Elizabeth	1	f	"

2304 Farmer

ENGLISH, J. J.	49	m	Ga
Viney	50	f	"
Sampson (Farmer)	20	m	"
James "	18	m	"
Lumpkin "	15	m	"
Martha	13	f	"
Frances	10	f	"
Elizabeth	6	f	Ala
Mary	4	f	"
Francis	2	m	"

1224 Farmer ($1,400)

ENGRAM, Oliver C.	37	m	NC
Maria	27	f	Ga
Mary	10	f	"
Charlton	9	m	"
Ann	6	f	Ala
John	4	m	"
Judson	2	m	"

163 Farmer ($1,500)

ETHRIDGE, Richard C.	50	m	NC
Elizabeth	45	f	SC
Shadrac (Farmer)	17	m	Ga
Meshac "	11	m	Ala
Abednego	8	m	"
Esta	2	f	"
JOHNSTON, John (Laborer)	19	m	Ga
MUNCUS, Micajah (Laborer)	25	m	"

1451 Farmer ($250)

ETHERIDGE, Thomas	60	m	NC
Jane	49	f	Ga
John (Farmer)	21	m	"
Stephen "	19	m	"
James "	18	m	"
Seaborn "	15	m	"
Daniel	11	m	"
Mary	8	f	"
Emeline	7	f	"
Caroline	7	f	"

EUBANKS, Charles
(See John Harrison)

1797 Laborer

EUBANKS, John	30	m	Ga
Louisa	28	f	"
Elijah	6	m	"
John	4	m	"
Mary	1	f	Ala

2121 ($800)

EUBANKS, Nancy C.	47	f	Ga
Frances	20	f	"
Franklin (Farmer)	19	m	"
Rebecca	17	f	"
Edward (Farmer)	15	m	"
Nancy	13	f	"

1163 Farmer ($375)

EVANS, E. M.	22	m	Ala
Mary	17	f	"
Alexander	1	m	"
Mary	48	f	Ga

EVANS, Georgiann
(See John P. Glover).

528 Farmer ($450)
EVANS, J. L. C. 29 m Ga
Martha 34 f "
HARDWICK, Alfred H. 13 m "
George W. 20 m "

322 Farmer ($425)
EVANS, James 48 m Ga
Melinda 50 f "
Andrew (Farmer) 21 m Ala
William " 18 m "
Sarah 15 f "
Jane 17 f "

456 Farmer
EVANS, John 34 m SC
Mary 24 f Ala
Jane 9 f "
Elizabeth 7 f "
Rhody 5 f "
Sylvester 2 m "

EVANS, T.
(See Henry M. Tompkins).

1081 Farmer
EVANS, William 38 m Ga
Sarah 14 f Ala
Arritto 11 f "
Crawford 10 m "
Elizabeth 7 f "
Rebecca 5 f "

1448 Farmer
FAIL, Thomas * 62 m SC
CUNNINGHAM, Jas B. (Farmer) 22 m "
Elizabeth 26 f "
Thomas 2 m Ala
James 1 m "
SULLIVAN, Elizabeth 17 f Ga

FAIRCLOTH, Benjamin
(See J. T. Hood).

828 ($2,000)
FAISON, Nancy 54 f Ga
Thomas J. (Farmer) 21 m Ala
Alexr. M. " 19 m "
James D. " 16 m "
Nancy 14 f "
Sarah 16 f "

348 Farmer ($300)
FARMER, Abel 45 m NC
(Cont.)

(# 348 FARMER cont.)
Molsey 40 f SC
Margaret 18 f Ala
William (Farmer) 15 m "
Martha 13 f "
Mary 11 f "
Jane 9 f "
Caroline 7 f "
Sarah 3 f "

1966 Farmer ($150)
FARMER, Abram 48 m SC
Molsey 40 f "
Margaret 19 f Ala
William (Farmer) 16 m "
Martha 14 f "
Mary 11 f "
Jane 7 f "
Amanda 5 f "
Sally 3 f "

1965 Farmer ($100)
FARMER, Benjamin 40 m SC
Eliza 32 f Ala
Robert 14 m "
Sarah 11 f "
Squasha 8 f "
Mary 5 f "
John 2 m "

FARRER, George
(See Henry M. Tompkins).

1389 Harness Maker
FARRER, Hardeway 51 m SC
Sarah 46 f "
Harriet 17 f "
Geo. (Harness Maker) 22 m "
Malvina 13 f "
Emma 11 f "
Eugenia 8 f "
HAMNER, Sarah 16 f "

459 Farmer ($2,500)
FAULK, A. W. 37 m Ga
Charlotte 28 f SC
Nancy 15 f Ala
Charlotte 13 f "
Henry 11 m "
James K. P. 8 m "
Markey 6 m "
A. W. 2 m "
John 4/12 m "

* The above household of Thomas Fail almost illegible.

449 Farmer

FAULK, Henry	50	m	Ga
Sarah	50	f	"
William (Farmer)	23	m	Ala
Emeline	20	f	"
Sarah A.	18	f	"
Martha	17	f	"
Jane	15	f	"
Elizabeth	13	f	"
LaFayette	11	m	"
James	9	m	"

631 Farmer ($700)

FAULK, Henry L.	34	m	Ga
Sarah J.	26	f	SC
William	4	m	Ala
Henry R.	2	m	"

513 Farmer ($3,000)

FAULK, James	64	m	NC
Mary	36	f	Ga
Sarah (Idiot)	45	f	SC
GRIFFIN, Mary	8	f	Ga

632 Farmer

FAULK, James K.	28	m	Ala
Mary	18	f	Ga
Lucretia	1	f	Ala

781 Farmer ($1,000)

FAULK, Jesse	28	m	Ala
Nancy	29	f	Ga
Sarah	7	f	Ala
Mary	6	f	"
James	3	m	"

FAULK, Julia
Nancy
(See Francis Johns).

508 Farmer ($200)

Faulk, Levi	26	m	Ala
Savannah	25	f	Ga
Jasper	6	m	Ala
Rhody	4	f	"
Sophronia	3	f	"
Jane	5/12	f	"

2049 Farmer ($2,500)

FAULK, Lorenzo	38	m	SC
Mary	32	f	Ga
Mary	14	f	Ala
Martha	12	f	"
William	10	m	"
Richard	7	m	"
James	5	m	"

(Cont.)

(# 2049 FAULK cont.)

John	4	m	Ala
Daniel	1	m	"

1845 Farmer ($300)

FAULK, Mark W.	23	m	Ala
Riney	19	f	"

(Married within the year).

1844

FAULK, Nancy	60	f	Ga

2221 Farmer

FAULK, Thomas	50	m	Ga
Penny	35	f	"
Jane	15	f	"
Martha	8	f	Ala
Jeremiah	6	m	"
Rachel	4	f	"
James	3	m	"
Sarah	1	f	"

888 Farmer ($1,000)

FAVORS, William R.	27	m	SC
Tabitha	27	f	"
John C.	4/12	m	Ala
HERRING, James R.	14	m	Ga
George	13	m	"
Samuel	11	m	"
Amanda	9	f	"
Matilda	6	f	"

795 Farmer ($400)

FEAGIN, George W.	27	m	Ga
Dorothy	20	f	"

(Married within the year).

891 Farmer ($4,000)

FEAGIN, James M.	35	m	Ga
Elmira	27	f	Ala
Samuel	9	m	"
Noah	7	m	"
Martha	5	f	"
Wealthy	3	f	"

894 ($4,500)

FEAGIN, Mary	40	f	Ga
Isaac (Farmer)	16	m	"
Daniel	13	m	Ala
Nancy	15	f	Ga
Mary Ann	11	f	Ala

895 Carpenter

FEAGIN, Samuel	24	m	Ga
Julia	21	f	"

(Married within the year).

1149 Farmer ($6,400)
FENN, Matthew 52 m Ga
Matilda 43 f "
John 15 m Ala
Calvin 13 m "
Rebecca 12 f "
Matthew 9 m "
Matilda 7 f "
Sarah 5 f "
James 3 m "
Mary 1 f "
WILLIAMS, William 25 m "

1483 Harness Maker ($500)
FENN, William A. 30 m Conn
Jane 28 f "
Elizabeth 10 f Ga
Frances 7 f "
Jane 4 f Ala
William 1 m "
Hilliard 2/12 m "
Sarah 18 f Conn

2004 Brickmason ($2,500)
FERGUSON, Robert 38 m Ire

1467 Farmer ($1,400)
FIELDS, Bennet B. 35 m SC
Amanda 26 f Ga
Martha 7 f Ala
John W. 6 m "
Charles R. 4 m "
Mary 3 f "
Amanda 1 f "

1281 Clerk
FIELDS, Henry H. 22 m SC
McDOUGALD, A. B. 30 m NC
(Clerk)

881 Farmer ($6,000)
FIELD, H. H. 47 m Va
Mary 35 f "
Fanny 7 f Ala
Rosa 4 f "
William 1 m "

2046 Farmer
FIGG, James 47 m NC
Margaret 41 f "
Sophia 18 f "
Frances 15 f "
John 14 m Ga
Martha 10 f "
Georgianna 7 f "
Jane 5 f "
Joseph 2 m "

877 Carpenter
FILLINGIN, A. 30 m Ala
Charity 21 f Ga

1611 Wheelwright ($60)
FINCH, William H. 35 m Ga
Mary 30 f "
John 13 m "
James 10 m "
Dudley 8 m "
George 5 m "
Mary 2 f "
BROOKS, James 27 m Ga
(Machinist).
GAFNEY, John 48 m Ire
(Laborer).

FINLEY, Benjamin
(See William R. Daffin).

1051 Farmer
FINNEY, Elisha 46 m Ga
Sarah 27 f "
Sarah A. 10 f "
Lucinda 6 f "
Nancy 2 f Ala
James H. 1 m "

926 Blacksmith
FITTS, H. B. 23 m Fla
Elizabeth 19 f Ala
(Married within the year).

1587 Machinist ($2,000)
FLAKE, Seaborn J. 49 m Ga
William 39 m "
Elmira 13 f "

1294 Physician
FLAKE, William 50 m Ga
Sarah 38 f "
Benjamin 19 m Fla
Florida 13 f Ga
William 11 m Ala
Martha 7 f "
Eugenia 5 f "

564
FLEMING, Caleb J. 21 m Ga
Colen 18 f NC
John 1 m Ala

FLEMING, William
(See John Powell).

565 Farmer
FLEMING, William 48 m Ga
Elizabeth 18 f Ala
(Cont.)

(# 565 FLEMING cont.)

Emily 18 f Ga
JOHNSTON, Jane 88 f Pa
CLARK, William 8 m Ala
Jane 5 f "
John 1 m "
(Wm. & Eliz. Fleming married within the year).

2165 Farmer ($10,000)
FLEWELLEN, E. R. 40 m Ga
Susan 33 f "
Junius J. (Student) 16 m "
George 14 m "
Charles 12 m "
Martha 10 f "
Randel 7 m "
Mary A. 5 f Ala
Georgia 3 f "
Pink 9/12 f "

824 Farmer ($2,500).
FLORENCE, Obediah 41 m Ga
Aramatta 28 f "
Charles B. 5 m Ala
Mary 4 f "
Martha 2 f "
Samuel 8/12 m "

819 Farmer ($2,000)
FLORENCE, Thomas J. 35 m Ga
Mary S. 32 f "
Mary J. 10 f "
Sarah 4 f Ala
Henry B. 9/12 m "

680 ($1,000)
FLOURNOY, Aley 45 f NC
Ann W. 30 f "
Harriet J. 27 f "
Joseph E. P. (Farmer) 25 m "
John W. (Farmer) 22 m "

1911 ($1,500)
FLOURNOY, Ann W. 50 f Ga
Ann 25 f "
Harriet 24 f "
Joseph P. (Farmer) 23 m "
John W. (Farmer) 21 m "

FLOURNOY, James Leander
(See Elias G. Dowling).

1689 Farmer ($900)
FLOURNOY, John 23 m NC
(Cont.)

(# 1689 FLOURNOY cont.)

Mary 18 f Ga
(Married within the year).

1355 Farmer ($1,280)
FLOURNOY, Robert W. 24 m Ga
Mary 24 f "
Virginia 2 f Ala
Jonathan D. 1/12 m "

1374 Farmer ($20,000)
FLOURNOY, Thomas 40 m Ga
Caroline 37 f "
Mary L. 17 f "
Robert (Farmer) 15 m "
Martha 12 f Ala
Caroline 10 f "
Frances 8 f "
Osborn 6 m "
Thomas 4 m "
William 1/12 m "

332 Farmer ($1,300)
FLOWERS, Abner 65 m NC
Rebecca 57 f "
Levin (Carpenter) 26 m Ga
William J. (Farmer) 19 m Ala
Abner (Farmer) 17 m "
Rebecca 15 f "

331 Farmer ($400)
FLOWERS, Harrel 23 m Ga
Julia 21 f Ala
Frances 2 f "
Cintha 1 f "
Harrell 2/12 m "

1961 Farmer
FLOWERS, Littleton 25 m SC
Martha 20 f "
John 5 m Ala
Mary 2 f "
Sarah 9/12 f "

596
FLOWERS, Mary 63 f NC
William H. (Laborer) 17 m Ala

FLOWERS, Penelope
(See William Horn)

1982 Farmer ($600)
FLOWERS, Right 28 m SC
Celia 25 f Ala
Thomas 8 m "
William 6 m "
(Cont.)

(# 1982 FLOWERS cont.)

Mary	4	f	Ala
Catherine	2	f	"

595 Farmer

FLOWERS, Willis	23	m	Ala
Ann R.	20	f	SC
Narcissa J.	6/12	f	Ala

141

FLOYD, Fadey	38	f	Ga
Sarah	8	f	Ala
Joseph	1	m	"

599 Farmer ($850)

FLOYD, Page	33	m	NC
Elizabeth	27	f	"
William	10	m	Ala
John	8	m	"
Molsey	6	f	"
Louisa	4	f	"
Joseph	14	m	"

1427 Peddler

FOLSOM, James J.	34	m	Ga
Elizabeth	28	f	"
James	8	m	"
Amanda	6	f	"
Mary	4	f	Ala
George	1	m	"

2091 Farmer

FORD, Eli N.	31	m	SC
Jane	23	f	Ga
Mary	4	f	Ala
Henry	3	m	"
PAUL, H. K. (Farmer)	25	m	SC

2090 Farmer ($3,000)

FORD, Gardner	65	m	SC
Elizabeth	61	f	"

794 Farmer

FORD, William G.	41	m	SC
Mary	29	f	Ga
Antonette	12	f	"
Thomas	9	m	Ala
Sidney	6	m	"
Oscar	4	m	"
Victoria	2	f	"
STEED, John (Teacher)	23	m	Ga

#1988 Farmer

FOREHAND, Henry	29	m	NC
Elizabeth	26	f	Ga
William	7	m	Ala
Stephen	5	m	"
Mary	3	f	"
Sarah	1	f	"

244 Farmer ($200)

FOREHAND, Stephen	55	m	NC
Martha	46	f	SC
Nancy	17	f	"
John	15	m	"
Jesse	11	m	Ala
Jeptha	9	m	"
Thomas	5	m	"

546 Overseer ($800)

FORT, Duncan	27	m	NC

89 Overseer ($250)

FORT, Duncan	24	m	NC

267 Overseer

FORT, Elias	25	m	NC

FORT, William H.
(See Zach. Roquemore).

FOSTER, Francis
(See Simeon Hammock).

FOSTER, James
(See Henry M. Tompkins).

1363 Wheelwright

FOUCH, William	40	m	Ga
Lucy	32	f	"
Franklin (Farmer)	15	m	"
George	11	m	Ala
William	8	m	"
Mary	4	f	"

1677 Laborer

FOUNTAIN, Benj.	30	m	Ga
Mary	27	f	"
Bersheba	20	f	"

FOWLER, Enoch
(See Lucy Eford).

FRANKLIN, David
(See Benj. Burnham)

1755 Farmer ($1,000)

FRANKLIN, Ed.	39	m	Ga
Sarah	35	f	"
Rebecca	14	f	"
Mary	12	f	"
Elizabeth	11	f	"
Sarah	9	f	"
Martha	7	f	"
Laura	5	f	"
John	2	m	"

FRASIER, James
(See James Atwell).

2097 Farmer
FRASIER, Silas 24 m SC
Frances 33 f "
Labun 4 m Ala
Henry 2 m "
Frances 1 f "
SMITH, Wm. (Laborer) 23 m SC

1364 Farmer ($20,000)
FREEMAN, William 48 m Ga
Lucy 44 f "
Obediah (Student) 18 m "
William 14 m "
Sarah 12 f "
James D. 9 m Ala
Lucy 7 f "
Josephine 5 f "
Gustavus 4/12 m "

1472 Farmer
FRENCH, Bennet 23 m Ga
Sarah 20 f "
William 1 m "

1718 Laborer
FRENCH, James 23 m Ga
George 4 m Ala

1471 Farmer ($1,200)
FRENCH, Jasey P. 38 m SC
Mary 33 f Ga
Elizabeth 16 f "
James 13 m "
Lidia 12 f "
John 11 m "
Emeline 9 f "
Marion 7 m Ala
William 6 m "
Richard 3 m "
Jane 2 f "
KEIL, Joseph(Farmer) 16 m Ga

FRY, Adeline
(See William Stuckey).

FRY, Edward
(See Solomon Spurlock).

861 Farmer ($1,900)
FRYER, G. W. 33 m SC
Matilda 35 f "
Eliza 13 f "
John 11 m "
Rachel 9 f "
Ludy 7 f Ala
William 5 m "
(Cont.)

(# 861 FRYER cont.)
Elizabeth 3 f Ala
Sidney 1 m "

864 Physician ($2,000)
FRYER, R. H. 31 m SC
Lucinda 21 f Ala
Ann 67 f SC
LARY, John R. 27 m Ga
(Carpenter)

1800 Farmer
FULTON, John 27 m Ala
Margaret 23 f "
James 3 m "
John 1 m "

1773 Laborer
FUQUA, David 25 m Ga
Sarah 22 f "

342 Farmer
FUQUA, Randolph 30 m Ga
Mary 18 f SC
HARTZOG, Catherine 14 f Ala

1957 Farmer
FUQUA, Sterling 35 m Ga
Mary 30 f "
William 10 m Ala
Nancy 7 f "
James 5 m "
Elizabeth 2 f "

1768 Brickmason
FUTCH, John 29 m Ga
Nancy 28 f SC
Stephen 5 m Ga
Mary 1 f "

857 Farmer ($18,000)
GACHET, James E. 45 m Ga
Levinia 33 f "
Charles 12 m "
Martha 13 f "
Henry 6 m Ala
Lucy 4 f "
Mary L. 2 f "
JONES, Martha J. 9 f Ga

GAFNEY, John
(See William H. Finch).

2087 Farmer ($1,000)
GAINES, John G. 30 m Ga
Susan 25 f "
Thomas 5 m Ala
Mary 2 f "

56 Farmer ($200)
GAINEY, James P. 29 m SC
Rosanna 24 f "
Mary A. 6 f "
Louis 3 m "
Nancy J. 1 f Ala

129 Farmer
GALBRAITH, D. 47 m NC
Sarah 49 f "
Mary A. 12 f Ala

354 Farmer ($1100)
GALLOWAY, James 43 m Ga
Elizabeth 35 f "
Mary 17 f "
George W. 15 m "
James 13 m "
Lovet 11 m "
Elizabeth 9 f Ala
Benjamin 7 m "
Leroy 5 m "
Wellborn 3 m "
Thomas J. 10/12 m "

1264 Laborer
GALLOWAY, Melvin 34 m SC
Caroline 32 f Ga
John 12 m Ala
Francis 9 m "
Andrew 4 m "
James 6 m "
Lucy 6/12 f "

1897 Farmer
GALLOWAY, William 48 m NC
Elizabeth 30 f Ga
Elizabeth 21 f "
Jordan (Farmer) 19 m "
William " 18 m "
Sira 15 f "
Harriet 13 f "
Armstead 11 m "
Henry 9 m "
John 6 m "
Sarah 4 f "
Crocket 3 m "
Jane 3/12 f "

1990 Farmer ($200)
GAMBLE, James L. 27 m Ga
Louisa 20 f Ala
Thomas 3 m "
Sarah 1 f "

1064 Farmer ($200)
GAMBLE, William J. 26 m Ala
(Cont.)

(# 1064 GAMBLE cont.)
Elizabeth 26 f Ga
William 2 m Ala

1349 Printer ($200)
GARDNER, Benjamin 36 m NC
Eliza 30 f Ga
Louisa 14 f "
John 11 m "
Frances 8 f Ala
Samuel 7 m "
JACKSON, Thomas 21 m Ga
(Printer).

1258 Merchant ($1500)
GARDINER, Colin 35 m NY
Jane 35 f Ga

1794 Farmer ($5,000)
GARLAND, Edward 39 m Va
Mary 29 f Ga
Lucy 10 f Ala
Elizabeth 7 f "
Emma 5 f "
Ailsey 3 f "
Josephine 1 f "

GARNER, James
(See Allen Smith).

1869 Farmer ($300)
GARNER, John 46 m Ga
Jane 42 f "
Elizabeth 18 f Ala
Sarah 16 f "
Jane 14 f "
India 12 f "
Arminda 10 f "
Martha 9 f "
George 8 m "
Dicey 7 f "
Mary 4 f "
John 2 m "
Catherine 6/12 f "

2092 Farmer ($800)
GARRET, David 24 m Ga
Elizabeth 23 f "
America 4 f "
Miranda 2 f "
JOHNSTON, James D. 22 m "
(Farmer)

2085 Farmer ($1,000)
GARRETT, W. D. 23 m Ga
Elizabeth 21 f "
America 4 f "
Miranda 2 f "
(Cont.)

(# 2085 GARRETT cont.)
SASSER, John 27 m Ga
(Laborer)

GARVIN, L. L.
(See Jno. N. Copeland).

2143 Farmer ($1,000)
GARY, James 36 m Ga
Sarah 25 f "
Roderick 10 m "
Mary 8 f "
William 6 m "
Benjamin 5 m "
Rebecca 3 f Ala
Virginia 1 f "
Ellen 1/12 f "

GASTON, Alpheus
(See Ransom Godwin).

1246
GASTON, Jane 42 f Ga
L. Q. C. (Clerk) 22 m "
(Property: $350)
Victoria 12 f "
William 8 m "

2273 Occp. not given.
GATES, Stephen 25 m SC
Sarah 28 f Ga
Missouri 9 f "
Benjamin 5 m Ala
William 2 m "
Sarah 6/12 f "

391 Farmer
GEORGE, Daniel B. 27 m Ala
Mary 27 f NC
Cinthia 3 f Ala
Daniel 5/12 m "

1293 Grocer ($1,600)
GERKE, Charles F. 36 m Ger
Sina 36 f SC
Caroline 11 f Ala
Louisa 7 f "
Mary 5 f "
Harriet 4 f "
SHORT, Wines S. 16 m NC
(Laborer)
SAWYERS, Jasper 20 m Ga
(Laborer)

238 Farmer ($600)
GIBBENS, Stephen 44 m NC
Eliza 44 f SC
(Cont.)

(# 238 GIBBENS cont.)
Savannah 9 f Ala
John 6 m "
BODEFORD, Drucilla 20 f NC

1470 Tanner
GIBBS, Henry 19 m Ga

1743 ($200)
GIBHART, Sarah M. 72 f SC
Eliza 40 f "
Camilla 38 f "
Agnes 34 f "

2118 Farmer ($2,000)
GIBSON, George M. T. 25 m Ga
Nancy 28 f "
Obediah 4/12 m Ala

793 Farmer ($800)
GIBSON, Wm. H. C. 26 m Ga
William C. 65 m "
(Occp. - none)
Mary 62 f "
Elizabeth 21 f "

869 Farmer ($500)
GIDDENS, Isaac 28 m NC
Gabriella 22 f Ala
John 1 m "
James 2/12 m "

2289 Farmer ($400)
GIDDINS, Jacob 57 m NC
Eliza 47 f "
Eliza Ann 17 f "
Jacob (Farmer) 15 m "
Elva 13 f "
Elizabeth 11 f "
Needham 8 m Ala

1184 Farmer ($100)
GIDDINS, Mitchell 22 m Ga
Eliza 22 f SC
Nancy 4/12 f "

GILCHRIST - see Kilchrist

260 Farmer
GILCHRIST, Daniel 27 m NC
Elizabeth 18 f Ga
Zachary T. 1 m Ala

1634 Farmer
GILCHRIST, Gilbert 70 m NC
Mary 49 f "
Caroline 18 f "
Nancy 16 f "
(Cont.)

(# 1634 GILCHRIST cont.)

Angus 15 m NC
Gilbert 13 m Ala
Adeline 11 f "

1633 Overseer ($1,000)
GILCHRIST, John 23 m NC

904 Farmer ($1,200)
GILCHRIST, Malcolm 33 m NC
Eliza 24 f Ga
William 3 m Ala
Benjamin 1 m "
Neill 2/12 m "

1589 Shoemaker
GILL, William 34 m NC
Mary 34 f SC
Thomas 13 m "
William 12 m "
Augustus 9 m "
George 6 m "
Robert 4 m Ala
Frances 3 f "
Daniel 6/12 m "

545 Farmer ($800)
GILLENWATER, James A. 19 m Va
Jane A. 17 f NC
(Married within the year).

547 Blacksmith ($800)
GILLENWATER, Thomas 43 m Va
Nancy 36 f "
John (Farmer) 17 m "
William 14 m "
Nathan 11 m Ala
Virginia 6 f "
Mary 4 f "
Thomas 1 m "

1231 Preacher, MES *
GILLESPIE, C. C. 28 m Ga
Caroline 22 f Ala
Charles S. 1 m "

1422 Farmer ($400)
GILLIS, Angus 23 m NC
McNAB, John C. 23 m "
(Farmer)
Lucy 20 f "
Mary 2 f "

1111
GILLIS, Catherine 43 f NC
(Cont.)

(# 1111 GILLIS cont.)

Neill (Farmer) 20 m SC
Roderick " 19 m Ala
John 14 m "
Norman 12 m "
Hugh 10 m "
Mary 7 f "

327
GILLIS, Christian 66 f Scot
Margaret 40 f NC
Mary 38 f "
Christian 32 f SC
John W. 12 m "

GILLIS, Christian
(See R. C. McSwain).

336 Farmer ($100)
GILLIS, Daniel 30 m SC
Catherine 24 f "
Sarah 7/12 f Ala
McLEOD, Sarah 60 f Scot
CAMPBELL, D. G. 34 m NC
(Physician)

325
GILLIS, Flora 62 f Scot
Charles (Farmer) 30 m SC
Hugh " 28 m "
Jane 20 f Ala
Nancy 25 f SC
John 2 m Ala

199 Farmer ($100)
GILLIS, John 46 m NC
Catherine 48 f "
John 16 m SC
Nancy 15 f "
Sarah 10 f Ala
Malcolm 9 m "
Effey 6 f "
Christian 60 f NC

324 Farmer ($500)
GILLIS, Neill 30 m SC
Nancy 20 f NC
West 1 m Ala
Ichabod 2/12 m "

GILLIS, Neill
(See Joel Winslett).

GILLIS, Sarah
Christian
(See John McGilberry).

* MES: Methodist Episcopal, South.

949 Farmer
GILMORE, George 68 m Va
Rachel 55 f NC
Amanda 21 f Ala
George 19 m "

GILMORE, Owen
(See James Hamilton).

1929 Farmer
GILMORE, William 30 m Ga
Martha 25 f "
William 13 m "
Jane 12 f "
John 11 m Ala
Daniel 9 m "
Warren 8 m "
Mary 6 f "
Elizabeth 4 f "
Sarah 6/12 f "

GINWRIGHT, Sarah
Canady
Martha
(See Stephen Hughes).

743
GIRLEY, Callin 27 f NC
Molsy 12 m Ga
Mary 10 f "
Hiram 8 m "
Andrew 6 m "
Henry 4 m "

418 Farmer ($150)
GIST, Count A. 28 m Ga
Martha 21 f "
Martha 4 f Ala

609 Laborer
GIVINS, John W. 22 m SC
Martha 20 f "
John 3 m Ala
Sarah 1 f "

2268 Farmer
GLASS, Jack 23 m Ga
Jane 20 f "
Mary 6/12 f Ala

2188 Laborer
GLASS, Jackson 23 m Fla
Jane 26 f Ga
John 3 m Ala
Mary 1 f "

1201 Laborer
GLASS, James 25 m Ga
(Cont.)

(# 1201 GLASS cont.)
Lidia 20 f Ga
(Married within the year).

273 Farmer ($900)
GLASS, Levi 46 m Ga
Elizabeth 30 f "
Margaret 22 f "
Olive 21 f "
Eliza 15 f "
Thomas 10 m Ala
John 8 m "
CREECH, David 10 m "
Wesley 6 m "
Franklin 1 m "
GLISSON, Henry 18 m Ga
(Laborer)
(Levi & Eliz. Glass married within the year).

2212 Farmer ($100)
GLASS, Littleton D. 43 m Ga
Nancy 30 f "
William 14 m "
Mary 12 f Ala
Matilda 10 f "
John 8 m "
Nancy 5 f "

GLASS, Rebecca
(See Nancy Bishop).

1623 Farmer ($600)
GLENN, A. T. 25 m SC
Thompson S. 76 m Va
(Minister, M. E. *)
Mary 60 f NC
John 30 m SC
Catherine 18 f "

1535 Preacher, M. E. *
GLENN, James E. 64 m SC
Elizabeth 54 f "
Algernon (Farmer) 28 m "
Elvira 22 f "
James 17 m "

1559 Farmer ($5,000)
GLENN, M. M. 34 m SC
Barbara 28 f "
Ellen 9 f "
Eugene 7 m Ala
Sarah 5 f "
Julien 3 m "

* Methodist Episcopal.

465 Farmer ($300)
GLENN, William M. 29 m Ga
Mary 20 f Ala
Adelbert N. 2 m "
William 8/12 m "

GLISSON, Henry
(See Levi Glass).

1701 Farmer ($400)
GLOVER, Alfred 29 m Ga
Elizabeth 20 f "
Henrietta 7 f Ala
Frances 5 f "
John 3 m "

GLOVER, E. E.
(See Robert Worthington)

1700 Overseer
GLOVER, Eli 27 m Ga
Susan 17 f "

826 Farmer ($1,000)
GLOVER, H. H. 39 m NC
Sarah 39 f Ga
Ann 12 f "
Ellen 8 f "
Lavina 6 f Ala
Missouri 2 f "

1462 Farmer ($2,500)
GLOVER, John P. 65 m NC
Drucilla 57 f Ga
Mary 20 f "
Samuel (Farmer) 18 m "
Andrew 12 m "
VINING, Washington 19 m "
(Farmer)
William 13 m "
George 12 m "
EVANS, Georgiann 18 f "
CAREW, Franklin 1 m "
GLOVER, James 9 m Ala

GLOVER, Lucretia
(See Louisa Barwick).

1463 Overseer
GLOVER, Nathan 24 m Ga
Elizabeth 20 f NC
Munroe 3 m Ala
Jane 1/12 f "

256 Farmer
GLOVER, Newton 25 m Ga
(Cont.)

(# 256 GLOVER cont.)
Sarah 14 f Ga
Elizabeth 11 f "

1702 Farmer ($400)
GLOVER, Thomas 30 m Ga
Rachel 22 f "
Jane 3 f Ala
James 1 m "

1209 Wheelwright
GLOVER, Thomas N. 60 m NC
Ellender 48 f SC

1939
GLOVER, Tildey 70 f Ala
Tildey (Blind) 58 f ---
Eliza 30 f Ala
Winney 18 f "
CARR, Mary 22 f "
James 7 m "

GLOVER, Wiley
(See Marshall Hunter).

1310 Merchant
GODWIN, Bansom 40 m NC
Eliza 24 f "
Ellen 4 f Ala
John 2 m "
Sarah 1 f "
GREGORY, Jas.(Clerk) 20 m Conn
GASTON, Alpheus 20 m Ga
(Clerk)
BESSON, J. A. B. 22 m Fr
(Tanner ?).
Ann 18 f NY

1476 Carpenter ($200)
GOFF, A. J. 31 m Ga
Martha 26 f "
Martha A. 2 f Ala
GRIFFIN, Peggy 31 f "

GOFF, Sarah
(See Ivy Morris).

706 Farmer
GOING, Jarret 40 m NC
Nancy 35 f "
James 14 m Ala
Jarret 8 m "

679 Millwright ($800)
GORMAN, William 42 m Mass
Sarah 32 f SC
(Cont.)

(# 679 GORMAN cont.)

Sarah E.	10	f	Ala
Martha	9	f	"
Iranna(?)	7	f	"
William	4	m	"

524 Farmer ($400)

GOUMILLION, Henry	57	m	SC
Jane	46	f	"
Ann J.	18	f	"
William H.	16	m	"
Elijah	12	m	Ala
CARTER, Salina	25	f	Ga

GOUMILLION, Joseph
(See Judge S. Williams).

GRAHAM, John
(See George W. Benson).

GRANGER, A. S.
(See William Hinson).

1574 Waiter (Negro)

GRANT, James	23	m	Ga

1690 Farmer ($400)

GRANT, John A.	66	m	NC
Elizabeth	60	f	"
Elizabeth	22	f	"
Caroline	18	f	"
John (Farmer - $300)	27	m	"

274 Farmer ($500)

GRANT, John H.	68	m	NC
Elizabeth	57	f	"
John A.(Farmer - $400)	26	m	"
Elizabeth	18	f	"
Caroline	16	f	Fla

GRANT, Squire (Colored)
(See Benjamin Screws).

451 Farmer ($400)

GRANT, Thomas M.	65	m	Va
Martha	50	f	Ga
Eliphar	21	f	"
STOKES, Salissa J.	13	f	Ala

81 Farmer ($200)

GRANTHAM, Edward	28	m	NC
John	10	m	SC
Johnston	8	m	"
Daniel	8	m	"
Edward	9	m	"
Mary	7	f	"

GRANTHAM, Edward J.
Mary J.
(See John Johnston).

1242 Farmer

GRANTHAM, James	52	m	NC
Lucy	47	f	SC
DAVIS, Nancy	27	f	"
Mary	7	f	Fla
Lucy	4	f	"

87 Farmer

GRANTHAM, James	52	m	NC
Lucy	47	f	SC
DAVIS, Nancy	27	f	"
Mary A. E.	6	f	Fla
Lucy	4	f	"

1126 Farmer

GRANTHAM, William	45	m	NC
Saleta	38	f	SC
Martha	13	f	"
Mary	11	f	"
Jesse	8	m	Ala
Jincey	6	f	"
Catherine	3	f	"
William	13	m	SC

1872 Farmer ($1,000)

GRAVES, Hardy	45	m	SC
Rhody	48	f	"
THOMPSON, Sarah *	21	f	Ala
Rhody *	18	f	"
Robert * (Farmer)	15	m	"
Adam *	13	m	"
THOMPSON, Thomas	24	m	"

1549

GRAVES, Harriet	35	f	SC
Mary	14	f	"
William	13	m	"
Caroline	10	f	"
Lavinia	7	f	"
Sarah	5	f	"
Thomas	2	m	Ala

GRAVES, Henry S.
(See Henry McCall)

GRAVES, William
(See Henry M. Tompkins).

1909 Farmer ($100)

GREEN, Alfred	24	m	Ga
Maria	18	f	"

(Married within the year).

878 Farmer ($400)

GREEN, Allen	46	m	SC

(Cont.)

* Children of Rhody Graves by her first husband, Robt. Thompson.

(# 878 GREEN cont.)
Mary J. 35 f NC
Aaron 14 m Ala
Lewis 12 m "
Frances 11 f "
Lidia 9 f "
James 7 m "
Bazil 5 m "
Barnebas 3 m "
Allen 1 m "

813 Farmer ($2,000)
GREEN, Amos 50 m Ga
Sarah 35 f "
Stith 10 m Ala
Ada 7 f "
Otis 4 m "
Austin 2 m "
JENNINGS, Sophia 17 f "

811 Farmer ($200)
GREEN, George 56 m NC
Elizabeth 47 f Ga
Joseph (Farmer) 18 m "
Nathan " 16 m "
Martha 10 f "

1214 Farmer
GREEN, John A. 32 m Ga
Elizabeth 40 f --

GREEN, Marion
(See George Scroggins).

GREEN, Robert
(See Nath. G. Holmes).

1156 Farmer
GREEN, Robert R. 30 m Ga
Mary 20 f "
Elizabeth 1 f Ala

526 Farmer
GREEN, Thomas 30 m Ga
Sarah 18 f Ala
Elizabeth 2 f "
William 1 m "

928 Farmer
GREEN, Thomas 60 m --
Mary 35 f Ga
Nancy 12 f Ala
Jane 10 f "
Thomas 8 m "
Elizabeth 6 f "
George 4 m "
John 2 m "

511 Farmer ($400)
GREEN, Thomas C. 30 m SC
Emeline 28 f "
Nancy 11 f Ala
William H. 7 m "
Amanda 2 f "

1910 Farmer
GREEN, William 22 m Ga
Jane 20 f "
(Married within the year).

1211 Farmer
GREEN, William 66 m NC
Margaret 30 f Ga
Thomas J. (Farmer) 18 m "
DAVIS, Martha 15 f Ala
Eliza 7 f "

1212 Farmer
GREEN, William F. 28 m Ga
Elizabeth 22 f "
John 3/12 m Ala

910 Farmer
GREENWOOD, Samuel 47 m Ga
Elizabeth 24 f "
Lucy 16 f "
Leonora 7 f Ala
Ann 3 f "
Elizabeth 2 f "
Calla 9/12 f "

GREGORY, James
(See Ransom Godwin).

671 Farmer
GRICE, Robert 33 m SC
Musell(?) 30 f "
Eliza 12 f "
Mary J. 10 f "
Levina 8 f "
Rebecca 5 f "
Martha 3 f Ala

2120 Farmer
GRIER, George 50 m Ga
Emily 40 f "
Catherine 13 f "
Sarah 8 f "
Retiniha 5 f Ala
James G. 2 m "

2063 Merchant
GRIFFIN, Eli 35 m SC
Martha 23 f Ga

GRIFFIN, Julia A.
Jane, Franklin, Eliz.,
Nancy and Martha
(See Smith Ham).

1991 Laborer

GRIFFIN, J.(or I.)	32	m	Ga
Martha	27	f	"
William	9	m	Ala
John	7	m	"
Mary	5	f	"
Susan	3	f	"
Thomas	8/12	m	"

1489 Laborer

GRIFFIN, Lewis	48	m	SC
Delilah	37	f	Ga
Hezekiah (Laborer)	15	m	"
Washington	12	m	"
John	10	m	"
Elizabeth	7	f	"
Jeremiah	4	m	"
Mary	3	f	"
Daniel	1	m	"

240 Farmer

GRIFFIN, Lewis	48	m	SC
Delilah	40	f	Ga
Hezekiah	15	m	"
George	12	m	"
John	10	m	"
Elizabeth	6	f	"
Jeremiah	5	m	"
Mary	3	f	"
Daniel	1	m	"
Joshua (Farmer)	37	m	SC

GRIFFIN, Mary
(See James Faulk).

GRIFFIN, Peggy
(See A. J. Goff).

#1583 Farmer ($300)

GRIFFIS, Henry	52	m	Ga
Rebecca	45	f	"
Emily	20	f	"
Mary	18	f	"
Joseph (Farmer)	16	m	"
William	10	m	"
Massillon	6	m	Ala
Sarah	2	f	"
Jane	8/12	f	"

GRIFFIS, M. M.
(See Wm. A. Barham).

GRIFFITH, Moses
(See G. W. McGinty).

2294 Farmer ($600)

GRISSETT, Daniel M.	37	m	NC
Eliza	33	f	"
James	12	m	Ala
Sarah	9	f	"
William	6	m	"
Mary	3	f	"
William	1	m	"

973 Farmer ($1,800)

GRUBBS, Adam	48	m	SC
Demaris	52	f	"
Samuel (Farmer)	15	m	Ala
Green	12	m	"
LISTER, Thomas (Overseer - $200)	24	m	"
HENRY, James (Physician)	22	m	Ga
Amanda	14	f	Ala

(Jas. & Amanda Henry married within the year).

1861 Farmer ($500)

GRUBBS, Friendly	30	m	Ala
Caroline	35	f	Ga
Josiah (Laborer)	24	m	Ala

115 Laborer

GRUBBS, Henry	33	m	SC
Rebecca	38	f	"
Louisa	17	f	"
Larana	15	f	"
Rosanna	12	f	"
Lucius	10	m	"

889 Farmer ($1,000)

GRUBBS, J. T.	26	m	Ala
Lucetta	28	f	Ga
Catherine	21	f	Ala

GRUBBS, James
John - Wm. - Francis - Green
and Morgan
(See John McNair).

GRUBBS, Marthena
(See Wm. Andrews).

974 Physician

GRUBBS, Morgan M.	26	m	SC

643 ($600)

GRUBBS, Polly	40	f	Ga
Winney	20	f	Ala
Elizabeth	15	f	"
Enoch (Farmer)	18	m	"

GRUBBS, Stephen
Caroline, - John, - Edward,-
Elizabeth -
(See Edward Cox).

663 Farmer ($2,500)
GRUBBS, W. J. 30 m SC
Mary 27 f Ga
Hepsey 9 f Ala
Mary 7 f "
William 5 m "
James 4 m "
Seth 2 m "
Elizabeth 72 f SC
THORN, Joseph 30 m Ga
(Overseer)

872 Farmer ($3,000)
GRUBBS, William 46 m SC
Nancy 38 f Ga
Mary 20 f Ala
Elizabeth 18 f "
Emeline 16 f "
Amanda 14 f "
Green 12 m "
Hetty 10 f "
Savannah 8 f "
Lidia 5 f "
John 1 m "

818 Farmer ($375)
GUERRY, William L. 24 m Ga
Sarah 21 f Fla

GUILFORD, Allen
(See James Mabry).

GUILFORD, Margaret
William A.
Mary
(See Mary A. Miles).

1433 Carpenter ($200)
GURIN (Gavin?) John 37 m Fr
Amy 39 f Ga
Jane 10 f "
William 5 m "
John 1 m Ala
MINGER, John 40 m Ger
(Carpenter)

1896 Farmer ($200)
GURNELS, Pitman L. 49 m Ga
Dilley 49 f "
Eveline 23 f "
Julia 21 f "
Henry (Farmer) 18 m "
(Cont.)

(# 1896 GURNELS cont.)
Dilley 16 f Ga
Malita 14 f "
Martha 12 f "
Elizabeth 10 f "
Jefferson 7 m Ala

1055 Farmer ($600)
GUTHRIE, William 39 m Ga
Dolly A. 32 f "
Elizabeth 8 f "
Sarah 4 f Ala

753 Blacksmith ($600)
HAGOOD, Appleton 43 m Ga
Mary 41 f "
Henry (Blksmith) 17 m "
Allen " 15 m "
Appleton 12 m "
Mary 10 f "
Emory 7 m Ala
Martha 5 f "
James 3 m "
Ellen 1 f "

1954
HAIGLER, Charles 30 m NC
Mary 30 f Ala
Charles 10 m "
William 8 m "
Elizabeth 6 f "
Mary 4 f "
John 2 m "

395 Farmer ($200)
HAIGLER, Charles 36 m NC
Nancy 35 f "
Hiram 14 m Ala
Jane 12 f "
Abijah 9 m "
Martha 8 f "
Elizabeth 6 f "
Charles 9/12 m "

754 Farmer
HAIGLER, Francis M. 23 m NC
Martha 23 f Ga

755 Farmer ($800)
HAIGLER, Henry 54 m NC
Elizabeth 45 f "
John (Farmer) 19 m Ga
William " 17 m "
Ephriam " 15 m "
Philip 13 m "
Nancy 13 f "
(Cont.)

(# 755 HAIGLER cont.)

Henry	10 m Ga
Margaret	8 f Ala
Sarah	5 f "
Barnet	4 m "
Zial (Lial?)	2 m "
HAIGLER, G. W.	23 m NC

1684 Farmer ($100)

HAIGLER, Jacob	35 m NC
Catherine	33 f "
Elizabeth	3 f "
Sarah	19 f "
Margaret	16 f "
Adam	14 m "
Jeremiah	12 m "
Henry	11 m "
Mary	10 f "
Martha	9 f "

2270 Laborer

HAIGLER, James	23 m NC

HAIGLER, James
(See James Morris).

1685 Farmer ($1,000)

HAIGLER, Peter	70 m NC
Margaret	40 f "
COOLEY, Sarah	70 f "

428 Farmer ($300)

HAIGLER, Thomas	30 m NC
Lydia	30 f "
Wellborn	10 m Ala
Josiah	9 m "
James M.	8 m "
Moses W.	7 m "
Mary	6 f "
Milton	5 m "
Frances	1 f "

1817 Farmer

HAILEY, Holden	75 m NC
John	28 m "

752 Farmer ($125)

HAILEY, James	48 m NC
Elizabeth	26 f --
George (Farmer)	21 m NC
Hiram "	19 m Ga
Curron	16 m "
Rachel	14 f "
James	12 m "
Martha	11 f "
John	5 m Ala

(Cont.)

(# 752 HAILEY cont.)

Nancy	4 f Ala
Caroline	6/12 f "

1269 Tinner ($1,200)

HAILEY, William D.	33 m NC
Emily	24 f Ga
Harriet	3 f Ala
John	1/12 m "
BOOTH, Jos. (Tinner)	21 m "

1981

HAIR, Milbra	25 f Ga
Molsey	4 f Ala
John	6/12 m "

1227 Clerk

HALL, David	34 m SC
Adeline	27 f Ga
Mandana	1 f Ala
CANNON, Thomas J. (Merchant)	23 m SC
TISON, Henry C. (Merchant - $800)	29 m SC

159

HALL, Florina	44 f Ga
Caroline	15 f "
Jackson	12 m "
William	9 m Ala
JACKSON, Thomas (Occp. - none).	84 m SC

HALL, Goodwin
(See V. H. Tate).

2184 Laborer

HALL, Henry	33 m SC
Daniel	30 m "
Elisha	26 m "
Martha	24 f "
Eliza	13 f Ala
William	10 m "
Emeline	8 f "
CRAULEY, Patience	19 f SC

132 Farmer ($50)

HALL, Hiram	47 m SC
Epsey	46 f "
Mary A.	21 f Ga
Chappel	20 m SC
Elizabeth	19 f Ga
Margaret	17 f "
Charity	14 f "
Sarah	11 f "
HARRISON, William	8 m "
Harriet	7 f "

1177 Farmer ($900)
HALL, John W. 38 m SC
Polly 40 f "
Mary 15 f Ala
Amanda 12 f "
William 11 m "
James 9 m "
Almira 8 f "
Eugenia 7 f "
Irwin 5 m "
John 4 m "
Eudora 3 f "
Luison 1/12 m "

HALL, Mary
Wesley
(See George W. Jackson).

783 Farmer ($6000)
HALL, Matthew 45 m Ga
Atha 37 f "
James M. (Student) 18 m "
John T. 6 m "?
Franklin C. 6 m Ala?
Sarah E. 4 f "
Rachel P. 1 f "

780 Farmer (1,500)
HALL, R. G. 29 m Ga
Sarah 28 f "
Sarah J. 8 f "
John 6 m "
Matthew W. 3 m "
Samuel 8/12 m Ala

HALL, Samuel
(See Joseph Whigham, Jr.)

1178 Farmer ($300)
HALL, William 55 m SC
Effy 25 f "
Frances 23 f "
William 21 m "
Sampson 19 m "

362 Laborer
HAM, Jesse 65 m SC
Mary 67 f "
Esquire (Laborer) 28 m "
David " 26 m "
Fanny 30 f "
Polly 25 f Ala
Patrick 5 m "
Sally 3 f "
Betty 3/12 f "
CARR, Solomon 40 m Pa
(Laborer)

137 Farmer
HAM, Smith 47 m SC
Sarah 29 f Ga
William (Farmer) 19 m "
Allen " 16 m "
Eliza 14 f "
Henry 12 m "
Jackson 9 m "
Elizabeth 7 f "
Benjamin 5 m "
Augustus 3 m "
Jacob 2 m Ala
Martha 9/12 f "
GRIFFIN, Julia A. 20 f SC
Jane 5 f Ga
Franklin 4 m "
Elizabeth 3 f "
Nancy 2 f "
Martha 1 f "

31 Millwright ($1,900)
HAMILTON, James 46 m NY
GILMORE, Owen 28 m Ire

HAMILTON, John S.
(See Mary Mixon).

1297 Drayman
HAMILTON, R. P. 42 m Va
Elizabeth 41 f "
James M. (Clerk) 21 m "
William N. (Student) 19 m Ala
Frances 2 f "

2171 Farmer ($9600)
HAMMETER, Joel 43 m SC
Elizabeth 42 f "
Julia A. 11 f "
Carolina 5 f Ala
Elizabeth 2 f "
CAUGHMAN, Isaisa 30 m SC
(Overseer).

HAMMOCK, Ross
(See Edward S. Ott).

114 Farmer ($250)
HAMMOCK, Simeon 40 m Ga
Jane 26 f "
Mary A. 3 f Ala
Jeremiah 1 m "
Angelina 14 f Ga
FOSTER, Francis 50 m "
(Laborer)

560 Farmer ($1,500)
HAMMOCK, Thomas 52 m Ga
(Cont.)

(# 560 HAMMOCK cont.)

Mary	50	f	NC
Sarah	22	f	Ga
Thomas	14	m	"

HAMMOCK, Uriah
(See William Ott).

2112 Farmer ($150)

HAMMONS, Henry M.	60	m	NC
Elizabeth	50	f	"
Ann	17	f	"
Mary	73	f	"

HAMNER, Sarah
(See Hardeway Farrer).

1148 Carpenter

HANCOCK, E. S.	32	m	NC
Rebecca	22	f	"
George	6	m	Ala
James	3	m	"
John	2	m	"
William	4/12	m	"

2084 Farmer ($2,800)

HANCOCK, Josiah	44	m	NC
Mary	37	f	Ga
James	14	m	"
Sarah	12	f	"
Laura	9	f	Ala
Isham	8	m	"
Emily	7	f	"
Georgiann	5	f	"
Susan	3	f	"
Joseph	1	m	"

2398 Farmer ($200)

HANDLEY, Irwin	33	m	Ga
Martha	24	f	Ala
James	6	m	"
William	4	m	"
Sarah	2	f	"

1443 Overseer

HANEY, Augustus B.	30	m	Ga
Mary	21	f	"
William	6	m	"
Eldridge	1	m	Ala

HANLEY, Thomas
Emeline
(See David Hartzog).

1388 Cabt. Maker ($1,200)

HANSON, F. J. C.	39	m	Den *

(Cont.)

(# 1388 HANSON cont.)

Catherine	31	f	SC
Sarah	9	f	Ala
Donald	5	m	"
Elizabeth	4	f	"
George	2	m	"

2305 Clerk ($1,000)

HARDMAN, Jack	43	m	Ga
Eugenia E.	35	f	SC
Mary A.	13	f	Ala
Thomas L.	11	m	"
Rosalie A.	9	f	"
John J.	6	m	"
William P. P.	4	m	"
Arthur S.	1	m	"

HARDWICK, Alfred H.
George W.
(See J. L. C. Evans).

HARDY, Elizabeth
Susan
Jacob
(See Acton Nash).

139 Farmer

HARDY, Richard J.	33	m	NC
Phoebe	27	f	Ga
John	6	m	"
James	5	m	"
Louisa	3	f	Ala
Argen	2/12	f	"

347 Farmer ($1,700)

HARGROVES, Henry	51	m	NC
Elizabeth	47	f	"

HARGROVES, Lemuel
(See Charles Petty).

1686 Laborer

HARLIN, Thomas	21	m	SC

2283 Farmer

HARP, Allen	36	m	Ga
Emeline	24	f	"
Sarah	9	f	Ala
William	2	m	"

827 Farmer ($1,500)

HARPER, William	55	m	NC
Margaret	43	f	SC
William (Farmer)	16	m	Fla
Hannibal	13	m	"
LaFayette	11	m	Ala

(Cont.)

* Denmark

(# 827 HARPER cont.)

Thaddeus	9	m	Ala
Eliza	6	f	"
Cincinnatti	4	m	"
Franklin	3	m	"
Sarah	1	f	"

918 Overseer

HARPER, William F.	45	m	Ga
Rebecca	30	f	"
WOOD, Mildred	16	f	"
Benjamin (Student)	17	m	"

1036 Farmer

HARPER, Willis E.	26	m	NC
Elizabeth	22	f	Ga
Harriet	1/12	f	Ala

HARRALL, William
(See C. J. M. Andrews).

913 Farmer ($600)

HARRASS, Thomas	45	m	Ga
Maranda	28	f	"
Martha	1	f	Ala
Mary	1/12	f	"

3 Farmer

HARRUP(Harrass?),Wm. I.	25	m	Ga
Angeline T.	23	f	"
James S.	7/12	m	Ala

1933 Tailor

HARRELL, E. S.	35	m	NC

HARRELSON, Nancy
(See George W. Benson).

HARRIS, Matilda
(See G. B. Williams)

HARRIS, Thomas
(See Arch'd. Carmichael)

380 Farmer

HARRISON, Alfred	20	m	NC
Catherine	28	f	"
BLANCHETT, Lemuel (Farmer)	15	m	Ala
John	8	m	"
Caroline	6	f	"
Sharp (?)	2	m	"
Jane	1	f	"

2122 Farmer ($800)

HARRISON, John	29	m	Ga
Martha	28	f	"

(Cont.)

(# 2122 HARRISON cont.)

Martha	5	f	Ga
William	2	m	Ala
Charles	1	m	"
EUBANKS, Charles	26	m	"

510 Farmer

HARRISON, John	35	m	Ga
Rebecca	36	f	"
Elizabeth	15	f	"
Margaret	13	f	"
Eliza J.	11	f	"
Serena	9	f	"
Susan	6	f	Ala
Frances	4	f	"
Thomas J.	2	m	"

1312 Merchant ($4000)

HARRISON, L. C.	44	m	Va
Sarah	39	f	SC
Mary	15	f	Ga
William	13	m	"
Virginia	11	f	"
Augusta	9	f	Ala
George	7	m	"
John	5	m	"
Leonard	3	m	"
Sarah	1	f	"

HARRISON, L. L.
Charles
(See Neill McDonald).

2196 Farmer ($200)

HARRISON, Thomas	38	m	Ga
Nancy	29	f	"
Mary	14	f	"
Thomas	12	m	"
William	11	m	Ala
Elizabeth	9	f	"
James	7	m	"
Martha	5	f	"
Eliza	2	f	"
Susan	3/12	f	"

1940 Farmer ($300)

HARRISON, Thomas	25	m	NC
Mary	20	f	Ala
William	2	m	"

HARRISON, William
Harriet
(See Hiram Hall).

923 Farmer ($300)

HARROD, James	36	m	Ga

(Cont.)

(# 923 HARROD cont.)
Martha 31 f Ga
Mary 11 f Ala
Nancy 9 f "
Margaret 7 f "
Martha 5 f "
Sarah 3 f "

1110 ($400)
HARROD, Sarah 40 f NC
Elijah (Farmer) 17 m Ala
Margaret 16 f Miss
Jane 14 f "
John 12 m Ala
William 10 m "
Elizabeth 7 f "

HART, Edward
(See E. M. Herron).

1266 Marchant ($7000).
HART, John 46 m NH
Elizabeth W. 37 f RI
Henry (Clerk) 21 m "
John B. " 19 m "
Charles " 17 m "
Ann E. 16 f "
Mary 14 f Ala
Sarah F. 11 f "
Harrison 9 m "
Francis 7 m "
Maria 5 f "
George 3/12 m "

1796 Carpenter
HARTLEY, George 40 m Ire
Catherine 30 f Ga

HARTZOG, Catherine
(See Randolph Fuqua).

339 Farmer ($300)
HARTZOG, David 56 m SC
Rebecca 36 f "
William 6 m Ala
Rachel 3 f "
Tabitha 2 f "
John 2/12 m "
HANLEY, Thomas 15 m "
(Farmer)
Emeline 14 f "

1415 Farmer
HARTZOG, Francis 26 m SC
Rebecca 28 f "
Sarah 5 f Ala
(Cont.)

(# 1415 HARTZOG cont.)
George 4 m Ala
Jane 2 f "

HARTZOG, Isaac
(See James Bexley).

376 Laborer
HARTZOG, James 17 m SC
Martha 18 f "
(Married within the year).
William 2/12 m Ala

1782 Farmer ($650)
HARVELL, David 45 m Ga
Mahala 43 f "
Augustus 14 m "

445 Farmer
HARVELL, Joshua 26 m Ga
Sarah 20 f SC
(Married within the year).

142 Farmer
HARVELL, Needham 72 m NC
Elizabeth 47 f Ga
Frances 13 f "
Lucy 11 f "
Emily 8 f "
Sally 6 f "

543 Farmer
HARWELL, James 32 m Ga
Caroline 28 f SC
Martha 4 f Ala
Mary 3 f "
Henry 8/12 m "

542 Farmer ($2,500)
HARWELL, Samuel 72 m Va
Burchet 62 f "
HARWELL, Warren 22 m Ga
(Farmer)
Martha 17 f Ga
(Last two married within the year).
BIRDSONG, Martha 14 f Ga

HARWELL, William J.
(See George Rachel).

HATCHER, Rebecca
Priscilla
(See Green Smith).

2061 Farmer ($400)
HAWKINS, James L. 22 m Ga
Catherine 22 f NC
Benjamin 3/12 m Ala

HAWKINS, Pinckney
(See B. H. Brantley)

HAWKINS, Robert
(See John P. Brown)

262 Overseer
HAWKINS, Thomas A. T. 20 m Ala

1039 Farmer ($300)
HAYGOOD, J.W.A.E. 25 m Ga
Sarah 20 f Fla
William 1 m Ala

2126 ($400)
HAYS, Clarissa 46 f Ga
John 14 m Ala
Epsey 12 f "

1912 Carpenter
HAYS, James 33 m SC
Prudence 28 f NC
Margaret 10 f Ga
Asbury 9 m "
Susan 4 f Ala
Elvira 2 f "

64 Farmer ($1,000)
HAYS, Jesse L. 27 m Ala

303 Farmer ($700)
HAY, John 41 m Ga
Jane 26 f "
Lucy 7 f "
Mary A. 5 f "
William T. 3 m "
John 1 m Ala
RICKS, Louisa N. 9 f Ga
MOBLEY, Mary 68 f "

2182
HAYS, Martha 28 f SC
Sarah 10 f Ala
Louisa 6 f "
Sidney 3 m "
Elizabeth 2 f "

HAYS, Mary
(See James Morris).

1698 Farmer
HAYS, Thomas 30 m Ga
Vicey 32 f "
Nancy 13 f "
Jackson 7 m "
Jonathan 5 m "

2051 Farmer ($800)
HEAD, James M. 25 m Ga
(Cont.)

(# 2051 HEAD cont.)
Mary 20 f Ga
Matthew 1 m Ala

2050 Farmer ($100).
HEAD, Richard 32 m Ga
Epsey 27 f Ala
Elizabeth 4 f "

2227 Occupation not given
HEAD, Thomas 30 m Ga
Eliza 25 f "
Richard 4 m Ala
Mary 2 f "

124 Farmer ($1,400)
HEAD, William 67 m NC
Epsey 59 f Ga
Edwin 22 m "
Robert M. 20 m Ala
Ucal 16 m "
Eliza 7 f "

2099 Farmer ($600)
HEATH, Britton 42 m Ga
Rebecca 38 f "
Green (Farmer) 19 m Ala
Miles " 16 m "
Charles 14 m "
William 10 m "
Caroline 8 f "

371 Farmer
HEATH, Emanuel 28 m Ala

355 Farmer
HEATH, Green 29 m Ala
Bethena 25 f "
Mary 10 f Miss
Margaret 3 f Ala
Sarah 1 f "

377 Miller ($400)
HEATH, Isaac 63 m NC
KELLY, William 46 m Ga
(Farmer)
Sarah 20 m Ala
Martha J. 11 f "

HEATH, Lemuel
(See William Baxley).

357 Farmer
HEATH, Miles 31 m Ala
Jane 31 f NC
Sarah 7 f Ala
Isaac 6 m "
Edy 4 f "
(Cont.)

(# 357 HEATH cont.)
John 3 m Ala
Willis 1 m "

1822 Laborer
HEATH, Thomas 25 m Ala

HEATH, William
(See Nathan Horn).

1943 Physician
HEIDLE, J. B. 33 m Ga
Martha 32 f "
Florida 6 f Ala
Louisianna 4 f "
Elizabeth 2 f "
Ann 1 f "
WESCOTT, Hampton 8 m Fla

838 Farmer
HEIDLY, William 46 m SC
Susan 29 f "
Susan 17 f "
James 6 m Ala
Moses 5 m "
William 6/12 m "

1391
HEIDT, Sarah 52 f SC
Ann 25 f Ga
Almira 24 f "
Wiley (Cabinet Maker) 19 m "
BART, Sarah A. B. 22 f "
John W. 1 m Ala

1245 Merchant
HEINEMAN, S. 28 m Ger
Adelaide 26 f "
Hannah 3 f Ala
Eli 2 m "
SCHWARTZ, Lewis 29 m Ger
(Merchant).

431 Farmer ($600)
HELMS, Aaron 33 m NC
Mary M. 28 f Ga
William 13 m Ala
Frederick 10 m "
Judge 4 m "
Matilda 3 f "
Alexander 6/12 m "

389 Farmer ($400)
HELMS, Abraham 34 m NC
Nancy 32 f "
Emily 12 f Ala
Martha 12 f "
(Cont.)

(# 389 HELMS cont).
William 10 m Ala
Aaron 8 m "
Joel 6 m "
Adam 2 m "
Abraham, Sr. 79 m NC

650 Farmer ($500)
HELMS, Hilliard 33 m NC
Mahala 31 f "
Louisa 13 f Ala
William T. 12 m "
Jesse 9 m "
Mary J. 6 f "
Elizabeth 5 f "
Russell 4 m "
Lucinda 2 f "
Rachel 1 f "
Arch'd.(Cancer Doctor) 22 m NC

606 Farmer ($400)
HELMS, John 39 m NC
Halley 33 f "
Zilpha 15 f "
William 14 m Ala
Martha 13 f "
John J. 11 m "
George W. 10 m "
Sarah 9 f "
Joel 8 m "
Aaron 2 m "
Halley 6/12 f "

HENDERSON, David
Leroy
(See William Edge).

636 Farmer ($500)
HENDERSON, John 26 m Ala
Eliza 24 f "
Martha 1 f "
Mary 1/12 f "

1930 Farmer ($400)
HENDERSON, Joseph 25 m Ala
Margaret 25 f NC
William 1 m Ala

HENDRIX, Benjamin
(See D. Sylvester).

1181 Farmer
HENDRIX, Henry 48 m SC
Mary 27 f "
Margan 4 f Ala
Perry 2 m "
MARSHALL, Elias 30 m SC

1426 Drayman ($800)
HENDRIX, John, Sr. 53 m NY
Lucinda 42 f SC
John D. (Student) 25 m "
Whitfield " 23 m "
George " 15 m "
Mary J. 9 f Ala

212
HENDRIX, Mary M. 78 f Va

HENDRIX, Reuben
(See L. F. Stow).

177 Farmer ($100)
HENLEY, Adam 26 m SC
Letty 24 f "
John Q. 6 m Ala
Hezekiah 4 m "
George A. 10/12 m "

2291 Farmer ($200)
HENLEY, James 47 m NC
Elizabeth 30 f Ala
George (Farmer) 24 m NC
Curran " 16 m "
James 14 m "
Richard 9 m Ala
Nancy 5 f "
Sarah 3 f "
Rachel 15 f NC
John 6/12 m Ala

92 Farmer ($100)
HENLEY, John 31 m SC
Nancy 28 f NC
James 11 m Ala
Dixon H. L. 9 m "
Jefferson 7 m "
William 5 m "
Sarah 4 f "
Jane 3 f "
Joseph 2 m "

HENRY, James
Amanda
(See Adam Grubbs).

1713 Physician
HENRY, John D. 30 m Ga
Catherine 20 f "
John 1 m Ala

HERRING, C. A.
(See William King).

976 Farmer ($3,000)
HERRING, George 24 m NC
(Cont.)

(# 976 HERRING cont.)
Mary 48 f NC
DANFORD, Eli M. 25 m NC
(Laborer).

HERRING, James
(See James A. Parker).

HERRING, James R.
George
Samuel
Amanda
Matilda
(See William R. Favors).

665 Farmer ($1,000)
HERRING, John 56 m NC
Priscilla 24 f SC
Riley 10 m Ala
Julia A. 6 f "
Martha 4 f "
Hepsey J. 3 f "
George W. 2 m "

HERRIN, Joseph
(See George Scroggins).

1233 ($400)
HERRING, Mary 64 f Ga
James (Clerk) 45 m "
Henry (Silversmith) 26 m "
Thomas (Student) 16 m Fla

HERRING, Mary
(See Jeremiah Warren).

2177 Farmer ($300)
HERRING, Stephen 35 m Ga
Elizabeth 32 f "
James 10 m "
Mary 8 f Ala
William 3 m "
Martha 1 f "

2297 Laborer
HERRING, W. 27 m NC
Elmira 24 f Ala
Eliza 6 f "
James 4 m "
William 3 m "
Sarah 1 f "

1176 Farmer ($3,500)
HERRING, West 45 m NC
Charity 47 f "
Lewis 16 m Ala
Stephen 13 m "
Elizabeth 10 f "
(Cont.)

(# 1176 HERRING cont.)
Emanuel 8 m Ala
Martha 3 f "
Jackson 2 m "

1164 Farmer ($1,000)
HERRING, William 41 m NC
Sarah 24 f Ga
Martha 8 f Ala
James 6 m "
Mary A. 4 f "
Francis M. 9/12 m "
LESTER, Wm. (Farmer) 20 m "

470 Physician ($2,000)
HERRON, E. M. 40 m SC
Caroline 27 f "
Mary 7 f Ala
Harriet 5 f "
Derrel 4 m "
Edward 2 m "
HART, Edward 12 m "

HICKS, Adam
(See Samuel Wilkinson).

1455 Laborer
HICKS, Mathew 24 m Ga
Anna 22 f Ala

2287 Laborer
HICKS, Newton 47 m Ga
Nancy 40 f "
Morgan (Laborer) 18 m Ala
Jefferson " 16 m "
Elizabeth 10 f "
Sarah 8 f "
William 5 m "
Nancy 3 f "

310 Farmer ($400)
HIGHT, Felix 31 m Ga
Jane 28 f "
Robert 11 m "
Martha 10 f "
Frances 3 f Ala
Henry 6/12 m "
SAULS, John 10 m "

770 Farmer ($500)
HIGHTOWER, A. W. 30 m Ga
Sarah 24 f "
James 8 m Ala
Francis 6 m "
Amanda 4 f "
William 3 m "
Jane 1 f "

772 Farmer ($300)
HIGHTOWER, Isaac O. 24 m Ga
Rebecca 20 f Ala
Moly E. 7/12 f "

773 Farmer ($300)
HIGHTOWER, John T. 23 m Ga
Sarah 19 f "

1115 Farmer
HIGHTOWER, Robert F. 38 m Ga
Elizabeth 17 f SC
Elizabeth 3/12 f Ala
TAYLOR, George 18 m SC
(Farmer)
CHANEY, James O. 14 m Ala

905 Farmer ($1,500)
HIGHTOWER, Thomas A. 44 m Ga
Emma C. 39 f NC
Charles (Farmer) 20 m Ga
John " 18 m "
Sarah F. 17 f "
William S. (Farmer) 16 m "
Anna 13 f "
Amelia 11 f "
Mary J. 3 f Ala
Polk 2 m "
(John & Sarah F. married
within the year).

233 Farmer ($800)
HILL, B. W. 30 m SC
Catherine 25 f NC
John 8 m Ala
Mary 5 f "
Emily 3 f "
Catherine 7/12 f "

902 Insane (In poorhouse)
HILL, Charlotte 40 f --
Austin 4 m Ala

130 Farmer ($400)
HILL, Ephriam 43 m Ga
Ava 42 f NC
Martha 17 f Ga
Woodruff 6 m Ala
MINCHEW, Margaret 17 f Ga

1899 Farmer ($500)
HILL, Felix 46 m SC
Ann 36 f "
Jane 15 f Ala
John 13 m "
Sarah 12 f "
(Cont.)

(# 1899 HILL cont.)
Caroline 10 f Ala
William 4 m "
Felix 6/12 m "

78 Farmer ($500)
HILL, Francis W. 49 m Ga
Edney 47 f "
Edward (Farmer) 22 m "
John W. " 20 m "
James R. 17 m "

HILL, Hulda
(See Eliza C. Daniel).

258 Overseer
HILL, James R. 26 m Ga
Elizabeth 23 f Ala
Lorenzo 11/12 m "
SMITH, Ellen 13 f Ga

HILL, John M.
(See Joshua H. Danforth).

1736 Farmer
HILL, Lewis 70 m Va
Mary 62 f SC
Julia 20 f "
Wm. M. D. (Farmer) 18 m Ala

1400 Farmer
HILL, Martin 45 m SC
Sene 35 f NC
Isaiah 18 m Ala
Jane 15 f "
Maria 13 f "
Drusilla 10 f "
Bishop 7 m "
Hiram 5 m "
Elerlu 4 m "

HILL, Richard
(See Barney Ivey)

HILL, Sion
(See J. T. Hood).

HILL, William
(See Harmon H. Adams).

HILL, William M.
(See Samuel Nixon).

2148 Farmer ($100)
HINES, Lawrence 30 m Ga
Mary 25 f "
Willy 2 m Ala
Eliza 4/12 f "
John 5 m "
(Cont.)

(# 2148 HINES cont.)
PILANDER, Nancy 20 f Ga
Henry M. 6/12 m Ala

384 Farmer ($1,000)
HINOTE, Benjamin F. 54 m Ga
Elizabeth 51 f "
Frances 16 f "
Artemisia 14 f Ala
Benjamin F. 12 m "
Philip E. 9 m "

434 Farmer
HINOTE(?), Greenberry 21 m Ga
Sarah 21 f Ala
Ann E. 2/12 f "
DUNAWAY, Rhoda 16 f "

432 Farmer
HINOTE(?), Henry 27 m Ga
Margaret 27 f "
Elijah 1 m Ala

718 Shoemaker ($900)
HINSON, William 42 m NC
Maria 39 f NC
Jas. (Shoemaker) 16 m Ala
Jesse " 15 m "
Abraham S. 11 m "
William F. 8 m "
Albena 3 f "
Charles 3/12 m "
GRANGER, A. S. 21 m Ga
(Occp. not given).
HINSON, Jesse 66 m NC
(Occp. not given).
JOHNSON, Mary 56 f "
SUMMERSET, Joseph 24 m Ga
(Carpenter)
McCRARY, Alexander 23 m SC
(Grocer)
James A. (Grocer) 22 m "

140 Farmer ($250)
HIX, Francis 49 m Ga
Edney 48 f "
Edward (Farmer) 22 m "
John R. " 20 m "
James " 17 m "

2030 Farmer
HODGES, Elias G. 38 m Ga
TYE, John (Overseer) 20 m "

1048 Farmer ($10,000)
HODGES, George C. 52 m SC
Holliday (Farmer) 21 m Fla
(Cont.)

(# 1048 HODGES cont.)
George 14 m Ga
Sarah 1 f Ala
NEELY, Andrew G. 30 m Tenn
(Farmer)
Louisa 23 f Fla
George 5 m Tenn
Jesse 2 m Ala

2031 Farmer ($2,000)
HODGES, Pulaski 35 m Ga
Margaret 41 f "
William 10 m Ala
Robert 8 m "
James 6 m "
Jane 7/12 f "
Margaret 3 f "
TURK, George (Student) 19 m "
Lillis 14 f "

1013 Farmer ($800)
HOLDER, Abraham 40 m Ga
Silla 37 f "
Felix (Farmer) 20 m "
Mary 18 f "
David (Farmer) 16 m "
Thomas 14 m Ala
Jasper 13 m "
HOLT, Samantha 8 f SC

307 Farmer ($225)
HOLDER, John 32 m Ga
Mary 26 f "
Columbus 6 m "
Mary 1 f Ala

607 Farmer ($150)
HOLLAND, Jerse 52 m SC
Arpy 47 f NC
John (Farmer) 16 m Ala
Jerse 14 m "
Elizabeth 12 f "
Spencer 9 m "
Mary 7 f "
Thomas E. 5 m "
Abnela 3 f "

2128 Physician ($1,400)
HOLLAND, Joseph A. 30 m Ga
Sarah 26 f "
Charlotte E. 1 f Ala

608 Farmer
HOLLAND, William 24 m SC
Lucy 26 f Ala
Nancy 3 f "
Mary 1 f "
Charlotte 19 f SC

102 Farmer
HOLLAND, William 40 m Ga
Leonida 25 f "
Josiah 10 m Ala
BRYANT, Annis 56 f Ga

1341 Occp. not given ($3,000)
HOLLOMAN, A. B. 50 m Va
Amanda 29 f Ga
Mary 6 f Ala
Robert 3 m "
Henry 10/12 m "
BIRDSONG, Simanthe 18 f Ga

1373 Carpenter ($9,000)
HOLLOMAN, Eli C. 49 m Va

1454 Farmer
HOLLEMAN, William 63 m Ga
Margaret 42 f SC
John (Farmer) 24 m Ga
Mary 19 f "
Sarah 18 f "
Elizabeth 14 f "
Thomas 12 m "
Matthew 11 m "

184 Farmer ($150)
HOLLEY, Bricey 58 m Ga
Elizabeth 45 f SC
Mary A. 25 f Ga
Martha 22 f "
William 21 m "
Thomas 15 m "
Penney 12 f "
Jane 10 f Ala
John 8 m "

1796 Overseer
HOLLY, John 28 m Ga

HOLLEY, John
(See T. R. Sylvester).

990 Farmer ($300)
HOLLINGSWORTH, John K. 23 m Ga
Mary 17 f "
Mary 52 f Va
Ellender 25 f Ga
Mary 20 f "
James 18 m "
(John K. & Mary married
within the year).

937 Laborer
HOLMAN, John 39 m Ga
Amanda 22 f "
Winfield S. 2/12 m Ala

2241 Farmer
HOLMES, Hardy 45 m NC
Amanda 30 f "
Sarah 1 f Ala

1838 Farmer ($100)
HOLMES, Henry 52 m NC
Martha 25 f Ga
Barsheba 18 f "
Henry (Farmer) 16 m "
Matilda 12 f "
Benjamin 9 m "
Sarah 6 f "
Josephine 4 f Ala

1919 Farmer ($1,000)
HOLMES, N. G. 73 m SC
Jerusha 62 f "
WARD, Mary 60 f "
GREEN, Robt. (Farmer) 17 m Ga

1050 Farmer ($1,000)
HOLMES, Nathaniel G. 73 m SC
Jerusha 53 f "
GREEN, Robt. (Farmer) 18 m Ga
WARD, Mary 55 f "

170 Farmer ($1,200)
HOLMES, William 47 m NC
Sarah 40 f "
Arthur (Farmer) 16 m Ala
Elizabeth 13 f "
Melinda 11 f "
Sarah 9 f "
Amanda 7 f "
Edney 5 f "
Marion 3 m "
Margaret 2 f "

HOLSEY, Antionette
(See William T. Upshaw).

1495 Overseer
HOLSEY, James H. 29 m Ga

1803 Overseer
HOLSTON, John 27 m Ga
Lucy 21 f Ala
Mary 1 f "

1033 Farmer ($7,000)
HOLT, A. A. 27 m Ga
A. A. 18 f "
J. L. (Farmer) 20 m "
C. A. (Student) 19 m "

HOLT, Jane M.
(See Wingate M. Turner).

48 Farmer ($350)
HOLT, Randolph 50 m Va
Andrew 11 m Ala
Ann 9 f "
Scipio(Negro laborer) 65 m --

HOLT, Samantha
(See Abraham Holder).

1619 Overseer
HOLT, William M. 26 m Ga

527 Farmer ($600)
HOOD, J. T. 50 m NC
Elizabeth 39 f "
Bold R.* (Farmer) 19 m "
Sarah 9 f Ala
Elizabeth 5 f "
John T. 2 m "
FAIRCLOTH, Benj. 23 m NC
JOHNSTON, Sarah 14 f Ga
HILL, Sion (Laborer) 30 m NC
WILKS, Sarah 29 f SC
(* Bold Robin Hood married Sarah Johnston within the year. Will recorded Dec. 12, 1854, O. C. R. Book VI, p. 284, Barbour Co., Ala.)

HOOKER, James D.
(See Arch'd. Browning).

1302 Merchant ($1,500)
HOOLE, B. J. 37 m SC
Violetta W. 28 f "
James L. 9 m Ala
Sarah J. 6 f "
Mary J. 4 f "
Victoria S. 2 f "
McNAB, Robert(Clerk) 30 m SC

HOOLE, E. S.
(See Leroy L. Ryan).

1082 Farmer ($800)
Hooten, H. T. 33 m Ga
Rachel 23 f NC
Joseph 12 m Ga
Elizabeth 5 f "
Henry 3 m "
Tryphine 2 f "
James 1 m Ala

HOPE, Charlotte
(See Anthony Windham).

1088 Farmer
HOPKINS, Jackson 23 m SC
(Cont.)

(# 1088 HOPKINS cont.)
Rachel 21 f Ga
Caroline 6/12 f Ala

2017 Farmer ($1,100)
HORN, Joseph 26 m SC
Sarah 24 f Fla
Sarah 7 f Ala
Cordelia 5 f "
Ann 2 f "

HORNE, Judy
(See L. B. J. Parmer)

724 Farmer
HORN, Nathan 44 m NC
Margaret 35 f "
Elizabeth 13 f Ala
Mary 10 f "
Martha 7 f "
Eady 4 f "
Henry 2 m "
HEATH, William 5 m "

2018 Farmer ($2,300)
HORN, William 31 m SC
Nancy 45 f "
FLOWERS, Penelope 65 f "

223 Farmer
HORNE, William A. 31 m Ga
Missouri 21 f Ala
BRASWELL, Letty 21 f Ga

1902 Farmer
HORTON, James 36 m Ga
Eliza 26 f "
Mary 6 f "
John 3 m Ala
James 1 m "

2282 Farmer
HOULIN, Elisha 35 m Ga
Sarah 30 f "
William 7 m Ala
John 5 m "
Harriet 2 f "

HOUSE, Jackson
Irwin
Emily
Lewrana
(See William Weathers).

319 Farmer ($600)
HOUSTON, Edward, Sr. 65 m NC
Sarah 45 f "
Washington (Farmer) 22 m "
(Cont.)

(# 319 Houston cont.)
John (Farmer) 20 m NC
William " 18 m Ala
Hopkins " 16 m Ala
Charles 14 m "
LaFayette 12 m "
Samuel 1 m "

320 Farmer
HOUSTON, James 32 m NC
Nancy 25 f Ala
Hannah 6 f "
Mosely 5 m "
Edward 3 m "
Julia 2 f "

1955 Farmer ($200)
HOVEY, James 46 m Mass
Mary 31 f SC
James 12 m Ala
Frances 4 f "
Henry W. H. 1 m "

HOWARD, Emma S.
(See Martha Lamar)

566 Farmer ($80)
HOWELL, Joseph 26 m Ga
Martha 18 f "
Samuel 4 m Ala
Caroline 1 f "

1977
HOWELL, Sarah 60 f Ga
Washington 24 m Ga
(Farmer - $150)
Turner (Farmer) 19 m "
Mary 16 f Ala
Elizabeth 14 f "

1397 Farmer ($160)
HUDSON, Elijah 61 m NC
Elizabeth 57 f "
Adeline 22 f "
Nancy 20 f "
Elijah (farmer) 15 m "
Nelly 12 f "
Lissey 3 f Ala

1945 Farmer ($600)
HUDSON, G. H. 45 m Ga
Louisianna 35 f "
Needham (Farmer) 18 m "
Elizabeth 16 f "
Jonathan 14 m "
Abigail 10 f Ala
Amazon 8 f "
(Cont.)

(# 1945 HUDSON cont.)
Irwin 4 m Ala
Missouri 7/12 f "

37 Sawyer
HUDSPETH, Columbus 42 m Ga
Jane 28 f Ga
Ann E. 3 f Ala
Missouri 1 f "
BECK, Letty 16 f Ga

151 Laborer
HUFF, Terrel 24 m Ga
Elizabeth 26 f "
Martha 5 f "
Madison 3 m "
Cinderella 1 f "
Maria 2/12 f "

HUGENON, Sarah
(See Benjamin Craps).

1324 Farmer ($1,000)
HUGGINS, R. H. 35 m Ga
Frances 24 f "
David 1 m Ala

HUGGINS, Robert
(See Samuel W. Strange).

480 Farmer
HUGHS, Daniel 37 m SC
Elizabeth 38 f Ga
Nancy 16 f Fla
Elizabeth 12 f Ala
Margaret 9 f "
William W. 7 m "
Daniel 5 m "
infant 1/12 m "

158 Mason
HUGHS, George W. 28 m SC
Rebecca 22 f Ga
Washington 2 m "
Elvira 5/12 f "

676 Farmer ($300)
HUGHS, John 55 m SC
Elizabeth 52 f "

28 Farmer ($250)
HUGHES, Stephen 37 m SC
Ellender 38 f NC
Francis 13 m Ga
Elizabeth 12 f "
Sarah 2 f Ala
GINWRIGHT, Sarah 16 f NC
Canady 13 m Ala
Martha 11 f "

133 Farmer ($400)
HUGHS, Willis 50 m SC
Julia A. 48 f "
Joseph (Farmer) 20 m Ga
Ellison " 16 m "
Lorenzo D. " 15 m "
Willis M. 11 m "
Martha V. 8 f "

698 Farmer ($100)
HULEN, Thomas 39 m SC
Elizabeth 36 f "
Caroline 13 f Ala
William 11 m "
Adeline 9 f "
John 7 m "
Elizabeth 5 f "
Wiley 2 m "

1799 Overseer
HUNT, Henry 45 m Ga
Martha 40 f "
Robert 18 m "
Martha 17 f "

1402
HUNT, Nancy 30 f Ga
Wyatt 11 m "
Lucy 9 f "
Edna 7 f "
James 5 m "

1843 Farmer
HUNT, Richard 28 m SC
Elizabeth 25 f "
Evanilda 4 f "

HUNT, William
(See Milton A. Browder).

1588 Physician ($2,600)
HUNTER, James W. 37 m Ga
Julia E. 30 f "
Caroline 11 f "
James 9 m Ala
Hope 7 f "
Julia 2 f "
JACKSON, Emily 10 f "

1670 Farmer ($8500)
HUNTER, John L. 52 m SC

488 Farmer ($700)
HUNTER, Marshall 50 m SC
Sarah 41 f "
James H. (Farmer) 17 m "
Ebenzer " 15 m "
Daniel 12 m Ala
(Cont.)

(# 488 HUNTER cont.)
Beauchamp 10 m Ala
Green 8 m "
Caroline 6 f "
William 1 m "
GLOVER, Wiley 12 m SC
(Farmer)

835 ($1,800)
HUNTER, Sarah E. 31 f Ga
Sarah B. 8 f Ala
Mary 4 f Ga

285 Farmer ($1,200)
HUNTER, William A. 23 m SC
MERRILL, Elizabeth A. 37 f SC
Eliza 7 f Ala
Allen K. 5 m "

HURD, Aaron
(See Sherrod N. Parker).

1182 Teacher
HURD, R. W. 45 m SC
Matilda 40 f "
Edna 24 f "
DeKalb (Student) 15 m Ala
St. Helena 9 f "
Matilda 3 f "
Robert 1 m "

HURD, William
(See Washington Taylor).

1038 Farmer
HURST, James 35 m SC
Temperance 26 f Ala
John 11 m "
Jefferson 8 m "
James 6 m "
Joseph 4 m "
Susan 2 f "

2024 Laborer
HUTCHINSON, A. B. 40 m Ga
Elizabeth 40 f "
Abraham (Laborer) 21 m "
Jacob " 20 m "
John " 18 m "
Wellborn " 15 m "
Isaac 13 m "
James 10 m "
Mary 25 f "

HUTCHINSON, John
(See Duncan Cunningham)

1273 Merchant ($1,300)
HYATT, N. M. 38 m NY
(Cont.)

(# 1273 HYATT cont.)
Sarah 26 f Ala
Mary 6/12 f "
McKINNON, Alexander 25 m NC
(Clerk)

2151 Laborer
HYSMITH, W. B. 30 m Ga
Epsey 23 f "
Matthias 1 m Ala

INGLET, Georgia
(See Thomas Steedman)

IVES, Mary
(See Austin Williams).

1616 Farmer ($20,300)
IVEY, Barney 54 m NC
Ailsey 49 f "
James (Student) 19 m Ga
Josephine 13 f "
Barney 12 m Ala
Louis Emma 10 f "
HILL, Richard 20 m Ga
(Overseer).

1191 Farmer
IVEY, John 34 m NC
Elizabeth 22 f SC
Jane 1 f Ala

1795 Farmer ($6,000)
IVEY, Malichi 34 m Ga
Sarah 20 f SC
John B. 5 m Ala

#1751 Farmer
IVEY, Robert 23 m Ga
Virginia 19 f "

1837
JACKSON, Asa 26 m NC
Susan 25 f SC
Lucinda 4 f Ala
Malinda 4/12 f "

JACKSON, Emily
(See James W. Hunter).

2183 Miller ($150)
JACKSON, George W. 50 m Va
Matilda 33 f SC
Charles (Miller) 16 m Ga
William 9 m Ala
Nancy 6 f "
George 4 m "
Daniel 2 m "
(Cont.)

(# 2183 JACKSON cont.)
HALL, Mary 19 f SC
Wesley 2 m Ala

1836 Farmer ($200)
JACKSON, Gillis 55 m NC
Rachel 52 f "
May 22 f "
Laney 16 f "
Elizabeth 13 f "
William (Farmer) 15 m Ga

515 Farmer
JACKSON, Gilmer 19 m Ga

514 Farmer ($9,000)
JACKSON, J. W. W. 41 m Ga
Elizabeth 39 f "
Margaret 17 f "
Walker (Farmer) 15 m Ala
Wellborn 13 m "
George 11 m "
Louisianna 5 f "
Priscilla 5 f "

1166 Farmer ($600)
JACKSON, Jasper N. 26 m Ala
Mary A. 21 f Ga
James T. 2 m Ala
Moses T. 1 m "

995 Farmer ($2,500)
JACKSON, John 63 m Mass
Rhoda 33 f Tenn
Wallen(?) 13 m Ala
Stanley 11 m "
William H. 10 m "
Rowena 8 f "
Jane 7 f "
Virginia 5 f "
Glaucus 2 m "

1165 Farmer ($600)
JACKSON, Jordan A. 30 m Ga
Elizabeth L. 23 f "
Jacinth O. 4 m Ala
Mary J. 3 f "
Jasper N. 2 m "
John 1/12 m "

1766
JACKSON, Mary 22 f Ga
Elizabeth 4 f "

638 Farmer ($150)
JACKSON, Starling 34 m NC
(Cont.)

(# 638 JACKSON cont.)
Margaret 35 f NC
Juliann 12 f Ala
Nathan F. 9 m "
Lucy 7 f "
Sarah A. 4 f "
Mary 2 f "

JACKSON, Thomas
(See Benjamin Gardner)

JACKSON, Thomas
(See Florina Hall).

1327 Carpenter
JACKSON, Thomas 50 m Ga
Martha 22 f "
SAWYER, Joshua 18 m Ga
(Laborer)
Eudocia 14 f "
James 11 m "

JACKSON, William
(See John Wilder).

2140 Laborer
JAMERSON, John 34 m SC
Nancy 20 f Ga
John 1 m Ala

1809 Farmer ($2,000)
JAMES, Edwin 63 m SC
Mary 47 f "
Daniel D. (Boatman) 23 m "
James E. (Farmer) 22 m "
Robert 20 m "
Lucy 12 f Ala
Thomas 10 m "
Green 8 m "
Susan 4 f "
Jonas 1/12 m "
COX, Green S. 40 m Va
(Engineer)
Ann 26 f SC
Georgia A. 10 f Ala
William 8 m "
Mary 6 f "
James 4 m "
Cleopatra 2 f "

413 Merchant ($220)
JAMES, John B. 30 m SC
Mary E. 21 f Ala
Carleton 4 m "
Roxanna 2 f "
Claudia 8/12 f "
JAMES, James 22 m SC
(Farmer)

144 Farmer ($700)
JAMES, William 41 m SC
Ann 42 f "
William H. (Farmer) 19 m "
Louisa 18 f "
Elizabeth 15 f "
Amanda 13 f "
Sophronia 11 f Ga
Enos 9 m "
Wesley 7 m "
Lucinda 4 f "
Jane 3 f "
Samantha 1 f Ala

1786 Farmer
JARRETT, Joseph 47 m Ga
Maria 40 f "
George (Farmer) 18 m "
Felix " 16 m "
Mary 15 f "
Thomas 13 m "
Alexander 11 m "
Sophia 9 f "
Franklin 7 m "
James 5 m "
Amanda 3 f "
Joanna 5/12 f Ala

2075 Farmer ($800)
JENKINS, Daniel 63 m NC
Nancy 54 f "
Elisha (Farmer) 20 m "
Isham " 16 m "
Daniel 14 m "
Nancy 10 f "

2076 Farmer ($600)
JENKINS, Richardson 36 m NC
Delilah 33 f "
Martha 14 f "
Riley 12 m "
Sarah 9 f "
Daniel 5 m Ala
Jesse 1 m "

800 Farmer ($400)
JENKINS, Riley 30 m NC
Lucretia 25 f "
William 6 m Ala
George 5 m "
Samuel 2 m "
William 22 m NC

JENNINGS, Sophia
(See Amos Green).

1524 Farmer
JERNIGAN, C. H. 21 m Ga
(Cont.)
Caroline 43 f Ga
Frances 19 f "
James (Student) 15 m "
Albert 13 m "

JERNIGAN, Fereby M.
(See Peter Cunningham).

JERNIGAN, Milly
(See William Jernigan).

25 Farmer ($600)
JERNIGAN, William 25 m Ala
Martha 22 f Ga
Jason J. 4 m Ala
Stephen D. 3 m "
Mary J. 1 f "
JERNIGAN, Milly 60 f NC

1121 Laborer
Jewell, Otis 41 m Me
Mary 30 f Ala
William 3 m "
Fabius 5 m "
Rosaline 1 f "

2139
JIMMERSON, Sarah 40 f SC

627 Farmer ($2,000)
JOHNS, Francis 42 m SC
Nancy 45 f Ga
FAULK, Julia 10 f Ala
Nancy 8 f "

1446 Laborer ($200)
JOHNSON, John 48 m Sc
Martha 18 f Ga
Nancy 16 f "
Jacob 14 m Fla

1168 Farmer ($200)
JOHNSON, Lawson 22 m Ala
Mary 16 f "
Virginia 1/12 f "

JOHNSON, Mary
(See William Hinson).

JOHNSON, Aleniren(?) 24 f Ga
(See John W. Raines).

1150 Farmer ($350)
JOHNSON, Alexander 36 m SC
Elizabeth 25 f Ala
Alexander 12 m "
Amanda 9 f "
Wilson 8 m "
Martha 4 f "

JOHNSTON, Alexander P.
(See Jared P. Barber).

2261 Laborer
JOHNSTON, Andrew 23 m Ala

1404 Farmer ($1,000)
JOHNSTON, Bynum 29 m SC
Martha 22 f "
Wm. W. 7 m "
Jane 5 f "
Mary 3 f "
Bynum 1 m "

726 ($500)
JOHNSTON, Catherine 37 f NC
William 13 m Ala
John 11 m "
Felix 7 m "
Julia 4 f "

1204
JOHNSTON, Clia 18 f SC
William 6/12 m Ala

1089 Farmer ($350)
JOHNSTON, David 28 m SC
Mary 18 f Ga
Cornelia 1 f Ala
Silla 1/12 f "

JOHNSTON, David
Martha A.
Thomas C.
Sarah E.
(See Martha Lamar).

521 Farmer ($600)
JOHNSTON, Isham 46 m SC
Mahala 45 f "
Alexander 17 m Ga
James 15 m "
John W. 12 m "
Catherine 5 f "

1403 Farmer ($2,000)
JOHNSTON, J. D. 36 m SC
Mary 40 f "
Martha F. * 17 f "
Mary E. * 16 f "
Virginia * 13 f "
William 4 m "
Rachel 70 f Va

941 Farmer
JOHNSTON, J. W. 28 m Ga
Louisa 23 f SC
Lurena 2 f Ala
WHITNEY, Francis 12 m Md
JOHNSTON, Mary 52 f Ga
Isham (Occp. none) 23 m Fla
David (Student) 17 m "
Joseph 14 m "
Mary 10 f "
William (Farmer) 20 m "

315 Farmer
JOHNSTON, James 22 m SC
Harriet 25 f Ala
Mary 2 f "
John 10/12 m "

JOHNSTON, James D.
(See David Garret).

JOHNSTON, Jane
(See William Fleming)

884 Farmer
JOHNSTON, Jefferson 38 m SC
Epsey 30 f "
Louisa 8 f "
Calvin 6 m "
Emeline 3 f Ala
Angeline 1/12 f "

1119 Farmer ($1,500)
JOHNSTON, Jesse 48 m SC
Sarah 43 f "
William (Farmer) 23 m Ala
Rachel 20 f "
Emanuel (Farmer) 18 m "
Louisa 16 f "
Mary 14 f "
Julia 12 f "
James 10 m "
Lidia 8 f "
Frances 6 f "
Sarah 4 f "
Jesse 2/12 m "

302 Farmer ($1,700)
JOHNSTON, John 66 m SC
Mary 54 f "
Patience 21 f "
(Cont.)

* Children of Mary Sylvester & John H. Peake. Second Marriage of Mary S. Peake to Jonathan D. Johnston. See O.C.R. III - ABSTRACTS OF WILLS & ESTATES, Barbour Co., Ala.

(# 302 JOHNSTON cont.)
John W. (Farmer) 18 m SC
George W. " 16 m "
GRANTHAM, Edward J. 9 m "
Mary J. 6 f "

JOHNSTON, John
(See Wiley Oliver).

JOHNSTON, John
(See Richard C. Ethridge)

1100 Farmer
JOHNSTON, John 70 m SC
Elizabeth 21 f NC
Ruth 3 f Ala

2300 Laborer
JOHNSTON, John A. 24 m NC
Martha 21 f Ala
Elizabeth 4 f "
Martha 2 f "
John 3/12 m "

1247 Merchant ($3,000)
JOHNSTON, L. F. 30 m Ala
Martha 21 f Ga
Claude 4 m Ala
Martha 9 f "

1078 Farmer ($400)
JOHNSTON, Lewis A. T. 33 m SC
Patience 32 f "
Nancy 11 f Ala
Felder 8 m "
Elizabeth 4 f "
Rosanna 3 f "
Thomas 1/12 m "

2260 Farmer
JOHNSTON, Philip 49 m NC
John (Farmer) 20 m Ala
Luison(?) (Farmer) 17 m "
Judge 14 m "
Martha 9 f "
Elmira 6 f "

2114 Farmer ($3,000)
JOHNSTON, R. S. 41 m Va
Asenith 35 f Ga
Martha 17 f "
George 14 m "
WILLIAMS, George 22 m "
(Overseer)

1237 Farmer ($5,000)
JOHNSTON, Richard M. 20 m Fla
Amanda 21 f "
Marshall 1 m Ala
Elizabeth 50 f Ga

2299 Farmer ($400)
JOHNSTON, Samuel 40 m NC
Jane 37 f "
William (Farmer) 18 m "
Thomas " 16 m Ala
Sarah 13 f "
Martha 11 f "
Eliza 9 f "
James 5 m "
Theresa 2 f "

JOHNSTON, Sarah
(See J. T. Hood).

750 Farmer ($800)
JOHNSTON, Timothy 52 m NC
Elizabeth 51 f SC
William (Farmer) 20 m Ala
Phillip R. " 17 m "
Jacob E. " 15 m "
Timothy 12 m "
Mary 7 f "

JOHNSTON, Turner
(See Benjamin Warner).

JOHNSTON, Turner
(See Franklin E. Baker).

1268 Laborer
JOHNSTON, William 21 m Ga
Susan 17 f SC
Mary 5/12 f Ala
BRADY, Elijah 12 m "

1673 Farmer
JOHNSTON, William L. 21 m Fla

134 Farmer
JOINER, Canady 41 m NC
Lucy 26 f "
Sarah J. 6 f Ga
Mary E. 4 f Ala
William C. 1 m "

1079 Farmer ($1,000)
JOINER, Nathan 48 m SC
Cinthia 47 f "
Allen (Farmer) 27 m "
H. P. " 22 m "
Jones(?) 15 m Ala
Julia 13 f "
Robinson 12 m "
Lewis 7 m

1986 Farmer ($800)
JONES, Aerial 30 m NC
Matilda 26 f "
(Cont.)

(# 1986 JONES cont.)
Retus 9 m Ala
Josephus 7 m "
Mary 5 f "
Americus 3 m "
Sarah 1 f Fla

JONES, Adaline
(See M. D. Williams).

1368 Laborer
JONES, E. J. 31 m Ga

JONES, Elijah
(See R. T. White).

211
JONES, Elizabeth 38 f Ga
William (Farmer) 21 m Ga
Macy (?) 19 f Ga
Joseph (Farmer) 16 m Ga
Melinda 14 f Ala
Penelope 12 f "
Elizabeth 9 f "
Eliza 6 f "

1882 Farmer ($ 600)
JONES, Henry 87 m Va
Ellender 40 f Ga
Joseph 12 m Ala
Benjamin 8 m "

1884 Farmer ($150)
JONES, Henry L. 59 m Ga
Elizabeth 45 f "
Mary 18 f "
Emily 16 f "

2173 Farmer ($2,500)
JONES, James A. 35 m SC
Mary A. 30 f Ga
Elizabeth 9 f "
William 5 m "
Ellen 2 f Ala

1987 Farmer ($700)
JONES, James W. 35 m NC
Maria 32 f "
Leroy 14 m Ala
Thomas 13 m "
James 11 m "
William 9 m "
Wiley 7 m "
John 5 m "
Martha 4 f "
Nancy 2 f "
Susan 1 f "

518 Farmer ($300)
JONES, John A. 42 m Ga
Martha 23 f "
Lewis 21 m "
James R. 11 m "
Mary C. 10 f "
John H. 8 m "
Miles J. 7 m "
Solomon 4 m "
Thomas L. 3 m "
Joseph C. 5/12 m Ala

1760 Physician ($1,000)
JONES, Joseph 35 m SC
Cornelia 26 f Ga
BETHUNE, Mary 15 f "

1017
JONES, Levicey 60 f SC
Seaborn 14 m Ga

JONES, Martha J.
(See James E. Gachet).

JONES, Orren
(See Clark Echols).

181
JONES, Penelope 30 f Ga
James 12 m Ala
Mary 10 f "
Sarah 9 f "
Jasper 8 m "
William 7 m "

615 Farmer
JONES, Perry H. 20 m Ga
Martha 19 f SC
John 6/12 m Ala

1730 Farmer
JONES, Robert N. 42 m SC
Penelope 33 f Ga
Jasper 4 m Ala
POPE, James 12 m "
Frances 11 f "
Sarah 7 f "
Henry 6 m "

1875 Farmer ($400)
JONES, Russell 34 m NC
Elizabeth 23 f "
Alexander 3 m Ala
Margaret 6/12 f "
McCLURE, Mathis C. 24 m NC
(Farmer)
(Cont.)

(# 1875 JONES cont.)
Isabella 20 f Ala
(Mathis & Isabella McClure married within the year).

JONES, Sarah
(See Early Everett).

2027 Farmer ($700)
JONES, Seaborn 35 m SC
Jane 29 f "
William 9 m "
Chloe 7 f "
John 5 m "
Wiley 3 m Ala
Benjamin 8/12 m "

60 Farmer
JONES, Seaborn 32 m SC
Mary A. 31 f Ga
Caroline 12 f "
Elizabeth 9 f "
Lucetta 8 f Ala
Matthew 6 m "
Narcissa 4 f "
Thomas 1 m "

1318 Farmer
JONES, Silas 30 m Va
Margaret 21 f Ga
(Married within the year).

1520 Farmer ($80)
JONES, Thomas 44 m NC
Martha 35 f SC
Sarah 18 f Ga
Benjamin (Farmer) 16 m "
Margaret 14 f "
Abner 10 m "
Louisa 8 f Ala
Thomas 6 m "
John 5 m "
David 1 m "

2204 Laborer
JONES, W. E. 30 m Ga
Cinthia 23 f SC

993 Overseer
JONES, William 39 m Va
Elizabeth 39 f Ga
Lucinda 14 f "
Marietta 12 f "
Daniel 8 m "
Nancy 5 f "

1883 Farmer
JONES, William 28 m Ga
Rebecca 20 f NC
William 5 m Ala
Louisa 3 f "
Hollinger 1 m "

7 Farmer
JORDAN, Eli 23 m Ga
Martha A. 24 f "
Sarah F. 5 f "
Thomas 4 m Ala
John 1 m "

JORDAN, Hardy A.
(See D. Sylvester).

1544 Merchant ($600)
JORDAN, Henry L. 29 m Va
Ann C. 20 f Ga
George 3 m Ala
CRIMES, Cornelia J. 12 f "
DANIEL, John L. 20 m Ga
(Clerk)

JORDAN, J. W.
(See Austin Cargill).

1541 Merchant ($1,500)
JORDAN, Junius 36 m Va
Frances 34 f Ga
Henry 9 m "
Julian 7 m "
Junius 5 m Ala
Frances 4 f "
Martha 2 f "
WEYMAN, Rebecca 36 f Ga

152 Farmer ($150)
JORDAN, Membrance 50 m SC
Melinda 35 f Ga
Francis M. (Farmer) 17 m "
James 12 m "
Joseph 11 m "
William 7 m "
Simeon 5 m "
Abraham 2 m Ala

JORDAN, Nancy
(See John Bailey)

1890 ($200)
JORDAN, Olive 48 f Ga
John (Farmer) 21 m "
Henry " 19 m Ala
Mary 16 f "
William 12 m "
(Cont.)

(# 1890 JORDAN cont.)
Martha 8 f Ala
James 5 m "

JORDAN, Olivia W.
(See Jesse Batts).

1865
JORDAN, Sarah 36 f Ga
Mary 15 f Ala
Sarah 11 f "

JOSEY, J. J.
(See Joseph Cobb)

1253 Merchant
JOYCE, E. C. 30 m Ga
Elizabeth 19 f "
Edward 1/12 m Ala
THOMAS, Aaron 18 m "
(Clerk)

1215 Merchant ($3,000)
JOYCE, M. H. 41 m Ga
Sarah 23 f "

JUSTICE, Adolphus
(See Miles McInnis).

621 Farmer
JUSTICE, Blake 41 m Ga
Rebecca 32 f "
Gustavus 16 m "
Athelston 14 m Ala
William H. 8 m "
Frances 3 f "

JUSTICE, Edward
Sarah
(See Robert Pickett)

JUSTICE, James
(See John R. Robertson).

JUSTICE, John J.
(See James A. Stringer)

88 Farmer ($120)
KAY, Hiram 47 m SC
Nancy 38 f Ga
Jasper 11 m "
Newton 11 m "
Ann 7 f Ala
Sarah 6 f "
Joseph 4 "
Rebecca 2 f "
William 2/12 m "

1260 Farmer
KEELS, Elias M. 32 m Ala
Martha 19 f Ga
Mary 4/12 f Ala
William (Farmer) 28 m "
Niecy " 59 m SC
($800)

KEELS, Martha
Joseph
(See Jonathan Brown).

KEILS, Joseph
(See Jasey P. French).

544
KEILS, Susan 32 f Ga
Elizabeth 10 f "
Susan 6 f "
Georgiann 2 f Ala

KEEN, Lucinda A.
(See John D. Caton).

2255 Farmer ($800)
KEENER, Tilman B. 46 m NC
Stacy 35 f "
William (Farmer) 19 m "
Eveline 13 f Ala
Lawson 11 m "
Harrison 8 m "
Tilman 6 m "
Eliza 5 f "
Gaines 4 m "
James 3 m "
John 2 m "
Thomas 1/12 m "
Linson 1 m "

KELLY, Elizabeth
(See Robert P. Banks).

1850 Farmer
KELLY, Marion 31 m SC
Sarah 30 f "
James 10 m Ala
John 8 m "
Travis 6 m "
Mary 4 f "
Dorcas 2 f "

KELLY, William
Sarah
Martha J.
(See Isaac Heath).

1938 Farmer ($1,000)
KELLY, William C. 40 m SC
(Cont.)

(# 1938 KELLY cont.)

Elizabeth	34	f	SC
James	12	m	"
Charles	10	m	"
Daniel	7	m	Ala
John	5	m	"
Mary	2	f	"

1846 Farmer

KEMP, Jesse	26	m	SC
Matilda	25	f	Ala
Elizabeth	5	f	"

203 Farmer ($300)

KENNEDY, Daniel	33	m	Scot
Nancy	31	f	NC
Sibby	5	f	Ala
Hugh A.	3	m	"
Hector	2/12	m	"
SIKES, John (Laborer)	32	m	"
Sarah	26	f	"
Needham	1	m	"

806 ($600)

KENNEDY, Fanny	47	f	NC
John	19	m	"
James	15	m	Ga
Alsey	10	f	"
Elizabeth	8	f	"

805 Farmer

KENNEDY, Isaac	24	m	NC
Isabella	17	f	Ga
Thomas	1	m	Ala

1356 Farmer ($1,500)

KENNEDY, John	62	m	NC
David (Farmer)	25	m	"
Joseph "	22	m	"
SHELBY, Harriet	23	f	"
Emeline	3	f	Ala
John	1	m	"

1107 Farmer ($600)

KENNEDY, John	36	m	NC
Ann	26	f	SC
James	11	m	"
Spencer	9	m	"
Lawrence	7	m	Ala
Sanford	5	m	"
Sarah	1	f	"

1357 Farmer ($800)

KENNEDY, John M.	33	m	NC
Mary	25	f	Ala

(Cont.)

(# 1357 KENNEDY cont.)

Susan	4	f	Ala
Mary	3	f	"
John	1	m	"

868 Farmer ($800)

KENNEDY, Thomas	39	m	NC
Catherine	40	f	SC
Martha	16	f	Ala
John	13	m	"
Thomas	11	m	"
Mary	9	f	"
Cornelius	7	m	"
William	4	m	"

1657 Farmer ($400)

KENNEDY, Tomnay	46	m	NC
John (Farmer)	20	m	"
James "	18	m	"
Alsey	11	f	Ga
Elizabeth	8	f	"

1358 Farmer ($300)

KENNEDY, William	30	m	NC
Clary	22	f	"
Joseph	2	m	Ala

1607 Farmer

KENNEDY, William	61	m	NC
Sarah	59	f	"
WOOD, Reuben J. (Farmer)	24	m	"
John	9	m	"

KENNON, Emily
(See Martha Bludworth).

KENNON, Jane
(See Green Beauchamp).

1622 Farmer ($800)

KENNYMORE, John C.P.	37	m	SC
Nancy	43	f	Ga
CRAPS, Jane V.	17	f	SC

294 Laborer

KENT, Green	28	m	Ga
Frances	22	f	"

2015 Farmer ($2,500)

KENT, Guilford	42	m	Ga
Susan	25	f	SC
Stephen (Idiot)	32	m	Ga

426 Farmer

KETCHUM, Bartley W.	26	m	Ala
Sarah	28	f	NC

640 Farmer ($350)
KETCHUM, David 57 m NJ
Mary L. 40 f Ga
David (Farmer) 18 m Ala
LaFayette 12 m "
Matilda C. 10 f "
Benjamin F. 6 m "
Ann E. 25 f "
Elizabeth J. 15 f "

KETCHUM, William W.
James K.
Gilbert M.
(See Tyron Carr).

KEY, Milley
(See Catherine Mitchell).

2214 Millwright ($1,500)
KEY, Thomas A. 37 m Ga
Eliza 25 f "
James (Farmer) 16 m "
Sarah 14 f "
Emily 12 f "
Thomas 10 m "
Sophronia 8 f "
Demarius 6 f Ala
Viney 4 f "
Watson 2 m "
Henry 1 m "

KIDD, Eliza
(See David Lore).

2001
KILCHRIST, Lucy 35 f Ga
Martha 9 f "
Catherine 7 f "
Solomon 6 m "
Thielder 4 f Ala

278 Farmer
KILPATRICK, Easler 31 m SC
Emily 27 f NC
William 14 m Ala
Melissa 11 f "
Lucinda 9 f "
Samuel 7 m "
Melinda 6 f "
Marion 5 m "
Franklin 2 m "
Mary 1/12 f "

531 Farmer
KILPATRICK, Isaac 27 m SC
Warry (Farmer, $600) 59 m "
Levina 34 f "
(Cont.)

(# 531 KILPATRICK cont.)
Warry (Farmer) 20 m Ala
Easler " 19 m "
James S. " 16 m "
Elizabeth 56 f SC

532 Farmer
KILPATRICK, J. A. 30 m SC
Elizabeth 34 f "
Easler 3 m Ala
Warry 2 m "
Isaac 8/12 m "

591 Farmer
KILPATRICK, Jesse 32 m SC
Nancy 18 f Ala
Marion P. 1 m "

737 Farmer ($1,000)
KILPATRICK, William H. 43 m SC
Elizabeth 42 f "
Harriet 21 f "
Abner (Farmer) 16 m Ala
Almas(?) 13 m "
Caroline 13 f "
Sarah Ann 12 f "
Mary 10 f "
Martha 8 f "
Rebecca 6 f "
Alexander 4 m "
Frances 3 f "

592 Farmer
KILPATRICK, William R. 25 m SC
Rebecca 15 f Ala

2056 Farmer ($2,000)
KING, Abner H. 31 m Ga
Elizabeth 29 f NC
Sarah 4 f Ala
Henry 2 m "
John 4/12 m "

KING, John
Gabriel
Nancy
Smithey
(See Elisha Rumley).

2042 Farmer ($1,500)
KING, Robert H. 25 m Ga
Mary 18 f "
Henry G. 1 m Ala

862 Farmer ($1,600)
KING, Robert H. 25 m Ga
Mary 18 f "
Henry 1 m Ala

862 Farmer ($1,600)
KING, Robert H. 25 m Ga
Mary 18 f "
Henry 1 m Ala

KING, Sheppard
Marshall
(See Martha Snipes).

KING, Sheppard
Marshall
(See E. Snipes).

997 Farmer ($500)
KING, T. C. 23 m Ga
Elizabeth 23 f Fla
Catherine 1 f Ala
Lurana 45 f Ga

2043 Farmer ($1,500)
KING, Tandy W. 22 m Ga
Tillitha 21 f Ala
(Married within the year).

1094 Farmer
KING, William 19 m Ga
Sarah 25 f "

498 Farmer ($1,500)
KING, William 39 m NC
Mary 34 f SC
Sarah 12 f Ala
James 6 m "
Susan 1 f "
HERRING, C. A. 10 f "

KIRKLAND, James
(See William N. Atkinson).

361 Farmer
KIRKLAND, Snowden 55 m SC
Mahaley 28 f NC
Everett 14 m Ga
Melinda 13 f "
William 12 m Ala
Joel 11 m "
Daniel 11 m "
Winston 6 m "
Martha 2 f "

2301 Farmer
KNIGHT, H. 35 m NC
Malinda 30 f "
Thomas 10 m Ala
Sarah 8 f "
William 6 m "
James 4 m "
Mary 2 f "

408 Farmer
KNIGHT, Nathaniel 28 m Ga
Dicey 28 f NC
Rollin 4 m Ala
Louisa 1 f "

1167 Farmer
KNIGHT, Thomas J. 38 m Ga
Sarah 28 f "
Martha 11 f "
Mary 7 f "
Susan 5 f "
John 4 m "
KNIGHT, Rolla J. 33 m "
(Farmer).

616 Farmer ($1,000)
KNIGHT, William 53 m NC
Mary A. 50 f Md
William (Farmer) 21 m Ala
Alexander " 17 m "
Winfield S. 12 m "

533
KNIGHTON, Catherine 28 f Ga
Polly 10 f Ala
John 8 m "
Celia 4 f "
Elizabeth 3 f "
William 2 m "
Colden 5/12 m "

855 Farmer
KNOWLES, Joseph 20 m Ga
Lucinda 20 f NC
(Married within the year).

1546 Overseer
KNOWLES, Wiley 30 m Ga
Martha 25 f "
Caroline 6 f Ala
Mary 2 f "

KOLB, R. F. C.
(See R. C. Shorter)

682 Physician ($400)
LACY (Lary?), John 45 m Scot
Mary A. 42 f "
James 13 m "
Mary 17 f "
Isabella 5 f Ala

1605 Farmer
LAMAR, John O. 30 m Ga
Elizabeth 17 f "
Henry 9 m "

1604 ($5,000)
LAMAR, Martha 46 f SC
BEDLE, Catherine 61 f Ga
LINES, Hannah 30 f Md
JOHNSTON, David 17 m Ga
(Student)
Martha 16 f "
Thomas C. 12 m "
Sarah E. 10 f "
HOWARD, Emma S. 10 f Ala

506 Farmer ($500)
LAMPLEY, J. R.(?) 29 m NC
Catherine 33 f "
Linton 4 m Ala
Laura 2 f "
John 2/12 m "
SHIPMAN, James 26 m NC

1687 Farmer ($4,500)
LAMPLEY, Jacob 68 m SC
Hannah 58 f "
Sarah 26 f NC
Hannah 20 f "
Cality(?) (Student) 21 m "
James 14 m Ala
Mary 12 f "
THOMAS, Orlando 9 m "

649 Merchant ($10,000)
LAMPLEY, John M. 30 m NC
Milly 18 f Ala
Harmon 1 m "
Harrison D. (Clerk) 16 m NC
Ira (Merchant) 32 m "

892 Farmer
LAMPLEY, Thomas 38 m NC
Charlotte 28 f SC
John 12 m Ala
James 8 m "

2154 Farmer
LANCASTER, William M. 26 m Ga
Tillitha 20 f "
Rotitia 4 f "
Thomas 2 m "
Ziphania 1 f "

700 Farmer ($150)
LANDON *, Samuel 37 m Ga
Missouri 25 f "
Roxanna 12 f "
Jane 6 f "
(Cont.)

(# 700 LANDON cont.)
Polly 4 f Ga
Daniel 2 m Ala

1257 Merchant ($500)
LANEY, Charles D. 38 m NC
Eliza 24 f Miss
Charles 1/12 m Ala

1532 Overseer
LANGFORD, Robert 48 m Va
Sarah 55 f Ga
Sarah 18 f "
Mary 15 f "
Robert 13 m "

1756 Farmer
LANGSTON, Reuben 25 m Ga

LARY, John
(See John Lacy).

Lary, John R.
(See R. H. Fryer).

907 Farmer ($1,100)
LASSETER, M. M. 22 m Ga
Jane 19 f Ala
Mary 1 f "

961 Farmer ($2,500)
LASSITER, Matthew 62 m NC
Henrietta 66 f Md

259 Farmer ($1,200)
LASSITER, Thomas J. 40 m Ga
Margaret 29 f "
James R. 19 m "
Sarah 17 f "
William 15 m "
Martha 14 f "
John 13 m "
Matthew 11/12 m Ala

965 Laborer
LATTIMORE, George 50 m Scot

306 Farmer ($400)
LAW, Robert 42 m NC
Mary 41 f Va
Martha 16 f NC
Ellen 14 f "
William 11 m "
Asa 9 m "
Selden 7 m Ga
John 4 m "
Missouri 3 f Ala

* (Note: This should be "Landrum".)

2155 Farmer ($1,200)
LAWLESS, Jones 62 m Ga
Cinthia 45 f "
Jonathan 22 m "
Sarah 12 f "
Jonas 9 m "

1251 Farmer ($5,000)
LEAIRD, L. J. 38 m SC
Mary 13 f Ala
Lewis 9 m "
Andrew 5 m "
SYLVESTER, Joseph A. (Clerk) 16 m SC

1797 Overseer
LEDBETTER, J. A. 26 m Ga

1923
LEDBETTER, Martha C. 31 f Ga
Elizabeth 14 f Ala
Seaborn 10 m "
Sarah 5 f Tex

18 Tailor (Insane)
LEDDY, Peter 28 m Ire

1080 Farmer ($650)
LEE, Andrew 40 m SC
Nancy 35 f "
Martha 13 f Ala
Mary 8 f "
Lucinda 6 f "
Arincey 4 f "

836-856 Farmer ($5,000)
LEE, Ferdinand 52 m SC
Susan 52 f "
Ira 27 m "
Amse(?) (Student) 21 m "
Edwin " 18 m "
Sumpter " 17 m "
Heyward 12 m Ga
Ophelia 15 f SC
Julia 11 f Ala
LEE, James A.(Farmer) 30 m SC
Mary 18 f Ala
COOK, Amanda 29 f SC
William 4 m Ala

359 Farmer ($400)
LEE, Godfrey 32 m Ga
Sarah 22 f "
William 11 m Ala
John 9 m "
Mary 8 f "
(Cont.)

(# 359 LEE cont.)
Molsey 7 f Ala
Lovard 5 m "
Lewis 3/12 m "

311 Farmer ($500)
LEE, James 43 m SC
Sarah 41 f "
Harvey 18 m "
Irving 12 m Ala
Thomas 4 m "

1691 Farmer
LEE, Levi 25 m NC
Martha 22 f "
Sarah 1 f Ala

337 Farmer ($1,000)
LEE, Lovard 58 m SC
Elizabeth 55 f Ga
Lewis J. 3/12 m Ala

1343
LEE, Mary 48 f NC
Lucinda 18 f Fla
Rufus (Laborer) 16 m Ala

1944 Farmer ($3,000)
LEE, Needham, Jr. 37 m Ga
Emeline 35 f NC
Mary A. 14 f Ala
Jefferson 12 m "
Nancy 10 f "
Lucurgus 8 m "
Sarah 6 f "
Robert 4 m "
George 1 m "
SKIPPER, John (Farmer) 18 m Ga

690 Farmer ($7,000)
LEE, Needham, Sr. 64 m SC
Sarah 49 f Ga
Martha 15 f Ala
Jane 9 f "
Sarah 8 f "
Columbus 6 m "
Winneford 4 f "
TERRY, John T. 25 m Ga

604 Farmer
LEE, Needham G. 25 m Ga
Alice 22 f SC
Ann L. 6 f Ala
Gen. Taylor 4 m "
Margaret 1 f "

183
LEE, Robert 27 m SC
Mary 30 f Ga
Needham 6 m Ala
Almira 4 f "
Matilda 2 f "

1411 Farmer
LEE, Robert 23 m SC
Harriet 15 f Ga

312 Farmer ($200)
LEE, Timothy 24 m SC
Nancy 22 f Ala
Narcissa 3 f "
Leman 1 m "

LEE, Willie G.
Adeline
(See James M. Pruitt).

688 Farmer ($400)
LEGGIT, John D. 38 m Ga
Elizabeth 32 f NC
John 13 m Ga
Thomas 11 m "
Jane 9 f "
Bennet 7 m "
James 5 m "
Isophena 2 f Ala

LENHORN, Mary
(See Edward Bird).

LEONARD, James
(See Lemuel Senn).

2215 Laborer
LEONARD, William, Jr. 21 m SC
Martha 27 f Ga
Mary 1/12 f Ala

1468 Farmer ($100)
LEONNARD, William 81 m SC
Charity 75 f "

1469 Farmer
LEONNARD, William D. 24 m Ga
Martha 24 f "
Mary 1/12 f Ala

LESTER, William
(See William Herring).

LEVERETT, Lively
(See John L. Williams).

LEWIS, Benjamin
John
(Cont.)

(LEWIS cont.)
Jackson
Harrison
(See David Powell).

1372 Farmer
LEWIS, Daniel G. 28 m Ala
Lucy 27 f "
Mary 7 f "
Victoria 5 f "
John T. 4 m "
Harrison 2 m "
Henry 1 m "

79 Farmer
LEWIS, David 40 m Ga
Melinda 26 f "
Mary A. 10 f "
Thomas J. 9 m "
William G. 8 m "
Sarah 4 f Ala
John 2 m "
James 2/12 m "

1046 Carpenter ($500)
LEWIS, Elias 39 m NC
Sidney D. 29 f Ga
Ann 7 f Ala
John 5 m "
James 3 m "
Nancy 65 f NC
VICKERS, Joseph W. 29 m Ga
(Farmer, $100)

1086 Farmer ($2,000)
LEWIS, Elvey 60 m Va
Nancy 54 f NC
BOTTOMS, John 22 m Ga
(Overseer).

2248 Farmer
LEWIS, Harrison W. 45 m Ga
Francis 17 m Ala

90 Farmer ($300)
LEWIS, Isaac R. W. 23 m Ga
Martha A. 19 f SC

LEWIS, James A.
(See John McAllister).

176 Blacksmith ($400)
LEWIS, John 40 m NC
Epsey 33 f "
John W. (Farmer) 18 m "
George W. 12 m "
William R. 10 m Ala
(Cont.)

(# 176 LEWIS cont.)

Lydia A.	8	f	Ala
James A.	6	m	"
Nancy	4	f	"
Rosetta	2	f	"
Angus	1	m	"

1085 Farmer ($1,000)

LEWIS, Joseph J.	24	m	NC
Elizabeth	14	f	Ga

(Married within the year).

1311

LEWIS, Margaret	45	f	Ga
Samuel W. (Clerk)	23	m	"
Harriet	16	f	"
Jane	15	f	"
Jefferson	8	m	Ala

LEWIS, Martha
(See Joel D. Warren).

LEWIS, Mary
(See T. C. Efurd).

485 Farmer

LEWIS, Musgrove	38	m	SC
Elizabeth	28	f	Ga
Francis	4	m	Ala
Jane	2	f	"

1947 Farmer

LEWIS, Neecy	40	m	NC
Rebecca	29	f	Ala
Nancy	15	f	"
Susan	13	f	"
William	11	m	"
John	9	m	"
James	7	m	"
Thomas	5	m	"
Robert	3	m	"
Mary	1	f	"

LEWIS, Penny
(See Munroe Crocker).

2247

LEWIS, Sarah	75	f	SC

LEWIS, Stephen B.
(See William R. Wood).

1480 Laborer ($500)

LEWIS, T. J.	30	m	Ga
Sarah	20	f	"
MULFORD, Frances	40	f	"

651 Farmer ($1,000)

LEWIS, William	60	m	NC

(Cont.)

(# 651 LEWIS cont.)

Catherine	50	f	NC
Hanson (Farmer, $100).	25	m	"
LaFayette (Farmer)	22	m	"
Robert "	18	m	"
John "	15	m	"
Archibald	12	m	Ga
Harriet	23	f	NC
Polly	17	f	"
CHAUNCEY, James (Laborer).	22	m	"

LEWIS, William
(See James Traywick).

943 Farmer ($600)

LIGHTNER, John M.	25	m	Ga
Martha	20	f	SC
Mary	5	f	Ala

1144 Farmer ($400)

LIGHTNER, Michael	56	m	SC
Sophia	40	f	Ga
Samuel (Farmer) (Property $1,000).	25	m	Fla
Sarah	28	f	Ga
William (Farmer)	20	m	Ala
WARREN, Rebecca	13	f	"
Susan	11	f	"
Thomas	8	m	"
James	6	m	"
Joseph	4	m	"

1032 Farmer ($1,200)

LIGHTNER, Thomas S.	27	m	Ga
Nancy	21	f	Ala
Sarah	4	f	"
Nancy S.	2	f	"
Frances	3/12	f	"

1558 Music Teacher ($800).

LIGNOSKI, Randolph	30	m	Pol
Caroline	25	f	SC
Randolph	8	m	Fla
Elizabeth	5	f	"
Charles	1	m	Ala
BRUCE, Eliza A.	50	f	SC
RICE, Elizabeth	18	f	Fla

1792 Farmer ($700)

LILLY, David	49	m	Va
Margaret	49	f	Ga
Savannah	16	f	"
David	12	m	"
Augusta	9	f	"
James	7	m	"

\# 1173 Farmer ($1,200)
LINDSAY, Jeptha 42 m NC
Lidia 32 f Ga
Nathan (Farmer) 16 m Ala
Amy 13 f "
Nancy 8 f "
Charity 2 f "
William 8/12 m "
REGISTER, Elizabeth 10 f "

\# 984 Farmer
LINDSAY, Lewis 18 m NC
Lidia A. 16 f Ga
(Married within the year).

\# 1199 Teacher
LINDSAY, Simpson S. 30 m SC
Martha 19 f Ala
William 4 m "
Elizabeth 2 f "
Serepta 1/12 f "

LINES, Hannah
(See Martha Lamar).

\# 1581 Farmer
LINSEY, Hiram 28 m Ga
Mary A. 20 f NC
NICHOLS, Jeremiah 12 m Ga

\# 469 Farmer
LISTER, Joshua 46 m SC
Diana 38 f NC
Crawford 16 m Ala
Caroline 15 f "
Mary 14 f "
Martha 13 f "
Cleopatra 12 f "
Elizabeth 11 f "
David 10 m "
Sarah 9 f "
Washington 8 m "
Marion 7 m "
Celia 6 f "
Jane 4 f "

LISTER, Thomas
(See Adam Grubbs).

\# 1904 Farmer
LITTLE, John 36 m Ga
Martha 33 f "
Henry 10 m "
Mary 8 f "
Martha 5 f Ala
Elizabeth 2 f "

\# 840 Farmer ($3,000)
LITTLE, Josiah 50 m NC
Ann 47 f "
George W. (Farmer) 19 m SC
Anna 18 f Ala
Sarah 16 f "
James (Farmer) 15 m "
Jemima 13 f "
Mary 12 f "
Jefferson 10 m "
Catherine 9 f "
Ann 3 f "
BURNETT, John 15 m NC
(Laborer)

\# 967 Farmer ($160)
LITTLEFIELD, Henry A. 36 m Ga
Susan 40 f "
John (Farmer) 16 m "
Amanda 12 f "
Elijah 10 m "
Absolom 2 m Ala
Margaret 1/12 f "

\# 2041 Overseer
LITTLETON, Noah 31 m Ga
Frances 26 f "
Friendabid 10 m "
Alfred 7 m "
Mary 6 f "
Eliza 2 f "

\# 1004 Farmer ($5500)
LOCKE, Jesse 37 m Ga
Sarah A. 28 f Ala
Andrew 4/12 m "
Michael B. 10 m "
William H. (Farmer) 18 m "

\# 1409 Merchant ($400)
LOCKE, Thomas S. 24 m Ala
Mary 20 f Ga
John 1 m Ala
COLE, Sarah 20 f "
RYAN, Lemon J. 23 m Ga
(Occp. - none).
WILLIAMS, Stephen 19 m Ala
(Clerk)

\# 814 Farmer ($800)
LOCKHART, Aaron 39 m SC
Frances 40 f Ga

\# 1614 (Property: $150)
LOCKLEY, Elizabeth 52 f NC

1772 Farmer ($400)
LOCKLEY, Thomas 30 m SC
Mary 27 f Ga
Frances 12 f "
Marion 11 m "
George 9 m Ala
Wesley 7 m "
Martha 5 f "
Mary 3 f "
Louisa 1 f "

1763 Farmer ($100)
LOFLEN, Daniel 62 m Va
Eady 60 f "

1764 Farmer
LOFLEN, Thomas 23 m Ga
Catherine 19 f "
James 3 m Ala

LOGUE, Sarah
(See Benjamin Warner).

265 Lawyer ($2,500)
LOMAX, Tennant 29 m SC

LONG, Ann
Jane
Catherine
(See Nancy McNeill).

LONG, Benjamin
(See Sheppard M. Streeter).

896 Farmer ($600)
LONG, Charles 39 m NC
Elizabeth 36 f "
William (Farmer) 17 m "
Thomas " 16 m "
Mary 14 f Ala
George 12 m "
Green 10 m "
Feriby 7 f "
Martha 4 f "
Mary J. 2 f "
Margaret 70 f NC

1656 Farmer ($500)
LONG, Charles P. 30 m NC
Margaret 12 f Ala
James 10 m "
William 8 m "

LONG, Martha A.
(See Hardy Bass).

LONG, Susan
(See M. S. Sears).

1152 Farmer ($700)
LORE, David 42 m NJ
Ann 32 f SC
Aramia 2 f Ala
Ann 8/12 f "
KIDD, Eliza 30 f SC

344 Farmer ($1,000)
LOTT, Arthur 60 m SC
Bidsey 47 f Ga
Ephriam G. (Farmer) 22 m "
James " 19 m "
Narcissa 9 f "
Artemissia 9 f "
Henry 6 m Ala
Catherine 7 f "
Matilda 4 f "

987 Miller
LOVELACE, Benj. B. 43 m SC
Elizabeth 33 f Ga
Mary 18 f Ala
Sarah 16 f "
Jordan 8 m "
Penelope 6 f "
William T. 3 m "
Sophronia 1/12 f "

1948 Farmer
LOVELACE, LaFayette 25 m Ala
Nancy 17 f "
Mary 1 f "
Cornelia 2/12 f "

2238 Farmer
LOVELACE, William 60 m SC

LOW, Robert
(See Robert Law).

1481 Farmer
LOWE, Isaac 58 m Ga
Leoner 54 f SC
John (Farmer) 20 m Ala

1205 Farmer
LOWMAN, G. W. 27 m SC
Julia 28 f "
George 3 m Ala
Adrian 1 f "

2021 Farmer ($1,200)
LOWMAN, James L. 28 m SC

2020 Farmer
LOWMAN, John E. 31 m SC
Mary 26 f NC
(Cont.)

(# 2020 LOWMAN cont.)
Franklin 6 m Ala
Adolphus 4 m "
Levonia 2 f "

2019 Farmer ($6,000)
LOWMAN, John J. 56 m SC
Mary 49 f "
Samuel (Student) 15 m Ga
Mary 12 f "
Llewellyn 11 m "
Edwin 9 m "
Laura 4 f Ala
BOSWELL, William H. 35 m Ga
(Occp. -- none)
Elizabeth 24 f SC

#2180 Farmer ($2,000)
LOWMAN, Joseph 45 m SC
Mary 42 f "
John (Farmer) 16 m "
William 13 m "
Elizabeth 11 f "
Mary 9 f "
Catherine 7 f "
Joseph 5 m "
Anderson 3 m Ga

1723 Farmer
LOWMAN, William H. 34 m SC
John F. 9 m Ga
Charles A. 5 m Ala

LUDEN, John
(See Grover Caldwell).

LUDLAM, Elizabeth
(See Daniel J. Atkinson).

LUDLUM, Wiley
Edward
Sarah
Elizabeth
(See William N. Atkinson).

LUND, Peter
(See George W. Rutledge)

150 Farmer ($400)
McADAMS, James 32 m SC
Lerina 27 f "
James W. 9 m Ala
Benjamin 7 m "
Martha 5 f "
Susan 3 f "
George A. 1 m "
BRASWELL, Martha 20 f SC
Eliza R. 8/12 f Ala

2134 Farmer ($300)
McALLISTER, Charles 35 m Ga
Margaret 27 f "
SMITH, Amanda 9 f "
Mary 6 f "

McALLISTER, James
(See James Mabry).

1479 Carriage Maker
McALLISTER, John 25 m Ga
Eudosia 26 f "
James 2 m Ala
Casper 1/12 m "
Martha 50 f Ga
LEWIS, James A. 28 m Ga
(Blacksmith).

2135 Farmer
McALLISTER, Vincent 30 m Ga
Nancy 15 f Ala
(Married within the year).
Margaret 74 f NC

1561 Farmer ($1,700)
McALPIN, Alexander S. 40 m NC
Frances 20 f "
John 8 m "
William 6 m "
Eliza 3 f "

717 Merchant
McANDREW, William A. 36 m Scot
Sarah 29 f Ga
Alexander 12 m "
William 10 m "
Isabella 7 f "
Manah 1 f "

1734 Farmer ($1,500)
McBRYDE, John 73 m Ga
Rachel 68 f "
CARLISLE, Sophia 72 f SC
VINING, Eliza J. 13 f Ala
Anna 5 f "
BARNES, Alberton 27 m Ga
(Overseer)

1735 (Propery: $1,000)
McBRYDE, Mary Ann 37 f Ga
Catherine 21 f "
Rachel 19 f "
Eliza 15 f "
Sarah 12 f "
Agnes 10 f "
Sophia 8 f "

McBRYDE, Robert
(See William Truet).

837 Farmer ($2,000)
McBRYDE, Samuel 45 m Ga
Mary 22 f "
Catherine 22 f "
John T. (Farmer) 19 m "
James F. 16 m "
Samuel 13 m "
William 11 m Ala
Robert 7 m "
Rachel 4 f "
Sarah 1 f "
MORRIS, Maranda 2 f Ga
WALTON, Wilson 14 m "

1510 Overseer
McBRYDE, Stephen 24 m Ala

1340 Merchant
McCALL, D. A. 34 m NC
Serena A. 21 f Ala
Henry G. 1 m "
Dougald (Clerk) 25 m NC

851 Farmer
McCALL, Daniel 30 m SC
Catherine 25 f "
George 6 m "
Elizabeth 4 f "
Nancy 2 f "
Calvin 2/12 m Ala

443 Farmer ($500)
McCALL, Daniel 52 m NC
Mary 47 f Ga
Hartwell (Farmer) 26 m Ala
Archibald " 25 m "
John " 19 m "
Anna 16 f "
Mary 10 f "
Duncan 5 m "
CARROLL, John(Farmer) 17 m NC
Benjamin 14 m "

978 Farmer
McCALL, Gilbert 29 m NC
Adeline 23 f SC
Daniel 3 m Ala

739 Farmer ($400)
McCALL, Henry 22 m NC
Graves, Henry S. 20 m Ga
(Farmer)

McCALL, Martha
(See Abraham Brumbels).

444 Farmer ($200)
McCALL, Paul 36 m NC
Mary 29 f SC
James 9 m Ala
Mary 7 f "
Thomas 4 m "
Sarah 2 f "
Nancy 6/12 f "

659 Blacksmith
McCALLUM, Duncan 40 m SC
Rosanna 30 f Ala
Margaret J. 7 f "
Mary A. 5 f "
Alexander W. 2 m "

2040 Overseer
McCARROLL, Perryman 45 m Ga
Hetty 40 f "
Sarah 9 f Ala
Martha 4 f "

1692 Farmer
McCARTY, James 30 m SC

McCAY, Flora
(See A. B. Starke)

1473 Farmer ($100)
McCAY, William N. 44 m Ga
Elizabeth 28 f SC
Mary 6 f Ala
David 4 m "
Thomas 2 m "
Jasper 1 m "

1653 (Propery: $1,500)
McCLARY, Mary E. 34 f NC
James (Farmer) 16 m Ga
Pamelia 14 f "
Virginia 12 f "
William 10 m "
Fletcher 7 m "
Nancy 4 f "

McCLURE, Mathis C.
Isabella
(See Russell Jones).

1874 Farmer
McCLURE, Thomas C. 50 m SC
Mary 46 f "

McCLUSKEY, Naomi
(See Allen Loveless).

1936 Teacher ($200)
McCORMICK, William 33 m NC
(Cont.)

(# 1936 McCORMICK cont.)
Ann 32 f Ga
John 9 m Ala
George 7 m "
William 2 m "

1072 Farmer ($500)
McCRACKEN, R. M. 56 m SC
Mary 46 f "
James (Farmer) 18 m "
William " 16 m Ga
John 14 m "
Catherine 9 f Ala
ELLIS, Thomas 25 m NC
(Farmer)
Ann 22 f SC
Georgianna 4 f Ala
Mandana 2 f "
Louisa 1 f "

858 Farmer ($150)
McCRACKEN, Thomas E. 45 m SC
Elizabeth 42 f "
Allen (Farmer) 20 m "
Spencer " 16 m "

326 Farmer ($600)
McCRANEY, Malcolm 43 m NC
Arabella 40 f SC
Calvin 14 m "
Murdock 12 m Ga
John 10 m "
Neill 8 m "
Margaret 4 f Ala
James K. 1 m "

McCRARY, Alexander
James A.
(See William Hinson)

328 Farmer ($60)
McCRARY, Daniel 30 m SC
Jane 30 f "
Murdock 3 m "
Isabella 1 f "

2236 Farmer ($800)
McCRARY, James 50 m Sc
Rebecca 38 f "
Alexr. (Grocer) 24 m "
Frances 16 f "
Thomas (Grocer) 18 m "
Warren 12 m Ala
James 10 m "
Alitha 7 f "
Mary 4 f "
McCRARY, Sam'l. 43 m SC
(Farmer)

329 Farmer
McCRARY, Norman 27 m SC
Edy 22 f "
Wesley 2 m "

2109 Farmer ($800)
McCRARY, Thomas K. 35 m Ga
Amanda 25 f "
Amelius 6 m "
William 4 m "
Jeremiah 2 m "
Mary 1 f "

330 Farmer ($160)
McCREE, D. W. 61 m NC
Judy 40 f SC
William F. (Farmer) 17 m Ala
James E. 14 m "
Marg. (Margaret) J. 9 f "
Lucinda 7 f "
David J. 4 m "

1753 Farmer
McDANIEL, Andrew 37 m Ga
Nancy 36 f "
Thomas 10 m "
Elizabeth 8 f "
Marion 6 m "
Lucy 4 f "
John 2 m Ala
George 1/12 m "

13 Farmer ($1,800)
McDANIEL, Arch'd. 55 m NC
Harriet 46 f "
Arch'd. 18 m Ga
Amanda 17 f "
Loutia(?) 16 f "
Joshua 13 m "
John C. 11 m "
James G. 9 m "
Martha E. 3 f Ala

McDANIEL, Daniel
(See James Mabry).

641 Farmer
McDANIEL, Daniel 40 m NC
Nancy 57 f "
John (Farmer) 19 m Ala
Mary A. 21 f Ala
Flora 17 f "
Catherine 15 f "

1010 Farmer ($800)
McDANIEL, Philip A. 35 m Ga
Jane 29 f "
(Cont.)

(# 1010 McDaniel cont).
William 12 m Ga
Sarah E. 9 f "
John 7 m Ala
Adeline 5 f "
Ann 4 f "
Henry 2 m "
Charles 3/12 m "
SKANES, Wm. (Farmer) 30 m SC

1552 M. E. Preacher
McDANIEL, Walter H. 40 m Tenn
Frances 29 f Ala
John 4 m "

1920 Merchant
McDONALD, Angus R. 34 m NC
Mary 25 f SC
Mary A. 4 f Ala
Donald W. 3 m "
McDONALD, John R. 36 m NC
(Cabinet Maker)

1217 Farmer
McDONALD, Colin 65 m NC
Elizabeth 45 f "
BASS, Sarah 23 f "

1876 Farmer ($1,200)
McDONALD, Daniel B. 64 m NC
Mary 48 f "
John (Farmer) 26 m "
Sarah 23 f "
Daniel (Farmer) 16 m Ala
Mary 19 f NC
Caroline 14 f Ala
William 11 m "
Hugh 9 m "

1877 Farmer ($1,500)
McDONALD, Malcolm 54 m NC
Martha 43 f "
Sarah 19 f "
Robert (Farmer) 17 m Ala
Eliza 15 f "
Catherine 12 f "
Hugh 9 m "
Daniel 6 m "
Mary 2 f "

2206 (Property: $1,000)
McDONALD, Martha 45 f Ga
MEARS, Emma D. 20 f Vt
Jane 22 f "

1125 Farmer ($1,6000)
McDONALD, Neill 55 m NC
(Cont.)

(# 1125 McDonald cont).
Mary 32 f SC
Sarah 7 f Ala
Euphemia 5 f "
Mary 3 f "
Celia 1 f "
HARRISON, L. L. 14 m Ga
Charles 12 m "

570 Ditcher
McDONALD, Thomas 38 m Ire

McDOUGALD, A. B.
(See Henry H. Fields).

McDOUGALD, S.
(See Hugh McLean).

McDOWELL, Eliza
(See John Sloan, Sr.)

1893 Farmer ($200)
McDOWELL, John 26 m Ga
Martha 21 f "
Emma 1 f Ala

1309 Farmer ($1,500)
McDOWELL, Thomas C. 57 m Ga
Eliza 57 f NC
Antoinette 24 f Ga
Caroline 18 f "
James (Student) 16 m "
Virginia 12 f Ala

McDUFFIE, George
(See Arch'd. Carmichael).

McDUFFIE, John
(See Nancy Bishop).

368 Farmer
McEACHERN, Daniel 27 m NC
Sarah 23 f Ga
(Married within the year).

353 Farmer ($1,000)
McEACHERN, Gilbert 58 m Scot
Catherine 55 f NC
Isobel 24 f "
Anna 21 f Ala
Catherine 20 f "
Malcolm 18 m "
John 14 m "
Gilbert 10 m "

2191 Farmer ($20,000)
McGEHEE, Abner 43 m Ga
Louisa 41 f "
(Cont.)

(# 2191 McGEHEE cont.)

Lucius (Student)	15	m	Ga
Rebecca M.	13	f	"
Sarah	10	f	"
Thomas	6	m	Ala
Jefferson	5	m	"
Loretto	3	f	Ga

1412 Farmer ($480)

McGEHEE, Alfred	39	m	Ga
Martha	39	f	"
Frances	14	f	"
Georgiann	12	f	"
Mary	10	f	"
William	8	m	"
Seaborn	6	m	"
James	4	m	Ala

1775 Farmer ($250)

McGEHEE, Edward M.	35	m	Ga
Mary	25	f	"
William	5	m	"
Joseph	3	m	Ala
Charles	1	m	"

2153 ($400)

McGILBERRY *, Chaney	64	f	Scot
Roderick (Farmer)	30	m	NC
Martha	22	f	Ga
RICHARDSON, Moses (Farmer)	21	m	"

338 Farmer

McGILBERRY *, Duncan	36	m	NC
John (Farmer)	34	m	"
Daniel "	32	m	"
Malcolm "	30	m	"
Mary	65	f	Scot

301 Farmer ($1,000)

McGILBERRY *, James	52	m	Scot
Fanny	26	f	NC
James	30	m	"

903 Farmer ($800)

McGILBERRY *, John	46	m	Scot
Margaret	32	f	"
Hugh (Farmer)	16	m	Ala
Norman	14	m	"
Malcolm	11	m	"
Mary	9	f	"
Margaret	6	f	"
GILLIS, Sarah	35	f	Scot
Christian	40	f	"

* McGilvary

335 Farmer ($300)

McGILBERRY, Martin	48	m	Scot
Sarah	33	f	NC
Daniel (Farmer)	21	m	"
Angus	12	m	"
Alexr.	9	m	Ala
John	4	m	"
Neill	2	m	"
Martin	4/12	m	"
Elizabeth	19	f	NC
Catherine	18	f	"
Flora	10	f	Ala
DAY, Jas. (Laborer)	23	m	NC

1252 Druggist ($600)

McGINTY, G. W.	29	m	Ga
Elizabeth	29	f	"
GRIFFITH, Moses	10	m	"

1924 (Property: $500)

McGUIRE, Tempey	40	f	NC
Friley (Farmer)	21	m	Ala
Washington "	19	m	"
Warren "	17	m	"
Aaron	14	m	"
Marietta	12	f	"
Ann	8	f	"
Catherine	6	f	"
McLEOD, William C. (Merchant).	30	m	NC

76 Millwright

McINNIS, Angus	42	m	NC
Unity	19	f	Tenn
Elizabeth	3	f	Ala

1420 Carpenter

McINNIS, Duncan	37	m	NC

660 Carpenter

McINNIS, Duncan	40	m	NC
John (Miller - $3000)	60	m	"
Christian	45	f	"
Daniel	12	m	Ala
John M.	10	m	"
Catherine	8	f	"
Jane	6	f	"
Elizabeth	4	f	"

626 (Property: $2,000)

McINNIS, Jane	40	f	NC
Peter (Farmer)	25	m	"
Malcom (Teacher)	24	m	Ala
Catherine	20	f	"
Jane	16	f	"
Margaret	12	f	"

464 Miller ($1,300)
McINNIS, John 56 m NC
Christian 49 f "
Daniel 13 m Ala
John M. 11 m "
Catherine 10 f "
Jane 8 f "
Elizabeth 4 f "

658 Farmer ($3,000)
McINNIS, Miles 50 m NC
Sarah 56 f "
JUSTICE, Adolphus 17 m Ga

833 Farmer ($550)
McINTOSH, Archibald 60 m Scot
Mary 55 f "
John (No Occp) 24 m SC
Angus " " 18 m "
John 13 m Ala

277 Farmer ($480)
McINTOSH, Daniel 70 m Scot
Sally 50 f SC
Mary 20 f "
Peggy 18 f "
Christian 16 f "
Sally 14 f "
Regnald 10 m Ala
Angus 8 m "

817 (Property: $800)
McINTOSH, Margaret 50 f Scot
Norman (Farmer - deaf) 30 m SC
John G. " 28 m "
Mary (?)19 f "

816 Farmer
McINTOSH, N. A. 27 m SC
Elizabeth 24 f Ala

492 Farmer ($550)
McKAY, Donald 38 m Scot
Winney 35 f NC
Philip 6 m Ala
Christian 4 f "
Alexander 1 m "
McRAE, Ann 27 f NC

1419 Farmer ($200)
McKAY, John W. 34 m NC
Harriet 35 f Ga
George 13 m "
Dougald 11 m "
John 9 m "
Daniel 7 m Ala
Angus 3 m "
James 1 m "

1834 Farmer
McKELLER, Neill 63 m NC
Sarah 54 f "
Martha 16 f "
John 11 m Ala
Jincey 9 f "
BUTLER, Solomon 35 m NC
(Laborer)

1908 Farmer ($200)
McKENLEY, Elijah 40 m SC
Margaret 40 f "
Martha 12 f "
Nathaniel 11 m "
Frederick 9 m "
Mary 7 f Ala
Joseph 4 m "

1332 Merchant ($1,000)
McKENZIE, Andrew 36 m Eng
Adelaide 32 f Ga
Andrew 10 m Ala
William 8 m "
Mary 6 f "

2249 Farmer ($8,000)
McKENZIE, Daniel 46 m NC
Amanda 30 f Ga
Bethune 13 m Ala
Susan 11 f "
Ann 10 f "
Louisianna 7 f "
Elizabeth 1 f "

201 Farmer
McKENZIE, John 25 m SC
Nancy 25 f "
William C. 7/12 m Ala

646 Farmer
McKENZIE, John G. 50 m Scot

1015 Farmer ($500)
McKINNEY, A. F. 33 m SC
Sarah 19 f "
Nancy 1/12 f Ala
Alexander 78 m Ire
Nancy 58 f Ire
(Alexr. Co. Surveyor).

280 Laborer
McKINNEY, Benjamin 58 m Ga
Lucinda 38 f "
Andrew 15 m "
Sophronia 13 f "
Letltia 10 f "
Joanna 8 f "

McKENNEY, Benjamin
(See Avery Nolen)

1160 Wheelwright ($100)
McKINNEY, John S. 37 m SC
Mary 26 f "
Leonidas 12 m "
Caroline 10 f "
William 8 m "
John 5 m "
James 2 m Ala

McKINNON, Alexander
(See N. M. Hyatt).

1777 Farmer
McLACHLIN, Daniel 52 m NC
Catherine 54 f "
Robert (Farmer) 19 m Ga

1968 Farmer ($350)
McLEAN, Alexander 27 m Scot
Sarah 23 f SC
John 6 m Ala
Rachel 4 f "
Hugh 2 m "

1070 Farmer ($400)
McLEAN, Alexander 33 m Scot
Sarah 22 f Ala
John 7 m "
Rachel 5 f "
Hugh 1 m "
Hugh (Farmer) 24 m Scot

613 Farmer
McLEAN, Archibald 21 m Ala
Mary 19 f "
OLIVER, James 11 m SC

2203 Farmer ($400)
McLEAN, Colin 44 m NC
Catherine 40 f "
Margaret 19 f "
Sarah 16 f "
Jane 12 f Ala
John 8 m "
William 4 m "

117 Farmer ($2,600)
McLEAN, Daniel 53 m Scot

McLEAN, Elizabeth
(See Mary Mixon).

190 Farmer
McLEAN, Hugh 67 m Scot
Peggy 50 f "
Christian 18 f "
(Cont.)

(# 190 McLEAN cont.)
Sarah 14 f Scot
McDOUGALD, S.(Laborer) 58 m NC
McLEAN, Nancy 10 f Scot
Mary A. 8 f NY

1974 Farmer ($1,500)
McLEAN, John 62 m Scot
Catherine 38 f "
Daniel 8 m Ala
Hector 7 m "
Nancy 6 f "

#1434 Farmer ($1,000)
McLEAN, John (W,) 55 m NC
Margaret 50 f "
Daniel (Farmer) 24 m "
Catherine (C.) 13 f Ala
Eliza (J.) 11 f "
John (W.) 8 m "
Angus (A.) 6 m "

1342 Blacksmith
McLEAN, L. 39 m NC
Mary 33 f Ga
Margaret 3/12 f Ala
Eugenia 8 f "

136 Farmer
McLEAN, Malcolm 30 m Ala
Mary 32 f NC
William 9 m Ala
Jane 7 f "
Martha 5 f "
Nancy 3 f "
Rhoda 2 f "
John 1/12 m "
John (Laborer) 18 m "

180
McLEAN, Margaret 65 f Scot
Isabella 21 f NC

476 Farmer
McLENDON, J. G. 46 m SC
Elizabeth 27 f NC
Moley A. 4 f Ala
John C. 1 m "
McRAE, Mary 75 f NC

1521 Farmer ($400)
McLENDON, John 53 m Ga
Wilton (Farmer) 27 m Ala
Mary 45 f Ga
William (Farmer) 23 m Ala
Matthew " 19 m "
James " 17 m "
(Cont.)

(# 1521 McLENDON cont.)
Ann 16 f Ala
Louisa 13 f "
Eliza 11 f "
LaFayette 10 m "
Jefferson 8 m "
Richard 6 m "
Jackson 3 m "

678 Cabinet Maker ($150)
McLENDON, M. 40 m Ga
Catherine 36 f NC
Loammi G. 15 f Ga
John T. 10 m Ala
Elizabeth 8 f "
Martha 5 f "
Harriet 3 f "
George 2 m "
Josephine 5/12 f "
Amanda 13 f "

1108 Farmer ($400)
McLEOD, Alexander 36 m NC
Catherine 29 f SC
Mary 7 f Ala
Neill 6 m "
William 3 m "

477 Overseer
McLEOD, Alexander 50 m NC
Pamelia 27 f Ga
Nancy 12 f "
Norman 3/12 m Ala

2186 Occp., none. ($1,000)
McLEOD, Angus 69 m Scot
Margaret 68 f "

471 Farmer ($1,500)
McLEOD, Angus 27 m NC
Mary 60 f "
Mary 22 f "
McRAE, John (Farmer) 25 m "

2187 Overseer
McLEOD, Daniel 26 m SC
Pamelia 20 f "
William 6/12 m Ala

568 Wheelwright
McLEOD, Daniel 35 m Ga
Nancy 29 f "
Margaret 8 f Ala
Sophronia 6 f "
Martha 4 f "
John 2 m "
Mary 2/12 f "
Sarah 72 f NC

197 Farmer
McLEOD, Daniel 27 m SC
Frances 20 f "
John 2/12 m Ala

1147 Farmer
McLEOD, Daniel, Jr. 26 m SC
Pamelia 18 f Ga
William 1 m Ala

1146 Farmer ($1,000)
McLEOD, Daniel, Sr. 45 m Scot
Catherine 40 f NC
William (Farmer) 24 m SC
Archibald " 18 m "
Jane 15 f Ala
McLEOD, Neill 22 m NC
(Farmer)

788 Farmer ($900)
McLEOD, John 26 m NC
Janet 25 f "
John 5 m "
McSWAIN, Catherine 35 f "
Nancy 33 f "
Daniel (Farmer) 32 m "

1474 Farmer ($1,200)
McLEOD, John 42 m NC
Sarah 35 f Ga
George 2 m Ala
Mary 4 f "
William 5 m "

1109 Farmer ($300)
McLEOD, John 30 m SC
Jane 24 f Ala
Catherine 7 f "
CUNNINGHAM, James 21 m "

McLEOD, Neill
(See A. B. Miles).

198 Farmer
McLEOD, Roderick 55 m NC
Catherine 46 f "
Abagail 17 f SC
Margaret 11 f Ala

McLEOD, Sarah
(See Daniel Gillis).

1351 Carriage Maker ($1,000)
McLEOD, William 40 m NC
Francis 21 f Ga
BIRDSONG, Josephine 4 f Ala
PUGH, Whitson 13 m "

McLEOD, William C.
(See Tempey McGuire).

1504 Farmer
McLOCHLIN, Duncan 45 m NC
Margaret 50 f "
Robert 18 m "

McMANN, Margaret
John
Thomas
(See Duncan McRae).

966 Blacksmith
McMICHAEL, George 38 m Pa
Mary J. 6 f Ala
Henry 1/12 m "
Narcissa 26 f SC

1641 Farmer ($2,500)
McMILLAN, Alexr. 47 m NC

798 (Property: $500)
McMILLAN, Catherine 30 f NC
Catherine 10 f Ala
Elizabeth 8 f "
Mary 6 f "
Jane 4 f "
Alexander 13 m "
Daniel 12 m "

796 Farmer ($2,000)
McMILLAN, Daniel 51 m Scot
Mary 52 f NC
Fairley * 18 f "
John (Farmer) 16 m "
Edward 14 m Ala
Charles 12 m "
Alexr. (Farmer) 28 m NC

936 Farmer ($300)
McMURRY, Samuel F. 46 m Ga
Mary 48 f "
Elizabeth 19 f "
L. F. (Blacksmith) 18 m "
Gabriel (Farmer) 16 m "
Martha 14 f "
Sarah 12 f Ala
Mary 11 f "
Margaret 8 f "

662 Farmer ($400)
McNABB, Duncan 54 m Scot
Isabella 40 f NC
William (Farmer) 18 m SC
Daniel 10 m "
Charlotte 12 f "
(Cont.)

(# 662 McNABB cont.)
Ellen 8 f SC
Elizabeth 6 f "
Robert (Clerk) 21 m "

1271 Merchant ($6,000)
McNAB, Duncan 32 m Scot

2207 Farmer ($10,500)
McNAB, John 42 m Scot
Jane 35 f "
James (Student) 15 m NC
John 11 m Ala
Flora 10 f "
Graham 4 m "
Jane 1/12 f "

McNAB, John C.
Lucy
Mary
(See Angus Gillis)

McNAB, Robert
(See B. J. Hoole).

654 Farmer
McNAIR, Alexander 44 m NC
Jane 38 f "
Jemima J. 11 f "
Isabella 10 f Ala
Sarah M. 7 f "
Julia A. 5 f "
Marietta 2 f "

McNAIR, Alexander
Margaret
Sarah
(See A. D. Whittle)

693 Farmer ($1,500)
McNAIR, John 28 m Ga
Mary 32 f "
Phoebe 2 f Ala
GRUBBS, James 14 m "
John 12 m Tex
William 9 m Ala
Francis 8 m "
Green 6 m "
Morgan 4 m "

1818 Farmer ($1,000)
McNAIR, John P. 40 m NC
Ann C. 30 f Ala
John D. 7 m "
David 6 m "
(Cont.)

* (Note: O.C.R. Book VI - Fairly listed as a son.)

(# 1818 McNAIR cont.)
Elizabeth 4 f Ala
Nancy 72 f NC

1819 Farmer
McNAIR, Randall 36 m NC
Susan 26 f Ala
Nancy 8 f "
Daniel W. 6 m "
Taylor 4 m "
Cinthia 1 f "
Margaret 60 f NC

1329 Overseer
McNAIR, Samuel D. 42 m Ga
Sarah 29 f NC
Nancy 9 f "
William H. 6 m Ala
Daniel 5 m "
Mary 1 f "

360
McNAIR, Sarah 55 f SC
Louisa 20 f Ga
John (Farmer) 20 m "
Winneford 18 f "

1823 Grocer
McNAIR, Turquill 25 m Ga
Amanda 21 f Ala

686 Farmer ($250)
McNAIR, William 21 m Ga
Polly 24 f SC
SIMS, Daniel J. 19 m Fla
(Farmer)
Mary 16 f Ala
(Both couples married within the year).

536 Farmer ($600)
McNEILL, Anderson 47 m Ga
Elizabeth 34 f "
Martha 17 f "
Harriet 14 f "
Andrew 13 m "
Anderson 12 m "
Lucy M. 10 f "

30 Farmer ($400)
McNEILL, Angus 30 m NC
Margaret 23 f "

91 Farmer ($100)
McNEILL, Asa 55 m Ga
Emily 39 f "
(Cont.)

(# 91 McNEILL cont.)
John J. 11 m Ga
James 5 m Fla
Andrew J. 3 m "
Harriet 2 f "
Jane 1/12 f Ala

1371 Farmer ($200)
McNEILL, C. N. 48 m NC
Neill (Farmer) 22 m "
Ann 18 f "
George 10 m Ala
John 8 m "
James 6 m "
Thomas 4 m "

604 Farmer ($150)
McNEILL, Hector 37 m NC
Mary 36 f "
Margaret 12 f "
Effy 10 f Ala
Mary 8 f "
Emeline 6 f "
Clementine 6 f "

842 Physician ($1,500)
McNEILL, J. C. 34 m Nc
Mary 26 f SC
Caroline 8 f Ala
Samuel 7 m "
Sarah E. 3 f "
Nancy J. 5 f "
John A. 1 m "
McRAE, Duncan, Jr. 24 m SC
(Overseer)

474 (Property: $1,000)
McNEILL, Nancy 65 f NC
LONG, Ann 40 f "
Jane 15 f Ala
Catherine 13 f "

108 Farmer $1,050)
McNEILL, Roderic 35 m NC
Flora 24 f Ala
SEMPLES, John 21 m Ga
(Farmer)

1492 Carpenter
McPHAIL, Daniel 50 m NC
Julia 30 f "
Louisa 14 f "
David 10 m "
Edward 8 m "
Margaret 6 f "
Daniel 3/12 m Ala

1491 Farmer ($2,000)
McPHAIL, Edward 35 m NC
STAFFORD, Moses 19 m Fla
(Farmer)
BASS, Sarah 20 f NC
ELLIS, Joseph 20 m Tenn
(Laborer)
STRICKLEN, Rufus E. 20 m NC
(Laborer)

1232 Silversmith
McPHAIL, Michael 43 m NC
WILLIAMS, Effy 39 f "
Ann 13 f "
Mary 12 f "
Eady 10 f "

494 Farmer ($1,200)
McRAE, A. D. 35 m NC
RUFF, Bill (Colored) 40 m Ga
(Farmer)

1333 Trader
McRAE, Alexander 33 m SC
DENNIS, Joseph F. 36 m Ga
(Clerk)

1886 Farmer
McRAE, Alexander R. 27 m NC
Winney 15 f Ala
John 5/12 m "

McRAE, Ann
(See Donald McKay).

683 Farmer ($1,200)
McRAE, C. C. 26 m NC
Nancy A. 18 f "
Catherine 20 f "
John C. 24 m "
(C. C. & Nancy A. married within the year).

661 Farmer ($500)
McRAE, C. M. 30 m NC
Abigail 29 f "
Nancy 6 f "
Catherine 5 f Ala
Christopher 3 m "

1035 Farmer
McRAE, Duncan 62 m NC
Catherine 65 f "
McMANN, Margaret 38 f SC
John 14 m Ala
Thomas 7 m "

McRAE, Duncan, Jr
(See J. C. McNeill).

957 Farmer ($1,500)
McRAE, F. C. 33 m Ala
William (Farmer) 52 m NC
Margie 59 f Scot
Catherine 20 f NC
Murphy (Student) 19 m Ala
Washington 13 m "

#479 Farmer ($2,500)
McRAE, Farquhar A. 54 m NC
Mary 54 f "
Philip (Student) 22 m "
John L. 21 m "
Gillian 17 f "
Christian 15 f "
Charles 10 m "

475 Farmer ($1,200)
McRAE, G. W. 39 m NC
Christian 35 f "
William 3 m Ala
Mary 3 f "
Duncan 1/12 m "

645 Farmer
McRAE, Harvey 26 m NC
Lucy 21 f Ala
James 3/12 m "

1878 Farmer ($3,000)
McRAE, Jabez 22 m NC

McRAE, John
(See Angus McLeod)

939 Farmer ($2,800)
McRAE, John 34 m SC
Virginia 25 f Ga
Mary 3 f Ga
Amanda 2 f Ala
Sarah 1 f "

1852 Farmer
McRAE, John C. 29 m Ala
Martha 25 f "
William 2 m "
Daniel C. 27 m "

493 Farmer
McRAE, John C. 30 m Ala
Martha 22 f SC
William H. 2 m Ala

981 Farmer
McRAE, John E. 66 m NC
Christian 56 f "
Elizabeth 25 f "
Harriet 17 f "
(Cont.)

(# 981 McRAE cont.)

Isabella 14 f NC
Christian 10 f "
John 23 m "

1885 Farmer ($ 500)
McRAE, John R. 65 m NC
Comfort 55 f "
George (Farmer) 20 m "
John P. " 17 m Ga
Elizabeth 15 f Ga
Margaret 12 f "

McRAE, Mary
(See J. G. McLendon).

McRAE, Sarah C.
Mary
Elizabeth
Martha
(See M. A. Patterson)

McSWAIN, Catherine
Nancy
Daniel
(See John McLeod)

McSWAIN, Colin
(See Cullen Battle).

398 Farmer ($800)
McSWAIN, Daniel 74 m Scot
Mary 72 f NC
Nancy 24 f "

433 Blacksmith
McSWAIN, Daniel 26 m NC
Julia A. 22 f Ga
Alexander 2 m Ala

McSWAIN, J. C.
(See Leroy L. Ryan)

McSWAIN, James
(See Joel D. Warren).

397 Farmer
McSWAIN, Malcolm 22 m NC

334 Farmer ($2,360)
McSWAIN, R. C. 56 m Scot
Mary 56 f NC
Angus (Farmer) 25 m "
Caroline 21 f Ala
Sarah 16 f "
GILLIS, Christian 18 f NC

2067 Farmer
McSWAIN, Daniel 36 m NC

2066 Farmer ($500)
McSWAIN, Roderick 38 m NC
Catherine 34 f "
Finley 12 m "
Mary 10 f Ala
John 7 m "
Daniel 4 m "
Catherine 3 f "
Archibald 6/12 m "

164 Farmer ($300)
McVAY, Elijah 31 m Ga
Lucinda 29 f "
Andrew 6 m Ala
Christian 4 f "
William E. 1 m "
Christian (Blind) 85 f SC

2237 Jailor
MABRY, James 22 m Ga
McDANIEL, Daniel 45 m NC
(Farmer)
McALLISTER, James 40 m --
(Shoemaker)
ADAMS, David F. 40 m Fla
THARPE, Windham A. 35 m Ga
(Last two farmers.
GUILFORD, Allen 25 m Ga
(Laborer)

714 Sheriff ($1,000)
MABRY, Seth 29 m Ga
James,Deputy sheriff 23 m "
Nancy 53 f Va
COLLINS, Hartwell 22 m Ala
(Clerk)
RIST, Calvin 28 m Mass
(Lawyer)

1097 Farmer ($2,000)
MADDOX, John P. 41 m Ga
Eliza 36 f "
Amanda 17 f "
Elizabeth 15 f Fla
Rachel 13 f "
Ann 11 f Ga
Lewis 8 m Ala
John 5 m "
Joel 3 m "
Buena Vista 1 f "

MADDOX, Matilda
(See William Anglin).

MAGRUDER, Elias
(See Dennis Nolen).

912 Blacksmith
MALLORY, J. 51 m SC
Jane 40 f "
Sarah 4 f Ga

791 Farmer ($4200)
MALLOY, Duncan 53 m SC
Mary 40 f Ga
Caroline 16 f Ala
Martha 14 f "
Franklin 12 m "
Mary 9 f "
William 7 m "
John 6 m "
Janet 4 f "

1308 Farmer ($4000)
MALONE, Green 43 m SC
TORRANCE, John 19 m Ga
(Student).

1801 Farmer ($800)
MANN, Gilbert 76 m SC

2277 Farmer ($150)
MANN, Robert 45 m SC
Harriet 42 f "

MANN, Thomas
(See Robert Dill).

2011 Farmer
MARGART, John P. 33 m SC
Nancy 34 f "
Franklin 6 m "
Caroline E. 4 f "
Samuel T. 2 m "

1820 Farmer ($500)
MARLEY, H. J. 50 m NC
Diana 37 f "
Shine (Farmer) 20 m "
Harriet 17 f "
Elizabeth 9 f Ala
Irabella 7 f "
John 4 m "

1821 Farmer
MARLEY, James T. 23 m NC
Margaret 29 f "
Ann 1 f Ala

MARSHALL, Elias
(See Henry Hendrix).

MARSHALL, Elias
(See R. W. W. Bell).

1292 Boatman ($300)
MARSHALL, Samuel 41 m Me
Amanda 30 f SC
DAVIS, David 75 m "
(Occp. - none).

1660 Laborer
MARSHALL, Thomas 22 m SC
Sarah 19 f Ga
William 6/12 m Ala

2141 Overseer
MARTIN, Benjamin M. 35 m Ga
Elizabeth 31 f "
Jane 8 f Ala
James 6 m "
Mary 4 f "
John 2 m "

1062 Farmer ($700)
MARTIN, C. O. 30 m SC

MARTIN, Elmira
(See Thomas J. Barnett).

1369 Farmer ($200)
MARTIN, Ezekiel 34 m Ala
Elizabeth 24 f "
Sarah 5 f "
Daniel 4 m "
Roxanna 2 f "
John 6/12 m "
TABER, John W. 9 m "

823 Farmer ($ 1100)
Martin, Felix 36 m Ga
Nancy 27 f Ala
Arminta 13 f "
Quintillian 10 m "

1396 Grocer ($5,500)
MARTIN, J. G. L. 39 m Fr
Eliza 21 f "
James 5 m Ala
Celina 3 f "
Charles A. 1 m "
Besson, William E. 14 m "

1437 Farmer ($3,000)
MARTIN, James L. 60 m SC
Sarah 45 f Ga
Andrew J. (Farmer) 26 m "
William " 21 m "
John " 20 m "
George W. 18 m "
Sarah 10 f "
Thomas 13 m "
Elizabeth 16 f "
(Cont.)

(# 1437 MARTIN cont.)
Harriet 9 f Ga
Samuel 7 m Ala
Mary 5 f "
Victoria 3 f "
Columbus 1 m "

1366 Farmer
MARTIN, James R. 37 m SC
Priscilla 31 f "
Nancy 9 f Ga
Sarah 5 f Ala
Mary 2 f "

1728 Farmer ($100)
MARTIN, John 60 m NC
Charity 58 f "

1303 Clerk ($500)
MARTIN, John C. 33 m NC
Eliza M. 23 f SC
Mary C. 1 f Ala

1900 Farmer ($450)
MARTIN, John F. 35 m Ga
Elizabeth 30 f SC
Sarah 12 f Ala
Ransom 9 m "
Alfred 7 m "
Susan 4 f "
Eliza 2 f "
Lucetta 1/12 f "

1715 Physician
MARTIN, John H. 27 m Ga
Amanda 24 f Ala
James H. 4 m "
Benjamin 2 m "
Mary J. 3/12 f "

854 Farmer ($500)
MARTIN, John T. 35 m SC
Hepsey 24 f NC
Mary 4 f Ala
John 3 m "

505 Farmer ($2,000)
MARTIN, Martin D. 39 m NC
Margaret 31 f "
Catherine 11 f Ala
Murdock 9 m "
Alexr. L. 6 m "
Mary 4/12 f "

109 Farmer ($1000)
MARTIN, Robert 58 m Ga
Charlotte 54 f "
(Cont.)

(# 109 MARTIN cont.)
Thomas (Farmer) 18 m Ga
Robert " 16 m "
Martha 10 f Ala

2158 (Property: $1,200)
MARTIN, Sipra W. 34 f Ga
Nancy 16 f Fla
Sarah 14 f "
Penelope 12 f Ala
Henry 10 m "
Mary 7 f "
Sileta 6 m "
Martha 3 f "
SPEARS, Henry G. (Farmer) 25 m Fla
Willis (Farmer) 20 m "

847 Overseer
MARTIN, Sylvester 35 m NC
Delia 33 f Ga
Sylvester 13 m "
Elizabeth 11 f "
Peyton 9 m "
Sarah 7 f "
Thomas 5 m "
Benjamin 3 m Ala
James 1/12 m "

1813 Laborer
MARTIN, William M. 21 m SC

670 Farmer ($700)
MATHIS, Abel 42 m NC
Jincey 35 f "
Mary 17 f Ala
Martha 15 f "
Amanda 12 f "
Fankey 10 f "
Susan 9 f "
Jackson 7 m "
William 5 m "
Charles 3 m "

1282 Grocer
MAY, George J. 31 m Eng

1203 Overseer ($900)
MAY, James 47 m Ga
Martha 45 f "
Mary 14 f "
Elizabeth 12 f "
Ann 10 f "
Martha 8 f "
Matilda 5 f Ala
William 1 m "

(# 1695 MAY cont.)

John	7	m	Ga
James	5	m	"
Martha	3	f	Ala
Mary	3/12	f	"

342 Farmer ($700)

MAYS, John	51	m	SC
Olive	36	f	Ga
Wesley (Farmer)	17	m	"
Harrison	14	m	"
Telitha	12	f	"
Charity	10	f	"
John	7	m	Ala
Marcus	4	m	"
Jesse	2	m	"

MAYS, M. G.(?)
(See James Clark).

MEARS, Emma D.
Jane
(See Martha McDonald).

2210 Teacher

MEARS, Joseph W. N.	32	m	Vt.

2047 Farmer ($1,200)

MEDLEY, Eldred	44	m	NC
Mary	37	f	Ga
Mary E.	15	f	Ala
William	13	m	"
Joseph	11	m	"
Sarah	8	f	"
Matilda	6	f	"
Eldred	4	m	"
Newton	8/12	m	"

2048 Farmer

MEDLEY, Hansel	40	m	NC
Judith	68	f	"
Jemima	38	f	"
Milley	35	f	"

MEHAN, Thomas
(See Thomas Barry).

MERRILL, Elizabeth A.
Eliza
Allen K.
(See William A. Hunter)

METON, Catherine
(See Jeremiah Paul)

959 Farmer ($1,000)

MILES, A. B.	42	m	Ga

(Cont.)

(#959 MILES cont.)

Nancy	20	f	Ala
Mary	4	f	"
Jesse	2	m	"
McLEOD, Neill (Laborer).	21	m	"

1925

MILES, Mary A.	40	f	Ga
Abraham (Apprentice)	15	m	Ala
William	12	m	"
Columbus	5	m	"
GUILFORD, Margaret	18	f	"
William A. (Farmer)	28	m	Ga
Mary	2	f	"

1725 Carpenter

MILES, William	29	m	Ga
Charity	37	f	NC
Mary	8	f	Ga
Jasper	7	m	"
William	4	m	"

23 Carpenter

MILES, William	27	m	Ga
Charity	24	f	NC
Mary J.	9	f	Ga
Jasper C.	6	m	"
William N.	3	m	"

639 Farmer

MILLER, A. J.	33	m	NC
Elizabeth A.	27	f	Ala
Nancy V.	5	f	"
John W.	4	m	"
Lucretia J.	1	f	"

1023 Farmer ($3,000)

MILLER, A. T.	45	m	NC
Elizabeth	21	f	Ala
Martha	3	f	"
Priscilla	1	f	"

MILLER, Benjamin
(See Z. W. Parmer).

1195 Physician ($3,000)

MILLER, David C.	32	m	SC
Mildred	24	f	Ga

999 Farmer ($2,500)

MILLER, J. L.	32	m	SC
Sophia	21	f	"
Ann	4	f	Ala
Mary	2	f	"
John	3/12	m	"

841 Farmer ($11,000)
MILLER, John H. 38 m SC
Ann C. 31 f "
John (Student) 15 m Ala
Edward 13 m "
Zenahia 9 f "
Thomas 7 m "
Albert 5 m "
Ann E. 3 f "
Levina T. 1 f "
STEARNS, Harris 38 m NC
(M.E. Preacher).
Elizabeth 38 f Ga

1323 Farmer ($375)
MILLER, Lewis 47 m NC
Hetty 35 f Ga
James 20 m Ala
Catherine 16 f "
Mary 14 f "
Cinthia 12 f "
Nancy 10 f "
Amanda 9 f "
Joanna 8 f "
Emeline 6 f "
Jinsey 5 f "
Jefferson 2 m "

193 Farmer ($250)
MILLER, Martin 38 m NC
Jane 35 f --
Lewis (Farmer) 16 m Ala
Molsey 14 f "
Jane 12 f "
Nancy 10 f "
Jefferson 8 m "
Joseph 6 m "
Lucinda 13 f "
John 1 m "

217 Farmer
MILLER, William 77 m NC
Arta (?) 25 f SC
Salina 13 f Ala
Cinthia 11 f "
Abraham 9 m "
William 7 m "
Thomas 6 m "
Riney 3 f "
Epsey 2 f "

784 Carpenter
MILLS, Stephen H. 45 m SC
Martha 19 f Ga
(Married within the year).

MILLS, William
(See Samuel Whitsett).

MIMS, Eliza
Benjamin
(See Robert Bryan).

MINGER, John
(See John Gurin).

1868 Farmer ($100)
MINSHEW, Isaac 32 m NC
Sarah 29 f Ga
Jane 5 f Ala
Isaac 3 m "
Jacob 1 m "

624 Farmer ($800)
MINSHEW, Jacob 42 m NC
Mary 33 f SC
Catherine 13 f Ala
Melissa 12 f "
Lorenzo 10 m "
Julia 9 f "
Alonzo 6 m "

420 Farmer ($900)
MINSHEW, John 50 m NC
Harriet 40 f Ga
Merrick (Farmer) 24 m Ala
Eliza 20 f "
Nicey 18 f "
Lawson (Farmer) 17 m "
Martha 15 f "
John 14 m "
Harriet 10 f "
Samantha 7 f "
Mary 5 f "
Sarah 4 f "
Jane 2 f "

1998 Farmer ($100)
MINSHEW, Joseph 41 m NC
Mary 40 f SC
Martha 23 f Ga
Lovely 21 f "
Oliver (Farmer) 20 m "
Henry " 19 m "
Missouri 17 f "
Daniel 16 m "
Mary 14 f "
Nathan 13 m Ala
Robert 12 m "
Clarissa 10 f "
Joseph 9 m "
Servilla 5 f "
(Cont.)

(# 1998 MINSHEW cont.)
William 3 m Ala
John 1 m "

620 Farmer ($100)
MINSHEW, Joseph S. 45 m NC
Mary 43 f SC
Martha 23 f Ga
Elizabeth 22 f "
Caleb O. (Farmer) 19 m "
Henry " 18 m "
Margaret 16 f "
Daniel (Farmer) 15 m "
Mary A. 13 f "
Robert 12 m "
Nathan 11 m Ala
Joseph 10 m "
Clarissa 8 f "
Gracey 6 f "
John 3 m "
William 1 m "

MINCHEW, Marg.
(See Ephriam Hill).

463 Farmer ($500)
MINSHEW, Nathan 47 m NC
Elizabeth 32 f "
Catherine 17 f Ga
Bryant 13 m "
Martha A. 12 f "
Margaret S. 11 f Ala
Mary E. 10 f "
Ailsey R. 9 f "
Virgil J. 8 m "
Clarey 7 f "
Charlotte 6 f "
Caroline 5 f "
James A. 4 m "
Huldy 4/12 f "
BRYON, Richard 47 m NC
(Farmer)

2168 Farmer ($25,000)
MITCHELL, Americus C. 30 m Ga
Mary 26 f "
Julius C. 7 m Ala
James 5 m "
William 2 m "

1584 (Property: $9,000)
MITCHELL, Catherine 52 f Ga
MITCHELL, Geraldine 22 f Ga
Patrick 2 m Ala
KEY, Milley 14 f Ga
PERSONS, Martha 9 f Ala

379
MITCHELL, Celia 39 f SC
Eliza 14 f Ga
William 10 m Ala
Martha 8 f "
Mary 7 f "
Hiram 5 m "
Julia A. 3/12 f "

1548 (Property: $3,500)
MITCHELL, Julia 35 f Ga
Abraham (Student) 16 m "
Martha 14 f "
Sarah 12 f Ala
Jordan 10 m "

MITCHELL, Martin
(See Levi Mothershead).

1579 Farmer ($2,000)
MITCHELL, Randolph 50 m Ga
Martha 30 f NC
Napoleon (Student) 20 m Ga
Leonidas " 15 m "
Randolph 9 m "
Martha 1 f Ala
MITCHELL, Benjamin 26 m Ga
(Physician).

882 Overseer
MIXON, Harvey 25 m SC

1969 Laborer
MIXON, John 46 m SC
Sarah 60 f "
Elijah (Farmer) 18 m "
Richard " 21 m "
Daniel " 16 m "
Elbert 13 m "

1248 (Property: $600)
MIXON, MARY 43 f NC
McLEAN, Elizabeth 10 f Ala
HAMILTON, John S. 26 m Md
(Printer).

MIXON, Richard
Sarah
(See John Yonn).

1151 Farmer ($1,000)
MOATS, Jonathan 54 m SC
Nancy 33 f Ga
Jesse 13 m Ala

1651 Farmer
MOATS, Simeon 38 m Ga
(Cont.)

(# 1651 MOATS cont.)

Mary	30 f Ga
Elizabeth	8 f Ala
Jane	6 f "
Mary	2 f "

975 Farmer ($600)

MOATS, William	26 m Ala
Sarah	25 f "
Madison	6 m "
Elizabeth	4 f Miss
Taylor	1 m Ala
Emily	22 m "

MOBLEY, Mary
(See John Hay).

MOCK, David
(See Robert Dill)

MOODY, John
(See Henry Urquhart)

239 Farmer ($300)

MOONYHAM, William	40 m Ga
Martha	40 f "
Eliza	17 f "
Rebecca	11 f "
Martha	6 f "
John	5 m "
Frances	3 f Ala

2083 Farmer ($1,000)

MOORE, George W.	27 m Ga

MOORE, Mary A.
(See Ann T. Seals).

1484 Blacksmith

MOORE, William	21 m NJ

2077 Occp. - none

MOORE, William	33 m NC
Martha	25 f "
Jane	9 f "
Nancy	7 f "
Sarah	5 f Ala
Rachel	3 f "

MOORE, William B.
Americus
James
Mary
(See A. T. Dawkins).

1162

MORELAND, H. H.	25 m Ga
Mary	25 f "

MOORELAND, James
(See Jesse Sutton)

MORGAN, James C.
(See John Colby).

1478 Shoemaker

MORRIS, Ivy	35 m NC
Susan	35 f Ga
James	11 m "
John	9 m "
Edward	5 m "
Sarah	3 f "
GOFF, Sarah	22 f "

1161 Farmer ($1,000)

MORRIS, James	60 m NC
Gatsey A.	52 f "
HAYS, Mary	15 f Ala
HAIGLER, James (Farmer)	23 m NC

MORRIS, Maranda
(See Samuel McBryde).

1345 Boatman

MORRIS, Richard	28 m Va

MORRIS, Richard
(See Thomas Barry)

MORRIS, W. F.
(See James Cole).

1848 Farmer

MORRISON, Benjamin	24 m SC
Tiercy	21 f "
James	1 m Ala

1927 Laborer

MORRISON, Benjamin	29 m Ga
Elizabeth	23 f Ala
John	4 m "
Jane	2 f "

2279 (Property: $1,600).

MORRISON, Catherine	65 f Scot
Margaret	38 f SC
Flora	24 f "
Murdock (Farmer)	22 m "
Mary	19 f "

1118 Farmer ($250)

MORRISON, Daniel	29 m NC
Amy	25 f Ga
Andrew	6 m "
Alexander	4 m "
John	2 m Ala

1243 Merchant ($1,300)
MORRISON, John M. 40 m SC
Elizabeth 36 f "
James 13 m Ala
Andrew 11 m "
Sarah E. 16 f "

1926 Laborer
MORRISON, William 27 m Ga
Mary 16 f Ala
Sarah 1 f "

2172 Farmer ($4,000)
MORTON, William 46 m Ga
Eliza 35 f "
Ulysses (Student) 18 m "
John " 15 m "
Mary 13 f "
Elizabeth 10 f Ala
Thomas 7 m "
Retintia 5 f "
Sarah 3 f "
Charles 1 m "

MOSELY, Angeline
(See Robert O. Dale).

2096 Farmer ($600)
MOSELY, F. M. 36 m Ga
Mary 35 f "
James J. 13 m Ala
William 10 m "
Susan 8 f "
Elizabeth 6 f "
Francis 5 m "
Mary 4 f "
Martha 1 f "

1618 M. E. Minister ($1800)
MOSELY, John A. 31 m Ga
Eliza 26 f "
Thomas 10 m "
Benjamin 8 m "
Malcolm 5 m "
John 3 m "
Mary 1 f "
DeWITT, Ann 66 f SC

1441 Laborer
MOSES, John 36 m Ga
Mary 35 f "
Alexander 11 m "
James 10 m "
Sarah 8 f "
Elizabeth 7 f "

1215 Farmer ($1500)
MOSHER, W. H. B. 27 m RI

1267 Brickmason ($400)
MOSS, William 42 m Eng
Harriet 36 f SC
Louisa 5 f Ala
William 1 m "

703 Farmer ($1,000)
MOTHERSHEAD, Levi 45 m SC
Lucy 47 f "
WALKER, John (Farmer) 18 m Ala
Joseph (Farmer) 15 m "
MITCHELL, Martin 25 m SC
(Farmer)

1287 Shoemaker
MUCKLERAINE, John 27 m SC
Nancy 35 f "
John 5 m Ala

MULFORD, Frances
(See T. J. Lewis)

160
MUNCUS, Cinthia 50 f SC
Richard (Laborer) 16 m Ga

MUNCUS, Micajah
(See Richard C. Ethridge).

1758 Farmer ($1,000)
MURPHY, O. H. 36 m Ga
Rebecca 32 f "
Elizabeth 13 f "
Samuel 12 m "
Ambrose 8 m "
Terrinda 6 f Ala
John 2 m "

MURPHY, Semantha
(See William Owens).

189 Blacksmith
MURPHY, William 49 m SC
Adeline 33 f Ga
Nicholas 15 m "
William 13 m "
Mary E. 11 f Ala
Narcissa 9 f "
Zachariah 4 m "
Joseph 1 m "

2275 Farmer
MYERS, Erasmus 40 m SC
Elizabeth 30 f "
Daniel 7 m Ala
Martha 6 f "
George 4 m "
Charles 1 m "

2276 Farmer
MYERS, J.(or I.?) 62 m SC
Elizabeth 45 f "
Ellender 15 f Ga
Martha 14 f "
Ellison 12 m Ala
James 9 m "
Cinthia 2 f "
BROWN, Elizabeth J. 18 f Ga
Mary 3/12 f Ala

2003 Farmer
MYERS, J. B. 50 m SC
Elizabeth 48 f "
Eliza 16 f "
Martha 14 f "
Ellison 11 m Ala
James 9 m "
Cinthia 3 f "
BROWN, L.(Carpenter) 27 m SC
Jane 18 f "
William 2/12 m Ala

853 Farmer ($200)
MYERS, James 60 m SC
Elizabeth 46 f "
Eliza 15 f Ala
Martha 13 f "
Ellison 10 m "
James 8 m "
Cinthia 6 f "
Mary 4 f "

1621 Laborer
MYERS, John C. 30 m NJ
Penelope 33 f NC
Alemedia 17 f Ga

MYERS, William
(See Orren Bennet).

1851 Farmer ($100)
NANCE, Sylvester 25 m SC
Catherine 27 f "
David 9/12 m Ala

95 Farmer ($150)
NASH, Acton 86 m Va
Margaret 83 f Ga
HARDY, Elizabeth 45 f "
Susan 18 f "
Jacob (Farmer) 16 m "

1765 Engineer ($150)
NASH, Hezekiah 35 m Conn
Catherine 22 f SC
Maria 1 f Ga

NEELY, Andrew G.
Louisa
George
Jesse
(See George C. Hodges).

1127 Farmer
NEESE, Davis 46 m SC
Margaret 35 f "
Mahala 18 f "
Thomas (Farmer) 16 m "
William 13 m "
James B. 8 m "
Dorus 6 m "
Henry 2 m Ga
Sarah 1 f "

1131 Farmer
NEESE, L. A. 40 m SC
Ann 32 f "
Mary 16 f "
James 13 m "
Allen 10 m "
Rachel 8 f "
Martha 6 f "
Eugenia 5 f "
Henry J. (Farmer) 18 m "

748 Shoemaker
NEICE, Henry 40 m SC
Nancy 65 f NC

NEICE, Henry
(See Benjamin A. Barron).

523 Farmer ($500)
NEICE, John 43 m SC
Mary 23 f NC
Jesse T. 4 m Ala
William 3 m "
John 3/12 m "

NELMS, John W.
(See John D. Turner)

116 Farmer ($2,000)
NELSON, Jacob B. 37 m Tenn
Catherine 31 f Ga
Elizabeth 6 f Ala
James S. 4 m "
John G. S. 2 m "
STEMBRIDGE, John 11 m Ga
Sarah E. 9 f "

NEWMAN, Clarissa
Angeline
(See Michael Carren).

NEWMAN, John
(See B. R. Barksdale).

NICHOLS, Jeremiah
(See Hiram Linsey).

1274 (Property: $1,000)
NICHOLS, Mary 47 f Ga
Bassianus (Stabling) 21 m Ala

1275 Merchant
NICHOLS, Theophelus 27 m Ga
Ann 20 f "
William 2 m Ala
Henry 1 m "

NIX, Thomas
(See Elisha Betts).

1208 Farmer ($225)
NIX, William R. 33 m SC
Sarah 32 f Ga
Elizabeth 9 f Ala
John 7 m "
James 5 m "
Frances 3 f "
Reuben 2 m "
George 4/12 m "

992 Farmer
NIXON, Samuel 60 m NC
Delaney 53 f "
William 13 m Ga
THARP, Chilly 14 f "
HILL, William M. 3 m Ala

1732 Farmer ($1,000)
NOBLES, Archibald 41 m NC
Eliza 37 f Ga
Lawrence 16 m "
Mary 14 f "
Martha 12 f "
Jane 9 f "
Eliza 8 f "
Celia 6 f "
Jackyann 3 f "
James 1/12 m Ala

253 Farmer ($3,000)
NOLEN, Avery 45 m SC
Milly 44 f "
Elijah 22 m Ala
Catherine 20 f "
Nancy 18 f "
McKENNEY, Benj. 56 m SC
(Laborer)

242 Farmer ($500)
NOLEN, Daniel 43 m SC
(Cont.)

(# 242 NOLEN cont.)
Elizabeth 35 f Ga
Eliza 16 f Ala
John 13 m "
Mary 10 f "
Nancy 8 f "
Daniel 6 m "
Amanda 2 f "

241 Farmer ($2,000)
NOLEN, Dennis 35 m Ga
Martha 22 f SC
Mary 67 f SC
Eliza M. 21 f Ala
(Dennis & Martha married within the year).
SPURLOCK, Green 15 m Ala
MAGRUDER, Elias 48 m Va
(Last two laborers).

1682 Farmer ($500)
NOLEN, Simpson 28 m Ala
Jane 22 f SC
(Married within the year).

1235 Farmer ($200)
NOLEN, W. S. 24 m Ga
Ruthey 20 f Ala
(Married within the year).

1814 Farmer
NOLEN, Wheat G. 28 m Ga
Caroline 21 f SC
Frances 4 f Ala
William 3 m "
Elizabeth 2 f "
John 8/12 m "

980 Farmer ($150)
NOLIN, James B. 48 m Ga
Mary 41 f SC
William A. (Farmer) 23 m Ala
Fair D. " 18 m "
Thomas 11 m "
Nancy 9 f "
John 8 m "
Daniel H. 6 m "
Marion 4 m "
Rowan 2 m "
James 1/12 m "

1580 Carpenter
NORELS, Hartwell 34 m SC
Pamelia 34 f SC
Tabitha 3 f Ga
Mary 1 f "

NORRIS, H. K.
(See William R. Stokes).

1056 Farmer ($800)
NORTEN, Daniel A. 37 m Ala
Lucinda 38 f SC
William A. 14 m "
James 13 m Ala
Mary E. 11 f "
Julia 10 f "
Lewis F. 7 m "
Aner(?) 4 f "
Josephine 2 f "

2023 Farmer ($650)
NORTON, Daniel A. 37 m SC
Lucinda 39 f "
William (Farmer) 15 m Ala
James 13 m "
Eliza 11 f "
Julia 9 f "
Lewis 7 m "
Elizabeth 5 f "
Josephine 3 f "

1135 (Property: $1,000)
NORTON, Isabella 40 f SC
Lucinda 18 f Ala
Amanda 16 f "
Caroline 14 f "
Nancy 12 f "
Franklin 11 m "
Thomas 10 m "
James 9 m "
Watson 8 m "

1052 Farmer
NORTON, J. J. 25 m SC
Nancy 26 f "
Elbert 7 m Ala
Amy A. 6 f "
Polly 4 f "
Erasmus 2 m "

619 Laborer
NORTON, James 54 m NC

1122 Farmer ($1,500)
NORTON, James R. 45 m SC
Margaret 40 f "
Mary 21 f Ala
Norman (Farmer) 18 m "
Catherine 16 f "
Lewis (Farmer) 15 m "
Russell 13 m "
Martha 12 f "
Daniel 11 m "
James 10 m "
(Cont.)

(# 1122 NORTON cont.)
Patience 9 f Ala
Fletcher 8 m "
Harriet 7 f "

2022 Farmer ($800).
NORTON, John K. 34 m SC
Christian 34 f "
John D. 13 m Ala
Andrew 12 m "
William 10 m "
Nancy 10 f "
Sarah 8 f "
Mary 6 f "
Viney 3 f "

880 Farmer ($1,600)
NORTON, John W. 56 m SC
Nancy 48 f NC
Charity 24 f SC
Wesley (Farmer) 23 m "
Jane 20 f Ala
Lucy 18 f "
Martha J. 15 f "
Albert 14 m "
Edward 12 m "
Wilbur 10 m "
Georgianna 8 f "
Thomas C. 4 m "
Cornelia 3 f "
PICKETT, Charles 26 m Ga
(Physician - $100).

1659 Farmer
NORTON, William A. 34 m SC
Eliza 29 f "
James 8 m Ala
Thomas 5 m "
Nathan 3 m "

281 Farmer ($600)
NORWOOD, Manassa 51 m Sc
Eliza 30 f "
William 21 m "
Jesse 17 m "
Caroline 12 f Ga
Louisa 14 f "
Henry 5 m "

1970 Laborer
O'BRYAN, Daniel 58 m NC
Catherine 54 f "
Elizabeth 25 f "
John (Laborer) 23 m "
Martin " 20 m "
Ann 17 f Ala
(Cont.)

(# 1970 O'BRYAN cont.)
Mary 14 f NC
ANDERSON, Fanny 29 f Ala
William 6 m "
John 2 m "
Mary 1 f "

OCHTERLONIE, David
(See John Quattlebaum).

1213 Farmer ($2,400)
ODUM, H. S. 41 m Ga
Marinda 28 f "
William M. 7 m Ala
Nancy 5 f "
Missouri 4 f "
Elisha 1 m "

1400 Farmer ($200)
ODUM, James 45 m SC
Clarissa 43 f Ga
Julia 11 f "
Clarissa 8 f Ala
James 4 m "

4-4 Farmer
ODUM, Lewis 47 m SC
Tabitha 43 f Ga
William 20 m Ala
James 18 m "
Cullen 15 m "
Jonathan 13 m "
Jacob 11 m "
Mary M. 6 f "
Henry 3 m "
Catherine A. 1 f "

1442
ODUM, Sarah 60 f Ga
Jackson 22 m Ala
Norman 20 m "
CAMERON, James 21 m Ga

1694 Farmer
ODUM, Seaborn A. 22 m Ala
Eliza 18 f "
William 3/12 m "

OLIVER, Augustus
Anna
(See Noah Wheeler).

1007 Farmer
OLIVER, Charles T. 39 m Ga
Lidia 22 f "

OLIVER, James
(See Archibald McLean).

2189 Laborer
OLIVER, James H. 21 m Ga
Lucinda 19 f "
Milbra 6/12 f Ala

2068 Preacher, M. E.
OLIVER, John L. 60 m Ga
Elizabeth 55 f "
Mary 21 f "
Caroline 19 f "
Wesley (Farmer) 17 m "
Lucy 12 f "

386 Wheelwright
OLIVER, Joseph 44 m SC
Catherine 30 f "
William(Wheelwright) 16 m "
Joseph 1 m Ala

612 Farmer
OLIVER, Joseph 77 m NC
Sarah 74 f "

777 Farmer ($3,600)
OLIVER, M. D. 24 m Ga
Nancy 17 f "
Sarah 1 f Ala

OLIVER, M. D.
(See S. S. Walkley).

611 Wheelwright
OLIVER, Samuel 32 m SC
Nancy 21 f Ga
John A. 11 m SC
Martha 4 f Ala
Sarah 6 f SC
William 1 m Ala

2032 Farmer
OLIVER, Thomas 28 m Ga
Lydia 22 f "

763 Farmer ($5,000)
OLIVER, Wiley 47 m Ga
Milbray 43 f "
Sarah 18 f "
Jasper (Student) 15 m "
Young 12 m Ala
Alexr. B. 10 m "
WAINWRIGHT, Charlotte 35 f "
Zach. T. 4 m "
JOHNSTON, John 24 m Ga
(Overseer)
ROBERTS, John L. 22 m Va
(Clerk).

1300 Merchant
OLIVER, William 22 m Ga
(Cont.)

(# 1300 Oliver cont.)

Mary	22	f	Ga

573 Farmer ($1,500)

ORR, James	29	m	Ire
Jane	20	f	Ala
William	1/12	m	"
BUSH, Mary	38	f	Ga
BRASWELL, Jeptha (Farmer)	21	m	Ala

1326 Farmer ($5,500)

OTT, Edward S.	34	m	SC
Amanda	22	f	Ga
Anna	3	f	Ala
William	1	m	"
HAMMOCK, Ross (Overseer).	23	m	Ga

1642 Farmer ($8,000)

OTT, William	61	m	SC
HAMMOCK, Uriah (Overseer)	25	m	Ga

382 Farmer

OWENS, Henry	48	m	SC
Flora	50	f	NC
Delilah	18	f	Ala
Greenberry	13	m	"
Queen E.	12	f	"
Jackson	10	m	"

OWENS, Jane
(See E. E. DuBose)

#2170 Farmer ($4,000)

OWENS, Thaddues C.	27	m	Ala
Emily (Deaf & dumb)	23	f	Ga
Henry " " "	5	m	Ala
Laura	3	f	"
Jarrod	2	m	"

2167 Farmer ($20,000)

OWENS, Whitman H.	56	m	NC
Eliza Ann	45	f	SC
Georgia Ann	15	f	Ga
Jane	11	f	"

118 Farmer

OWENS, William	24	m	Ga
Susan	24	f	"
Samuel	8	m	"
James	6	m	"
John	5	m	"
Jane	5/12	f	Ala
MURPHY, Semantha	10	f	Ga

1095 Farmer ($100)
(Cont).

(# 1095 OWENS cont.)

OWENS, William	26	m	Ga
Susan	22	f	"
Susan	10	f	"
Samuel	8	m	"
William	6	m	"
James	4	m	"
Eliza	4/12	f	Ala

2129 Farmer ($3,000)

OWENS, William J.	40	m	Ga
Elizabeth	35	f	"
Elizabeth	19	f	"
Sarah	15	f	"
Philemon	13	m	"
Rebecca	12	f	"
Julia	10	f	"
Mary	8	f	"
John	4	m	Ala

PADGETT, George W.
(See M. A. Patterson).

859 Farmer ($1,600)

PADGETT, Josiah	24	m	SC
Mary	21	f	Ga
John	2	m	Ala
Sarah	1	f	"

771 Merchant ($850)

PADGETT, M.	38	m	Ga
Sarah M.	39	f	SC
Elam J. M.	11	m	Ga
Elizabeth	8	f	"
Esther	6	f	Ala
John	4	m	"
Sarah	1	f	"

860

PADGETT, Penelope	65	f	SC
Lucinda	28	f	"
Charity	27	f	"
Pamelia	25	f	"

PAGE, Samuel
Allen
(See John Webb).

2081 Farmer ($2,500)

PALMER, M. G.	33	m	Ga
Susan	21	f	"
Frances	8	f	Ala
Mary	5	f	"
Susan	2	f	"

47 Farmer ($200)

PALMORE, Elbert	35	m	Ga
Elizabeth	35	f	"

(Cont.)

(# 47 PALMORE cont.)

Mary J. 13 f Ga
George W. 11 m "
John M. 9 m "
LaFayette 4 m Ala
Benjamin 1 m "

40 Farmer
PALMORE, Gazaway 33 m Ga
Nancy 12 f "
Elizabeth 10 f "
Celia 8 f "
James 6 m Ala
William 4 m "
Gazaway 7/12 m "

39 Farmer ($300)
PALMORE, Grief 80 m NC
Mary 82 f SC
DUKES, Sarah 16 f Ga

1407 Farmer
PARAMORE, John 51 m Ga
Aga 46 f "
Elizabeth 24 f Ala
James (Farmer) 20 m "
May 18 f "
Aga A. 16 f "
Reddin 11 m "
Martin 9 m "
Frederick 7 m "

PARHAM, John
(See James Talbot).

2029 Farmer ($150)
PARKE, Andrew L. 35 m SC
Ruthy 33 f "
William 5 m Ala
Mary 1 f "
Sarah J. 2 f "

1210 Physician ($2,400)
PARKE, Thomas D. 55 m Ire
Ann 55 f NC
Frances 28 f "
Mary 20 f "
Jane 18 f "
Ellender 16 f "

1914 Farmer ($400)
PARKER, Edward M. 25 m Ga
Martha 23 f "
Thomas 2 m Ala
Benjamin 2/12 m "

2009 Farmer
PARKER, Hiram 31 m Ga
(Cont.)

(# 2009 PARKER cont.)

Flora 28 f NC
Lucinda 14 f Ga
Serena 10 f "
Newton 6 m "
Rosaline 6/12 f Ala

746 Farmer ($200)
PARKER, James A. 24 m Ga
Catherine 22 f "
HERRING, James 18 m "

2306 Laborer
PARKER, Joel J. 26 m Ga

991 Farmer ($500)
PARKER, Kinchen 60 m NC
Martha 15 f Ga
Caroline 14 f "
Eliza 12 f "
Wesley 9 m "
Jackson 7 m "

745 Farmer ($600)
PARKER, Kinchen 65 m Va
Patsey 49 f Ga
Caroline 14 f "
Eliza 12 f "
Wesley 10 m "
Jackson 7 m "

1593 Farmer ($6,600)
PARKER, Milo B. 47 m Ga
John (Farmer) 19 m "
William 13 m "
Joseph 11 m "
Josiah 9 m "
Josephine 6 f Ala
Milo B. 4 m "
Lawrence 2 m "
Missouri 38 f Ga

1907 Farmer ($200)
PARKER, Seth 47 m NC
Evaline 35 f Ga
John 13 m "
Mary 11 f Ala
Cinthia 9 f "
Martha 6 f "
William 4 m "
Nancy 2 f "

1915 Farmer
PARKER, Sherrod N. 23 m Ga
Grace 23 f "
Charles 4 m "
Louisa 2 f Ala
William 1/12 m "
HURD, Aaron 17 m "

1913 Occupation - none
PARKER, Stephen 63 m Ga
Elizabeth 61 f Va

741 Farmer ($200)
PARKER, Walter B. 26 m Ga
Ann 22 f NC

224 Farmer ($100)
PARMER, Benjamin A. 30 m Ga
Sarah 30 f "
Sarah J. 9 f Ala
Lucinda 6 f "
Mary C. 3 f "
George 8/12 m "

298 Farmer ($500)
PARMER, Benjamin 50 m NC
Nancy 30 f Ga
Benjamin (Farmer) 18 m Ala
Mary 15 f "
Thomas 14 m "
Jacob 12 m Miss
George 10 m "
Marshall 6 m "
Eliza 11 f Ala
Henry 2 m "
William 3/12 m "

305 Farmer ($100)
PARMER, Benjamin, Sr. 69 m Md
Nancy 28 f SC
Jefferson (Farmer) 44 m Ga
George W. 11 m Ala
Sarah 9 f "
Amanda 6 f "
Andrew J. 4 m "
James L. 4 m "
John 2 m "

1629 Farmer
PARMER, George 53 m Ga
Nancy 37 f SC
Caroline 14 f Ala
William 10 m "

225 Farmer ($300)
PARMER, Jacob 24 m Ga
Adeline 24 f SC
James B. 1/12 m Ala

309 Farmer ($500)
PARMER, Jacob 56 m Ga
Martha 55 f SC
Rebecca 24 f Ga
Benjamin (Farmer) 19 m Ala
(Cont.)

(# 309 PARMER cont.)
Joseph 16 m Ala
William 12 m "
John 10 m "
STRIPLING, Benj. 24 m Ala
(Teacher).

873 Farmer ($300)
PARMER, Jacob H. 26 m Ala
Lidia F. 19 f "
Mary 1 f "

222 Farmer ($400)
PARMER, L. B. J. 32 m Ga
Elizabeth 30 f "
Amanda 11 f Ala
Barazade 9 f "
George 11 m "
Roxanna 4 f "
Jacob 1 m "
HORNE, Judy 102 f Va

32 Laborer
PARMER, Philip 21 m SC
Margaret 16 f Ga

584 Farmer ($600)
PARMER, Z. W. 30 m Ala
Mary 21 f "
James 4 m "
Henrietta 1 f "
MILLER, Benjamin 20 m "

1646
PARR, Elizabeth 33 f Ga
Nancy 15 f "
Martha 13 f "
Maria 11 f "
Gabriella 9 f "
George 7 m Ala
Janet 2 f "

1705 Farmer
PARRAMORE, Noah 27 m Ga
Mediah 22 f Ala
Frances 1 f "

963 Farmer ($100)
PARRISH, S. P. 40 m Ga
Martha 36 f "
Sarah 13 f "
Amy 11 f "
Mary 9 f "
Margaret 7 f "
Catherine 5 f Ala
Lidia 8/12 f "

\# 1798 Overseer
PARRISH, Thomas R. 36 m Ga
Sarah A. 30 f "
Eliza 10 f "
Thaddeus 8 m "
Georgia A. 6 f "
Mary 4 f "
Henry 2 m "
Laura 6/12 f Ala

\# 1596 Farmer ($300)
PARSONS, John 44 m Ga
Nancy 40 f "
John 14 m "
James 12 m "
William 9 m "
Pressley 6 m "
Elizabeth 1 f "

PARSONS, Thomas
(See James Bigham).

\# 1202 Farmer ($800)
PASSMORE, G. W. 38 m SC
Eliza 30 f "
Henrietta 12 f Ga
Versena 10 f "
Sylvannus 8 m "
Legrand 5 m "

\# 486 Farmer ($800)
PASSMORE, Lemuel 49 m Ga
Sarah 51 f SC
Samuel (Farmer) 20 m Ala
George W. " 17 m "
William " 16 m "
Martha 16 f "
Budy(?) (Farmer) 15 m "
Mary A. 13 f "
Caroline 10 f "
Elizabeth 8 f "

\# 496 (Property: $960)
PASSMORE, Mary 64 f Ga
J. R. A. (Farmer) 21 m "
B. M. (Occp. - none) 18 m "

\# 17 Farmer
PASSMORE, Stephen 30 m Ga
Elizabeth 25 f "
Jesse 7 m "
Samuel 6 m "
Edwin 2 m "
Stephen 1 m "

\# 1863 Farmer
PATE, William 42 m Ga
(Cont.)

(# 1863 PATE cont.)
Leonora 40 f Ga
Queenetta 18 f Ala
Drucilla 14 f "
William 12 m "
Harriet 3 f "

\# 497 Minister, O.Sl.P. ($600)
PATTERSON, M. A. 40 m NC
Ann 24 f "
Mary 5 f Ga
William C. 2 m Ala
Sarah 4/12 f "
McRAE, Sarah C. 20 f Fla
Mary 17 f "
Martha 15 f "
Elizabeth 12 f Ga
PADGETT, George W. 21 m Fla
(Occupation - none).

\# 1983
PATTERSON, Nancy 40 f Ga
Joseph (Farmer) 23 m "
John " 18 m "
William 14 m Ala
Mary 16 f "

PATTERSON, Newton
(See Henry M. Tompkins).

\# 1042
PATTERSON, Rebecca 40 f Ga
George (Farmer) 18 m Fla
Sarah 16 f "
Joanna 13 f "
Joseph 10 m "
Solomon 8 m "

PATTERSON, William T.
(See John S. Dobbins).

PAUL, H. K.
(See Eli N. Ford).

\# 1490 Laborer
PAUL, Jeremiah 23 m Ga
Elizabeth 28 f "
METON, Catherine 58 f Va

\# 1399 Farmer ($200)
PAULL, Jeremiah 22 m Ga
Elizabeth 23 f "
Louisa 3 f "
Leuysa 3 f "
Sidney 1 m "

\# 1263 Clerk
PAULLIN, William S. 38 m NJ
(Cont.)

(# 1263 PAULLIN CONT.)
Eliza 40 f SC
James S. 13 m Ala
WILLARD, Emma P. 11 f Ga

387 Farmer ($600)
PAYNE, Joseph 42 m SC
Lydia 35 f "
Frankey 16 f Ala
Rhody 14 f "
Sarah 12 f "
Absolom 9 m "
Nancy 7 f "
Judge 5 m "
Elizabeth 2 f "
Sarah 46 f SC
Elisha 14 m Ala

1424 Laborer
PEACOCK, James 39 m Ga
Rebecca 35 f "
Joseph (Laborer) 18 m "
Jane 14 f "
William 10 m "
Thomas 8 m "
Sarah 6 f "
Martha 4 f Ala
James 1 m "

364 Farmer ($150)
PEARCE, Jesse 55 m NC
Winneford 52 f SC
Missouri 12 f Ga
Nancy 10 f "
Elizabeth 8 f "
Louisa J. 6 f "

365 Farmer
PEARCE, Needham L. 27 m Ga
Mary 27 f NC
Mexcy 6 f Ga
Martha 5 f "

PEARSON, Green
(See Benjamin Dodd).

1680 Farmer ($5,000)
PEARSON, R.(B.?) T. 38 m NC
Harriet 27 f "
Herbert 10 m Ala
William 8 m "
James 5 m "
Robert 3 m "
Rosa 8/12 f "
SEAY, Calvin 33 m SC
(Overseer)

1440 Tavern Keeper
PEASE, Grave A. 60 m Conn
Harriet S. 52 f "
George A. 10 m Fla
BAIRD, Benjamin A. 40 m Ga
(Occupation - none)
CUNNINGHAM, James 46 m Ga
(Merchant)

PECK, H. K.
(See C. Rhodes)

1518 Farmer ($400)
PEDDY, James 50 m Ga
Jane 47 f "
Alexander (Farmer) 18 m "
Viney 15 f "
Adelaide 13 f "
Mary 6 f "
Sarah 4 f "

PEDDY, Jeremiah
(See Loderick Craig).

2093 Farmer ($900)
PENNICK, Lagurus 24 m Ga

2178 Farmer ($400)
PERKINS, James M. 32 m Ga
Rebecca 26 f "
Mary 5 f "
Elizabeth 4 f "
Susan 2 f "

12-13 Farmer ($400)
PERKINS, James M. 29 m Ga
Frances 29 f "
Frances 3 f Ala
Nancy 2 f "

PERRY, Elizabeth
(See John Stewart).

1360 Farmer $500
PERRY, John 58 m Va
Elizabeth 48 f Ga
James (Farmer) 15 m "
Eliza 10 f "
Frances 8 f "
Erie 6 f "

PERSONS, Emily J.
(See John M. Raiford).

PERSONS, Martha
(See Catherine Mitchell).

PERSON, Sarah
(See E. E. DuBose).

867 Physician ($8,000)
PETERSON, Batt 32 m Ga
Martha 9 f Ala
Eugenia 5 f "
RUSSELL, Wash. 25 m NC
(Overseer)

2262 Laborer
PETERSON, Duncan C. 24 m Ga
Elizabeth 21 f Ala
Mary 3 f "
John 1 m "

#1693 Farmer
PETERSON, William 24 m NC
Sarah 16 f "
(Married within the year)

PETTIGREE, James
(See James R. Upshaw).

722 Occp., none - ($7,600)
PETTY, B. F. 44 m NY
Catherine 22 f Tenn
Charles L. 11 m Ala
Benjamin F. 9 m "
Catherine 4 f "
Juliet 3 f "
Elizabeth 1 f "

709 Merchant ($4,000).
PETTY, Charles 30 m NY
Narcissa 26 f SC
Edward 5 m Ala
Anna 2 f "
HARGROVES, Lemuel 18 m "
(Clerk)
PETTY, Allen (Clerk) 21 m NY
DANFORTH, Laura 12 f Ga

453 Farmer ($300)
PHILLIPS, A. H. H. 23 m Ga
Martha 21 f Ala
Jesse 2 m "
Thomas C. 2/12 m "

458 Farmer ($1,000)
PHILLIPS, Burrel 27 m Ga

PHILLIPS, Caroline S.
Nancy E.
(See Jesse Sutton).

2138 (Property: $100)
PHILLIPS, Esther 69 f NC
Margaret 21 f SC
James (Farmer) 19 m "
Rebecca 14 f "
WENCH, William 14 m "
(Cont.)

(#2138 PHILLIPS cont.)
James (WENCH) 12 m SC
CARTER, Robert 9 m Ala

455 Farmer ($50)
PHILLIPS, Thos. P. C. 21 m Ga
Isham (Farmer) 65 m NC
Mary 53 f Ga

PICKETT, Charles
(See John W. Norton).

1678 Farmer
PICKETT, Robert 60 m SC
Sarah 50 f "
JUSTICE, Edward 19 m Tenn
(Student).
Sarah 9 f Ga
BELL, Samuel 24 m "
(Overseer).

789 Farmer ($900)
PICKET, Thomas 55 m SC
Mary 50 f Ga
Martha 16 f "
Sarah 15 f "
Thomas 14 m "
Richard 11 m "

792 Farmer
PICKETT, William 32 m Ga
Hany(?) 32 f "
John 12 m "
Georgia A. 10 f "
Ann 8 f "
Sarah 6 f Ala
Mary 4 f "
Robert 2 m "

345 Farmer ($325)
PIERCE, Lovard L. 25 m Ga
Anna 20 f "
Mary 4 f "
Thomas 2 m Ala
John 10/12 m "

1194 Laborer
PIERCE, Needham 28 m Ga
Mary 30 f NC
Winneford 7 f Ga
Martha 6 f "

1831 Shoemaker
PILOT, Samuel 27 m SC
Margaret 23 f "

61-62 (Property: $500)
PINKERTON, Catherine 60 f Ga
PINKERTON, Rebecca 30 f "
(Cont.)

(# 61-62 PINKERTON cont.)
Catherine 12 f Ala
Mahala J. 9 f "

73-75
PINSON, Mary 55 f SC

1712 Farmer
PIPER, William M. 42 m Ga
Melissa 41 f "
Mary 19 f "
John (Farmer) 18 m "
Elizabeth 15 f "
James 10 m "
William 8 m "
Ezekiel 2/12 m "

1219 Farmer ($500)
PIPKIN, Calvin 35 m NC
Sarah 32 f Ga
Lewis 13 m "
William 11 m "
Delaney 10 f "
Jackson 7 m "
Berrien 4 m Ala
Taylor 1 m "

1021 Farmer ($1,200)
PIPKIN, Haywood 38 m NC
Eliza 29 f "
Charles 13 m Ga
Mary 11 f Ala
Martha 8 f "
Frances 6 f "
Caroline 6/12 f "

PIPKIN, Jackson
(See Nicholas Crawford).

1666 Farmer ($2,000)
PITTS, N. W. 53 m NC
Maria 33 f Ga
John O. (Farmer) 25 m "
Columbus " 20 m "
Adaniram(?) " 18 m "
Noel 16 m "
Martha 3/12 f Ala

1331 Physician
POPE, C. J. 36 m Ga
Jane 27 f "
Sarah 8 f Ala
Ella 6 f "
Mary Stella 3 f "

668 Farmer
POPE, Hezekiah 34 m Ga
(Cont.)

(# 668 POPE cont.)
Milly 25 f Ga
Sarah 10 f "
John 9 m Ala
Nancy 6 f Ga
William 5 m Ala
Jeptha 3 m "
Mary L. 1 f "

POPE, James
Frances
Sarah
Henry
(See Robert N. Jones).

2303 Laborer
POPE, Simeon 39 m Ga
Martha 37 f "
Elizabeth 12 f "
John 10 m "
William 8 m "
Sarah 5 f "
Mary 2 f Ala
James 4/12 m "

PORTUS, John
(See C. J. M. Andrews).

2106 Farmer
POSEY, John 23 m Ga
Mary 21 f SC
Mary J. 5 f Ga
Martha 2 f "

2104 Farmer ($825)
POSEY, Lemuel 46 m Ga
Mary 46 f "
William (Farmer) 20 m "
Nancy 17 f "
James 15 m "
Aradna(?) 14 f "
Rachel 12 f Ala
Hope 10 f "
George 8 m Ga
Catherine 6 f "
Thaddeus 5 m "

2105 Grocer
POSEY, Pulaski 29 m Ga

1093 Millwright
POSTON, E. 47 m SC
Elizabeth 32 f Ga
James 7 m Ala
John 4 m "
Manfredonia 1 f "

1789 Peddler
POTTER, Augustus 34 m Ga
Hannah 34 f "
Mary 10 f Ala
Jackson 10 m "
James 9 m "
Susan 8 f "
Wesley 7 m "
Franklin 6 m "
Julia 1 f "

1671 Farmer
POTTER, James 38 m SC
Hannah 36 f "
John 15 m Ga
Elizabeth 13 f "
William 11 m "
Thomas 9 m Ala
Mary 7 f "
Hannah 4 f "
Robert 2 m "

2002 Toll Keeper ($135)
POURNELL, George W. 49 m NY
Amy 32 f Ga
Elmira 13 f "
George 8 m Ala
Alexander 6 m "

422 Farmer ($400)
POWELL, David 49 m SC
Eady A. 44 f Ga
Ransom (Farmer) 25 m SC
Sarah C. 23 f "
Martha 22 f "
Joseph (Farmer) 20 m "
Mary 16 f Ala
Margaret 13 f "
Susan 10 f "
Sally 10 f "
Eliza 8 f "
Matilda 6 f "
Ann M. 3 f "
Caroline 2 f "
Elliphar 3/12 f "
LEWIS, Benjamin 17 m "
(Farmer)
John 15 m "
Jackson 13 m "
Harrison 10 m "

1200 Farmer ($1,900)
POWELL, George 48 m SC
Bersheba 45 f "
Larkin W. 17 m Ala
Harriet 16 f "

1000 Carpenter ($3500)
POWELL, John 34 m Ga
George W. (Carpenter) 36 m "
ROCHESTER, Aaron 24 m SC
(Farmer)
FLEMING, William 40 m Scot
(Carpenter, - $500).

1615 Farmer ($4,500)
POWELL, Joseph P. 30 m Ga
Antionette 23 f "
Joseph 2/12 m Ala

POWELL, Milton
(See Charles T. Ziterour).

1158 Farmer
POWELL, William B. 24 m Ga
Elizabeth 21 f "
(Married within the year).

1562 Farmer ($1,700)
PRATT, William 40 m NC

998 Farmer
PRESCOTT, Zack. D. 42 m NC
Eliza 30 f Ga
Julia 10 f Ala
Francis 8 m "
John 6 m "

482 Farmer ($1,300)
PRICE, Burrel 43 m NC
Rebecca 42 f "
Riley A. 20 m "
Lemuel 16 m "
Elizabeth 14 f "
David E. 11 m Ala
John 8 m "
Leah A. 5 f "
Viney 1 f "

PRICE, Caswell
(See Ezekiel Wise).

PRICE, George W. F.
(See A. B. Seals).

1408 Farmer
PRICE, Hansford D. 52 m SC
Sarah 26 f Ga
John (Farmer) 20 m "
Elizabeth 16 f "
THOMAS, LaFayette 17 m "
(Laborer)

2264 Laborer
PRICE, Ira 22 m NC
(Cont.)

(# 2264 PRICE cont.)
Winny 18 f NC
(Married within the year).

729 Farmer ($700)
PRICE, Robert O. 38 m SC
Celia 35 f "
John (Farmer) 18 m "
William " 16 m "
Mary A. 14 f "
Martha J. 12 f "
Patience 9 f "
Margaret 7 f "
James K. 5 m "
Caroline 3 f Ala
Celia A. 1/12 f "

848 Farmer ($2,200)
PRICE, William 31 m SC
Emma M. 27 f Ga
WOOD, Jesse 10 m "

1956 Farmer
PRICE, William R. 34 m NC
Elizabeth 27 f "
Feribe 12 f "
Leeton 10 m Ala
Barrill 8 m "
Elizabeth 5 f "
Mary 8/12 f "

1519 Farmer
PRINCE, Henry 35 m NC
Lucy 25 f Ga

PRUETT, R. A.
Virginia
(See Keziah Coleman).

1706 Farmer ($5,500)
PRUITT, James M. 34 m Ga
Louisa 32 f "
Martha 11 f Ala
Sarah 10 f "
William (H.) 9 m "
John (E.) 7 m "
Samuel (T.) 4 m "
James (W.) 3 m "
DOSTER, Simeon J. 25 m Ga
(Teacher)
SEAY, Carville 25 m NC
(Overseer)
ALSOBROOK, Thomas 18 m Ga
(Student)
LEE, Willis G. 7 m Ala
Adeline 8 f "

1707
PRUITT, Mary 60 f Ga
SEAY, Adeline 20 f NC

1317 Lawyer ($2,000)
PUGH, J. L. 30 m Ga
Sarah S. 18 f SC
Laura T. 1 f Ala

PUGH, Whitson
(See William McLeod).

191 Farmer ($800)
PURSEWELL, Gabriel 40 m SC
Elizabeth 39 f "
William S. 20 m "
Frances J. 18 f "
Henry D. 14 m Ala
Rachel 12 f "

188
PURSEWELL, Henry 68 m Pa
Catherine 54 f SC

381 Farmer ($200)
PURVISS(?), David B. 38 m Ga
Elizabeth 38 f SC
Nancy 17 f Ga
John N. 14 m "
Mary 12 f "
Margaret 10 f "
Martha 8 f "
Sophronia 6 f "
David B. 1 m Ala
STEPHENS, Wesley 16 m Ga
(Farmer).

1045 Farmer ($440)
PYNES, Fair 46 m SC
Mary 40 f Ga
Francis (Farmer) 18 m Ala
Jasper " 16 m "
Daniel 13 m "
Lidia 11 f "
Calista 9 f "
Ruth 7 f "
Mary 4 f "
Columbus 2 m "

1608 Blacksmith ($250)
QUATTLEBAUM, John 48 m SC
Mary 27 f "
Amanda 8 f Ala
Wilkes 6 m "
Virginia 4 f "
Levi 1 m "
OCHTERLONIE, David 55 m Scot
(Carpenter).

1502 Farmer
QUICK, Jackson 30 m Ga
Mary 23 f "
Sarah 3 f Ala
John 6/12 m "

104 Farmer
RACHELS, George 77 m NC
Elizabeth 10 f Ga
HARWELL, William J. 21 m "
(Laborer)

103 Farmer ($800)
RACHELS, Hampton 49 m Ga
Sarah 29 f SC
Elizabeth 7 f Ala
Mary 6 f "
George D. 5 m "
James B.(?) 4 m "
Burril R. 3 m "
Effie 1 f "

#1545 Farmer ($15,000)
RAIFORD, John M. 46 m SC
Martha J. 32 f Ga
PERSONS, Emily J. 13 f "

RAINES, John G.
Lucretia
(See James Talbot).

36 Farmer ($5,000)
RAINES, John W. 43 m Ga
JOHNSTON, Aleniren(?) 24 m Ga
(Overseer)

33 Farmer
RAINES, Joseph G. 30 m Ga
Matilda C. 29 f "
Lucretia 6 f "
Henry 4 m "
Joseph L. 5/12 m Ala

1444 Laborer
RALEIGH, G. W. 68 m SC
Elizabeth 54 f NC
Sarah 32 f Ga
Eliza 26 f Ala
James (Clerk) 18 m "
John (Apprentice) 15 m "

898 Farmer
RALEIGH, J. W. 30 m Ga
Laney 33 f "
Amanda 8 f Ala
Nancy 6 f "
Mary 4 f "
(Cont.)

(# 898 RALEIGH cont.)
Josephine 2 f Ala
Ann 1 f "

2208 Cabinet Maker ($12,000)
RAMSER, Ursus 40 m Swit

RAMSEY, Margaret
(See E. D. Carter).

1509 Miller
RANTON, William 38 m NY

1804 Farmer ($75)
RASBERRY, John 64 m NC
Nancy 29 f "
Rachel 19 f Ga
Sarah 16 f "
Sanders (Farmer) 18 m "
Robert 13 m "
John 9 m Ala
James 7 m "
Calvin 2 m "

69 Farmer
RASH, Thomas 45 m NC
Ellen 55 f Ga
John L. 16 m "
Susan 14 f "

RAY, Archibald
(See William Boren).

72 Farmer
RAY, Elijah 26 m --
Denetta 24 f Ala
Thomas L. 6 m "
Susan E. 5 f "
Felix 4 m "
Joseph M. 3 m "
William N. 2 m "
Sullivan 3/12 m "

1780 Laborer
RAY, James 24 m NC
Dicey 24 f Ga
Mary 8 f "
Franklin 4 m Ala
William 2 m "
Margaret 1/12 f "

RAY, William
Sarah
(See Jacob Screws).

94 Farmer
REDDIE, Jonathan 49 m NC
Ann R. 23 f "
(Cont.)

(# 94 REDDIE cont.)
John F. 18 m NC
Elisha 16 m "
Esta 11 f Ga
Sarah 10 f "

Reddy, Stanmore
(See Young Wood).

2302 Farmer ($200)
REDING, Nathaniel 44 m SC
Elizabeth 38 f Ga
Jane 12 f Ala
Martha 9 f "
William 5 m "

1230 Overseer
REDMAN, Peter 30 m SC
Cinthia 25 f "
Frances 2 f Ala

1106 Farmer ($600)
REED, John 52 m Ire
Jane 50 f "
Margaret 21 f SC
James 17 m "
Sophia 15 f "
Thomas D. 11 m Ala
Caroline 8 f "
Josiah(Jonah?) 6 m "
Margaret 85 f Ire

REED, William
(See F. P. Boulware).

REES, Marietta
(See Eliza C. Daniel).

1683 Laborer
REES, Orlando 41 m Ga
Marena 37 f "
Munroe 15 m "
Sophronia 14 f "
Orlando 10 m Ala
Rebecca 7 f "

1113 Farmer ($500)
REES, William 38 m Ga
Luruney 37 f "
Edmund (Farmer) 18 m "
Josiah " 16 m "
Mary 14 f "
Elizabeth 12 f "
William 13 m "
Cornelia 9 f "
Aramantha 7 f "
John 4 m Ala
(Cont.)

(# 1113 REES cont.)
Jordan 2 m Ala
Posey 3/12 f "

316 Farmer ($2,000)
REEVES, Asher 51 m NC
Ellender 32 f Ga
Rebecca 15 f "
Wellborn 12 m Ala
Sithey(?) 9 f "
Nancy 3 f "
Martha 1 f "

123 Farmer ($200)
REEVES, David S. 28 m Ga
Mahala 22 f Ala
Thomas J. 5 m "
Cinthia J. 2 f "

293 Farmer
REEVES, H. T. 29 m Ga
Martha 27 f "
Columbus 8 m Ala
Walter 7 m "
Moses 6 m "
Julia 5 f "
Jane 3 f "
Minerva 5/12 f "

REEVES, Martha
Lugenia
(See Delilah Smith).

REEVES, Mary
(See F. S. Blakey).

REGISTER, Elizabeth
(See Jeptha Lindsay).

1662 Farmer ($700)
REYNOLDS, George 23 m Ala

1663 Occupation - none
REYNOLDS, James 70 m NC
Martha 58 f SC
Jesse (Idiot) 28 m Ala

269 Blacksmith
REYNOLDS, William 31 m Ala
Caroline 23 f Ga
Alfred 7 m Ala
Martha 5 f "
George 3 m "
Arrena 1 f "
RYAN, Reddic O. 46 m NC
(Blacksmith).

REYNOLDS, William
(See John Black)

1304 Merchant ($1,000)
RHODES, C. 27 m Conn
PECK, H. K. 25 m "
(Merchant).

RHODES, John
(See William T. Wells).

1464 Farmer ($800)
RHODES, William 35 m NC
Sarah 22 f Ga
Sarah J. 6/12 f Ala
CALLOWAY, James A. 24 m Ga
(Farmer)
Elizabeth 19 f Ga

863 Wheelwright
RHODES, Young H. 29 m NC
Catherine 22 f Ga
James 3 m Ala
Mildred 1 f Ga
ALLEN, Hansford 22 m "
(Wheelwright)

RIALLS, Eveline
John
(See Alfred Crowley).

RICE, Arthur
(See John Silas).

RICE, Elizabeth
(See Randolph Lignoski).

1279 Tailor
RICE, George W. 30 m Ga
Amanda 19 f "
Cinithia 4 f Ala
Mary 1 f "
BRITT, John H. 17 m "

43 Farmer
RICE, John 59 m NC
Nancy 58 f SC
Martha 33 f Ga

156 Farmer ($600)
RICHARDS, George W. 24 m Ala
Mary 20 f "
William 1 m "

26 Farmer ($600)
RICHARDS, James 39 m SC
Eliza 43 f "
Harriet J. 14 f Ala
Nancy E. 12 f "
Matilda 10 f "
William 7 m "
(Cont.)

(# 26 RICHARDS cont.)
James F. 5 m Ala
Robert D. 3 m "
Andrew 10/12 m "

166 Occupation - none
RICHARDS, Robert 74 m Ire

168 Farmer ($1,800)
RICHARDS, Thomas 51 m SC
Lucy 55 f Ga
Louisa 21 f Ala
Benjamin (Farmer) 20 m "
Robert E. " 18 m "
Giles 17 m "
Thomas 13 m "
William 9 m "
Lucy 6 f "
Joseph 3 m "
John 1 m "

157 Farmer ($350)
RICHARDS, Thomas W. 26 m Ala
Temperance 24 f Ga
James 6 m Ala
William 4 m "
Thomas 1 m "
Mary A. 28 f "

167 Farmer ($2,000)
RICHARDS, William 48 m SC
Matilda 43 f "
Melinda 20 f Ala
Mary 18 f "
James 11 m "
Louisa 9 f "
Dallas 7 m "
Robert 3 m "

RICHARDSON, Moses
(See Chaney McGilberry).

1547 Farmer ($24,000)
RICHARDSON, William N. 60 m Ga
Mary R. ($4,000) 56 f Va
Walker (Farmer) 25 m Ga
William (Student) 22 m "
THOMPSON, Louisa 27 f "

1124 Farmer
RICHBURGH, R. W. 26 m SC
Mary 22 f Ga
Rebecca 4 f Ala
William 2 m "
TATE, Henry D. 61 m NC
(Farmer)
Rebecca 57 f Ga

541 Butcher ($400)
RICKS, John 57 m Ga
Gatsey 49 f "
Lucien 15 m "
Florence 12 f "
George 10 m "
Rabun 8 m "
Haseltine 6 f "

RICKS, Louisa N.
(See John Hay).

2228 Farmer ($200)
RIGDEN, Ephriam 60 m NC
Martha 54 f "
David (Idiot) 23 m "
Frances 17 f Ala
Elizabeth 15 f "
Daniel 12 m "
William 20 m "
Sarah 7 f "

50 Farmer
RIGSBY, Thomas 32 m Ga
Mary 29 f NC
John T. 10 m Ala
Thomas 9 m "
Allen 7 m "
Wiley 5 m "
William 4 m "
James 2 m "

1026 Farmer ($450)
RILEY, Joseph 43 m Ga
Temperance 37 f "
Bartholemew (Farmer) 20 m "
John 16 m "
Morning 14 f "
Leonora 13 f "
Sophronia 10 f "
Lidia 9 f "
Elliphar 6 f "
Lucy 4 f "

RILEY, Mary A.
Martin
(See Alexr. Burnet).

RIST, Calvin
(See Seth Mabry).

567 Farmer ($5,000)
RIVERS, John F. 32 m Ga
Sarah 24 f "
William 2 m Ala
Marianna 3/12 f "
RIVERS, Joel 20 m Ga
(Overseer)

1554 Farmer
RIVERS, Robert T. 50 m Ga
Susan 50 f "

1553 Farmer ($20,000)
RIVERS, T. H. H. B. 39 m Ga
Nancy 35 f "
Rebecca 14 f "
Mary 12 f "
Thomas T. P. 10 m "
Sarah 7 f "
Caroline 5 f "
Frances 1 f "

815 Farmer ($2,100)
RIVERS, Thomas 71 m Va
Mary 59 f "
William W. (Farmer) 34 m Ga
Ann 20 f "
Alfred (Student) 16 m "
Rebecca 15 f "

622 Farmer ($200)
ROACH, Abner L. 30 m SC
Catherine 27 f --
ROWE, James F. 7 m Ala
Mary 4 f "

2218 Laborer
ROACH, James C. 25 m Ga
Clarissa 22 f "
John 3 m Ala
Nancy 1 f "

1606 Farmer
ROACH, Nathaniel 50 m NC
Nancy 42 f Ga
Milton 21 m NC
Nathaniel 13 m "
Sarah 10 f Ala
Ann 6 f "
Perry 6/12 m "
SCARBOROUGH, David F. 16 m Ga
(Farmer)
BRIGHT, Evelina 19 f "
Levi D. 3 m Ala

ROACH, William G. B.
(See Allen Stewart).

1054 Wheelwright ($100)
ROBERTS, Charles C. 34 m Pa
Jane 25 f SC
William 5 m Ala
Mary 4 f "
Sarah E. 2 f "
Catherine 6/12 f "

1299 Clerk ($1,600)
ROBERTS, George A. 24 m Va
Ann 24 f Ga
Ann E. 3 f Ala
Sarah 1 f "
ROBERTS, Eliza J. 45 f Va
Roberta 18 f "
Powell 2 m "

ROBERTS, James
(See Keziah Coleman).

ROBERTS, John L.
(See Wiley Oliver).

1482
ROBERTS, Pamelia 37 f Ga
Augustus (Laborer) 20 m Fla
John (Student) 15 m "
James 11 m Ala
William 7 m "

1390 Cabinet Maker
ROBERTS, Wiley 31 m Fla
Sarah 20 f Ga
Margaret 1 f Ala

1362 Farmer ($600)
ROBERTSON, A. S. 22 m Ga
Martha 18 f "
(Married within the year).

1249 Merchant ($1,200)
ROBERTSON, Foster 35 m Mass
Eliza 25 f SC
Clara 3 f Ala
Willard 1 m "

1027 Farmer ($1,800)
ROBERTSON, John R. 46 m NC
Frances 32 f Ga
Sarah 13 f "
JUSTICE, James 14 m "
ROBERTSON, Sarah 22 f "

2026 Farmer ($200)
ROBEY, Mathew 49 m Md
Mary 37 f Ga
Susan 16 f "
Elizabeth 12 f "
Mary J. 5 f Ala
Sarah 5 f "
Martha 2 f "

1568 Overseer
ROBEY, Willis 25 m Ga
Martha 21 f "
(Cont.)

(# 1568 ROBEY cont.)
Rosanna 4 f Ala
Martha 2 f "
John 3/12 m "

ROBINSON, Elizabeth
Sarah
(See Nancy Warren).

600
ROBINSON, Mary 50 f NC
Margaret 21 f Ga
Arpey 19 f "
Nathan (Farmer) 16 m "
Martha 14 f "
Henry 12 m "

ROBINSON, Nathan
(See Josiah Bass, Sr.)

2007 Farmer
Robinson, R. E. 29 m Ga
Martha 24 f "
Jane 8 f Ala
William 6 m "
Nancy 4 f "
John 2 m "

1298 Merchant ($3,000)
ROBINSON, Thomas 37 m NC
Sarah 31 f Ga
Cornelia 10 f Ala
Charles 8 m "
William 7 m "
Antonette 5 f "
Margaret 3 f "
Sarah 1 f "

ROCHESTER, Aaron
(See John Powell).

1307 Clerk
RODGERS, S. B. 33 m SC

1319 Farmer ($3,000)
ROGERS, B. A. 33 m Ga
Sarah 26 f Ga
Jemison 5 m "
WILLIAMS, Daniel 24 m NC
(Overseer)

ROGERS, James
(See C. Stephenson).

1320 Farmer ($8,000)
ROGERS, Osborn T. 25 m Ga
Louisa 24 f "
Anna 4 f "
(Cont.)

(# 1320 ROGERS cont.)
Sarah 2 f Ga
THOMPSON, Geo. W. 20 m "
(Overseer).

2213 Laborer
ROGERS, Robert H. 24 m Ga
Eliza 25 f "
Eveline 6 f "
Thomas 4 m Ala
Martha 2 f "
Sarah 2/12 f "
THOMAS, Elisha 10 m Ga
Nancy 7 f "

2159 Farmer
ROGERS, T. T. 30 m Ga
Lucy Ann 20 f "

2069 Farmer
ROGERS, William 50 m NC
Elizabeth 20 f "
William (Farmer) 17 m "
Margaret 14 f "
John 11 m "
David 9 m "
Catherine 7 f "

1450 Farmer
ROGERS, William F. 21 m Ga
Eliza 16 f "
(Married within the year).

1859 Farmer
ROLLIN, John 20 m Ga
Elizabeth 12 f Ala
(Married within the year).

1858 Farmer ($600)
ROLLIN, William J. 30 m Ga
Jane 20 f Ala
John 3 m "
James 1 m "
WATSON, David(Farmer) 50 m Ga
Jincey 40 f NC

ROLLINS, Sarah
John
(See E. B. Cowen).

44 Laborer
RONEY, John A. 25 m Ala
Catherine 26 f "
(Married within the year).
James M. 1/12 m "

537 Farmer
ROQUEMORE, John 30 m Ga
(Cont.)

(# 537 ROQUEMORE cont.)
Martha 33 f Ga
ARNOLD, Frances 14 f "

1225 Farmer ($12,800)
ROQUEMORE, T. J. 35 m Ga
Eliza 34 f SC
Cicero * 12 m Ga
George * 10 m Ala
Mary * 8 f "
Watsonia 6 f "
Jacksonia 4 f "
Leonia 2 f "
BENNET, Samuel 23 m Ga
(Teacher).

1635 Farmer ($4,000)
ROQUEMORE, Zack. 40 m Ga
Juliann 30 f "
Mary 16 f "
James (Farmer) 15 m "
Sarah 12 f Ala
Charles 10 m "
John 6 m "
Thomas 2 m "
FORT, William H. 22 m Ga
(Overseer).

ROSE, Caroline
Dorcas
(See John D. Caton).

ROSE, Hugh F.
(See Isham C. Browder).

601
ROSS, Martha 65 f --

1771 Minister, M.B. ($1,000)
ROSS, William 44 m Ga
Isabella 26 f "
John 10 m "
Mary 8 f "
Dorcas 6 f "
Jeter 4 m "
Francis 6/12 m Ala

ROUSE, Ann
Mary
(See C. B. Anderson).

* Children of George W. Stovall, dec'd., & wife Eliza, who later became Mrs. Roquemore.

2269 Farmer ($2,000)
ROUSE, Lewis 59 m NC
Mary 49 f SC
Thomas (Farmer) 19 m NC
Allen 12 m Ala
Irvin T. 10 m "
STAFFORD, Judith L. 20 f "
(Blind).

2080 Farmer
ROUSE, Lewis H. 30 m NC
Sarah 36 f "
Solomon 4 m Ala
Melinda 2 f "
John 1 m "

ROWE, James F.
Mary F.
(See Abner L. Roach).

1475 Overseer ($1,000)
ROWE, Thomas 49 m Ga
Malinda 52 f "

1189 Farmer
RUMLEY, Elisha 26 m SC
Winney 40 f Ga
KING, John (Farmer) 21 m Ala
Gabriel " 20 m "
Nancy 18 f "
Smithey 10 f "

2179 Occupation - none
RUNNELS, James 65 m SC
Martha 57 f "
Jesse (Farmer) 27 m "

1779 Farmer ($1,200)
RUSHING, Richard R. 38 m NC
Martha 33 f SC

1180 Farmer ($1,000)
RUSSELL, J. C. 36 m NC
Mary 36 f "
George (Farmer) 15 m Ala
Laura 10 f "
Helen 7 f "
Emma 4 f "
Joanna 2 f "

728 Farmer
RUSSELL, Joseph C., Sr. 67 m Va
Mary 55 f NC
Rachel M. 25 f "
Henry C. (Farmer) 23 m "
Malvina 19 f "

1138 Property: $1100.
RUSSELL, Ursula 45 f NC
(Cont.)

(# 1138 RUSSELL cont.)
William (Student) 15 m NC
Hartwell 13 m "
Ellen 11 f "
James 9 m Ala
Joseph 7 m "
Lucius 5 m "

RUSSELL, Wash
(See Batt Peterson).

111 Farmer
RUTHERFORD, Geo. M.T. 24 m Ga
Sarah 21 f "
Mary 1 f Ala
Robert 3/12 m "

2280 Farmer ($400)
RUTHERFORD, Patrick H. 30 m Ga
Ann 20 f "
Elizabeth 1 f Ala

#1029 Farmer ($200)
RUTHERFORD, Patrick H. 27 m Ala
Ann 22 f Fla
Louisa 1 f Ala

RUTLAND, Barbara
(See Andrew Saunders).

1499 Farmer
RUTLEDGE, Geo. W. 31 m Ga
Elizabeth 24 f "
William 4 m "
Mary C. 1 f Ala
LUND, Peter (Farmer) 65 m Mass

1932 Blacksmith
RYALLS, Owen 35 m Ga
Emily 33 f Fla
Ann 15 f Ga
Martha 12 f "
James 9 m "
Mary 7 f "
Emily 5 f Ala
Sarah 2 f "

296 Farmer ($2,000)
RYAN, Hampton 53 m Ga
Rachel 54 f "
Risden B. 28 m Ala

RYAN, Lemon J.
(See Thomas S. Locke).

297
RYAN, Leroy L. 29 m Ala
(Merchant)
McSWAIN, J. C. 22 m NC
(Clerk). (#297 cont.).

(# 297 RYAN cont.)
HOOLE, E. S. 29 m SC
(Physician)

RYAN, Reddic O.
(See William Reynolds).

694 Farmer
SANDERS, John 22 m Ga
Susan 15 f Fla
(Married within the year).
SIMS, Amy 55 f Ga

SANDERS, Penny
(See John W. Ellis)

1934 Laborer
SANDERSON, Thomas 28 m NC
Mary A. 21 f Ga

549 Carpenter ($1,200)
SANDIFORD, Samuel 36 m D.C.
Martha 26 f Ga
Emma 4 f Ala

1585 Farmer ($22,000)
SANFORD, A. W. 39 m Ga
Sophia 32 f "
Martha 15 f "
Octavia 1 f "

782 Farmer ($640)
SANFORD, William 40 m Ga
Sarah 40 f "
Newton (Farmer) 16 m "
Clayton 14 m "
Elizabeth 12 f "
Columbus 8 m Ala
Amanda 6 f "
Morgan 3 m "

1384 Laborer ($300)
SANTIFER, Jacob 22 m Tenn
Mary 22 f Ga
Amanda 2 f Ala

SAPP, Allen
(See Ryan Bennet).

255 Overseer
SAPP, William 23 m Ga

462 Farmer ($100)
SASCER, John 64 m Ga
Elizabeth 59 f "

SASSER, John
(See W. D. Garrett).

454 Farmer ($100)
SAUCER(?), William 26 m Ala
Martha 26 f "
Joseph 1 m "

SAULS, David
(See Edward Bird).

SAULS, John
(See Felix Hight).

2089 Farmer
SAULS, Reuben T. 33 m NC
Martha 34 f SC

1648 Merchant ($400)
SAULSBURY, Joseph 37 m Md
Mary 27 f Ga
Mary J. 10 f Ala
Caroline 5 f "
Joseph 1 m "

268 Teacher ($1200)
SAULSBURY, Joseph A. 35 m Ga
Sarah 35 f SC
Margaret 9 f Ala
Frances 7 f "
Laura 5 f "
Rosanna 4 f "
Louisa 1 f "

1129 Farmer ($200)
SAUNDERS, Andrew 25 m SC
RUTLAND, Barbara 16 f Ala

Saunders, Eliza J.
Mary
(See Turner Williams).

1128 Occp. - none ($200)
SAUNDERS, Francis E. 73 m NC
Barbara 60 f SC
Peter (Farmer,$200) 25 m "
Martha 12 f Ala

200 School Teacher
SAUNDERS, Gideon E. 23 m SC
Catherine 20 f "
Jane 4 f Ala
Martha 3 f "
John 1 m "

2057 Farmer
SANDERS, Isaiah 39 m SC
Elizabeth 35 f NC
Martha 11 f Ala
Henry 10 m "
(Cont.)

(# 2057 SAUNDERS cont.)
Mary 8 f Ala
James 7 m "
Priscilla 5 f "
Barbaretta 2 f "

185 Farmer ($125)
SAUNDERS, James 23 m SC
Mary 23 f "

1130 Farmer ($200)
SAUNDERS, William 38 m SC
Mary 25 f NC
Demaris 7 f Ala
Sarah 5 f "
Sena 3 f "
Jacob (Farmer) 22 m SC

21 Farmer ($200)
SAUNDERS, William B. 35 m SC
Rachel M. 23 f "

187
SAUNDERS, William C. 36 m SC
Mary A. 28 f Ga
Eliza 11 f Fla
Caledonia 7 f "
William B. 8/12 m Ala

SAVIME(?), Milbra
(See John Chaney).

SAWYERS, Jasper
(See Charles F. Gerke).

SAWYER, Joshua
Eudocia
James
(See Thomas Jackson).

SAWYER, Wilson
(See James W. Vann).

SAYRE, P. Tucker
(See Joshua H. Danforth).

SCARBOROUGH, David F.
(See Nathaniel Roach).

SCHWARTZ, Lewis
(See S. Heineman).

1359 Wheelwright ($200)
SCOTT, Alfred 29 m NC
Frances 27 f Ga
Martha 11 f "
Sarah 9 f "
William 5 m "
Sabra 1 f "

1393 Trader ($4,000)).
SCOTT, D. C. 36 m SC
Mary 22 f Ga
Walter 4 m Ala
Mary 2 f "

149 Farmer ($800)
SCOTT, James N. 44 m NC
Martha 48 f Va
Mary 12 f Tenn

994 Merchant ($1,500)
SCREWS, Benjamin 38 m NC
Morning J. 33 f NC
Harriet 13 f "
Mary 9 f Ala
William 11 m "
Benjamin 7 m "
Henry P. 5 m "
GRANT, Squire 40 m --
(Colored laborer).

1538 Merchant
SCREWS, Henry O. 29 m NC
Angeline E. 23 f SC
(Married within the year).

1790 Farmer ($500)
SCREWS, Jacob 45 m NC
Nancy 37 f "
John (Farmer) 18 m "
Samuel " 16 m "
Elizabeth 13 f "
Henry 11 m Ga
William 9 m "
Frances 6 f Ala
Laura 4 f "
Alonzo 1 m "
RAY, William(Farmer) 25 m Ga
Sarah 20 f NC
(Last two married within the year).

657 Farmer ($300)
SCROGGINS, George 26 m Ga
Elizabeth 30 f "
GREEN, Marion 22 m "
(Laborer)
HERRIN, Joseph 12 m Ala

#106 Farmer ($300)
SCROGGINS, Griffin 45 m Ga
Martha 35 f SC
Thomas 11 m Ga
Delitha 9 f Ala
Martha 6 f "
(Cont.)

(# 106 SCROGGINS cont.)
Jeremiah 5 m Ala
Andrew J. 4 m "
Nancy 1 f "

1234 Farmer
SEABROOK, Benj. W. 32 m SC
Harriet 27 f Ga
Martha 9 f "
John 7 m "
Mary 5 f "
Harriet 4 f Ala
Sarah 2 f "

1849 Farmer
SEAGERS, Ira 50 m SC
Elizabeth 45 f "
Southward (Farmer) 19 m "
Sally 25 f "
Emily 15 f Ala
James 12 m "
Mary 5 f "

1337 Clerk
SEALS, A. B. 24 m Ga
PRICE, Geo. W. F. 20 m Ala
(Teacher)

1564 Property: $500
SEALS, Ann T. 57 f Ga
Thomas (Farmer) 22 m "
MOORE, Mary A. 29 f "
SEALS, Archibald 67 m Va
(Occp. - none).
Eufaula 9 f Ala
Eugene 5 m "

539 Farmer ($750)
SEALS, James W. 42 m Ga
Nancy 38 f "
James (Farmer) 16 m "
Caroline 14 f Ala
S. J. J. 5 m "
John M. 2 m "

1432 Farmer ($800)
SEALS, John D. 34 m Ga
Ellena 30 f Ala
Ann 11 f "
Warren 9 m "
Laura 7 f "
Mary 4 f "
Martha 1 f "
Alexander 9 m Tenn

SEARCY, Harriet
(Cont.)

(SEARCY cont.)
Louisa S. Martha
Margaret Alcey
(See Needham Smith).

175
SEARCY, Rebecca 62 f NC
Wesley B. (Farmer) 22 m "

84 Farmer ($250)
SEARCY, William 43 m NC
Rebecca 45 f "
Martha 18 f "
Lemuel 19 m "
Elizabeth 14 f Ga
Wesley 13 m "
Thomas K. 11 m "
Jonathan 8 m Ala

1810 Property: $150
SEARLES, Elizabeth 48 f Ga

1612 Carpenter ($125)
SEARS, M. S. 24 m NC
Susan 16 f "
Julius 2 m "
LONG, Susan 50 f "

SEAY, Adeline
(See Mary Pruitt).

SEAY, Calvin
(See R. T. Pearson).

SEAY, Carville
(See James M. Pruitt).

2256 Farmer
Seay, H. M. 46 m SC
Ann 43 f "
Sarah 13 f Ala
Albert (Farmer) 16 m SC
John 11 m Ala
Maria 9 f "
Henry C. 7 m "
Zachary T. 3 m "

785 Farmer ($7,000)
SEAY, John W. 53 m SC
Barbara 44 f "
John W. (Student) 16 m Ga
Eliza 14 f "
Angeline 12 f "
Benjamin T. 6 m Ala
Harriet 4 f "
Caroline 2 f "

SEAY, Laura
(See Thomas Carr).

804 Overseer ($400)
SEAY, Munroe 25 m SC
Emily 21 f Ga
(Married within the year).

SEMPLES, John
(See Roderic McNeill).

870 Farmer
SENN, Lemuel 35 m SC
Mary 35 f "
Emma 16 f "
Martha 14 f "
Henry 12 m "
Daniel 10 m "
David 7 m "
Mary 4 f "
LEONARD, James 50 m "
(Laborer)

481 Farmer ($160)
SHANKS, George 28 m SC
Mary 23 f Ala
Drucilla E. 6 f "
Isabella M. 4 f "
Hilliard C. 2 m "
Eliza E. 3/12 f "

SHANKS, John
(See Arch'd. Carmichael).

SHANKS, Mary A.
Jeremiah
(See James K. Turner).

1995 Farmer
SHAW, B. M. 44 m SC
Matilda 44 f "
Julia 16 f Ga
Jane 14 f "
John 13 m "
Frances 11 f "
William 9 m "
Mary 7 f "
Martin 4 m "

550 Farmer
SHEFFIELD, R. 55 m Ga
WHITTAKER, Jackson 33 m "
(Farmer)
Matilda 30 f SC
Stephen 11 m Ga
John 9 m "
Frances 4 f "
WILLIAMS, John H. 75 m SC
(Farmer)

1741 Laborer
SHEHAN, Daniel 36 m Ire
Martha 36 f Ga
Catherine 8 f Ala
Merrill 6 m "
William 4 m "
Daniel 3 m Ga
Robert 1 m "
CRAYON, Mary F. 11 f Ala
James 9 m "

744 Farmer ($250)
SHELBY, Calvin 25 m NC
Emeline 21 f Ga
John W. 2 m Ala
Green 2/12 m "

SHELBY, Harriet
Emeline
John
(See John Kennedy).

742 Farmer ($500)
SHELBY, Moses 55 m NC
Harriet 50 f "
James M. (Farmer) 20 m Ga
Moses K. " 18 m "
Uzziel 16 m "
William 12 m "
Harriet 15 f "

1348 Physician
SHEPPARD, E. 57 m NJ
Sarah 42 f Pa
Preston W. 28 m NJ
(Physician)

SHEPPARD, James
(See Nicey Barefield).

1918 Farmer
SHEPPARD, John 28 m Ga
Molsey 24 f "
Lydia 8 f Ala
Elijah 5 m "
Joel 3 m "

1717 Physician ($200)
SHEPPARD, John * 39 m Ga
Ann 42 f "
William (Physician) * 16 m "
Joseph 13 m "
Solomon 10 m "
John 8 m "
* (Note: Believed to have been a farmer).

1380 Farmer ($200)
SHEPPARD, John H. 39 m SC
Susan 38 f "
Thomas 14 m Ala
James 10 m "
John 6 m "
Cinthia 4 f "
Amanda 2 f "
Henrietta 5/12 f "
James W. (Stabling) 30 m SC
Jane 23 f "

441 Farmer
SHEPPARD, Thomas 49 m Ga
Emily 45 f NC
Martha 18 f Ala
Elizabeth 16 f "
Emily 13 f "
William 12 m "
Benjamin 8 m Ala
Sarah 6 f "
Irena 2 f "

406 Farmer ($150)
SHEPPARD, Thomas 30 m Ga
Margaret 25 f SC
John W. 6 m Ala
Nancy 4 f "
Matthew 2 m "
Thomas 3/12 m "

1917 Farmer
SHEPPARD, William 60 m Ga
Jane 54 f "
William 17 m "
Elizabeth 16 f "
Harris 13 m "
Henry 11 m "
Dicey 6 f "

1613 Farmer ($500)
SHERMAN, Edwin T. 39 m Ga
Priscilla 30 f "
Nancy 12 f "
Thomas 10 m "
Rebecca 9 f "
Margaret 7 f "
John 5 m "
Martha 3 f "
George 1/12 m Ala
TURNER, Henry S. 22 m
(Farmer)

234 Farmer
SHIPES, Andrew 37 m SC
Christina 37 f "
Nathan (Farmer) 16 m "
(Cont.)

(# 234 SHIPES cont.)
Matilda 13 f SC
Josephine 6 f Ala

435 Farmer
SHIPES, Cornelius 23 m SC
Mary A. 21 f "
John 1/12 m Ala

436 Farmer
SHIPES, Mahaly 40 f SC
David 17 m "
Mary 15 f Ala
John 13 m "
Joseph 11 m "
William 9 m "
Julia 6 f "
Ellen 4 f "

1873 Farmer ($1500)
SHIPMAN, Alex 35 m NC
Mary 25 f "
Sarah 10 f Ala
Ann 9 f "
John 7 m "
James 5 m "
Alexander 3 m "
James 2/12 m "

503 Farmer ($4000)
SHIPMAN, James 61 m NC
Eliza 54 f "
Eliza 21 f "
George (Farmer) 18 m Ala
Lewis " 16 m "
Jerse(?) " 14 m "
Franklin 12 m "

SHIPMAN, James
(See J. K. Lampley)

1999 Baker
SHORT, William 24 m NC

SHORT, Wines S.
(See Charles F. Gerke)

119 Lawyer ($13,000).
SHORTER, Eli S. 26 m Ga
Marietta 21 f "
Anna 2 f Ala

535 Farmer ($3400)
SHORTER, R. C. 65 m Va
Mary B. 53 f Ga
Henry B. (Student) 17 m "
Laura M. 14 f "
KOLB, R. F. C. 11 m Ala

556
SIBLEY, Rebecca 57 f Mass

22 Brickmason
SIBLEY, S. S. 27 m SC
Nancy 24 f Ga
Caroline E. 4 f Ala
Lucretia C. 3 f "
Mary J. 1 f "

SIKES, John
Sarah
Needham
(See Daniel Kennedy).

154 Farmer ($350)
SIKES, Richard 45 m NC
Saleita 43 f Ga
Mary 12 f Ala
John 8 m "
Martha 7 f "
Hettie 5 f "
Jane 3 f "

1531 Farmer ($3,200)
SILAS, John 44 m Ga
Mary 46 f "
Patrick (Farmer) 21 m "
Elizabeth 17 f "
Lazurus (Farmer) 16 m "
RICE, Arthur 57 m SC
(Laborer)

SIMMONS, Augustus
(See Tristam Dalton).

1140 Farmer
SIMMONS, David 31 m Ga
Rachel 25 f "
Mary A. 7 f Ala
James 3 m "
Virginia 2 f "

SIMONS, Peter
(See A. G. Smith).

1711 Farmer
SIMPKINS, James 21 m SC
Mary 20 f Ga
(Married within the year).

1116 Farmer ($150)
SIMPKINS, Samuel 45 m NJ
Celia 46 f SC
James (Farmer) 21 m "
Eliza 19 f "
George (Farmer) 17 m Ala
Mary 15 f "

SIMPSON, Mary H.
(See James Cole).

1314 Clerk
SIMPSON, William T. 24 m Ga
BROWN, George H. 25 m NY
(Clerk)

672 Laborer
SIMS, Allen 19 m Fla
Mary 17 f Ga
(Married within the year).

SIMS, Amy
(See John Sanders).

SIMS, Daniel
Mary
(See William McNair).

2065 Farmer
SIMS, Henry 22 m Ga

919 Farmer ($400)
SIMS, Joel 50 m Ga
Jane 49 f "
Mary A. 21 f "
Martha 20 f "
Thomas (Farmer) 22 m "
Minerva 18 f "
Samuel (Farmer) 16 m Ala
Eveline 14 f "
COLE, Mary 22 f "
James 12 m "
Daniel 10 m "
Harriet 8 f "
Andrew 3 m "

63 Farmer
SIMS, Joel A. 30 m Ga
Elizabeth 22 f "
William F. 5 m Ala
Henry R. J. 3 m "
Emily 2 f "
Nancy J. 1/12 f "

2064 Carpenter
SIMS, M. R. 27 m Ga
Frances 26 f SC
James 6 m Ga
Mark 4 m Ala
Mary A. 3 f "
John 3/12 m "
BOTTOMS, Mary A. 30 f SC

1025 Farmer ($225).
SIMS, William W. 27 m Ga
(Cont.)

(# 1025 SIMS cont.)
Caroline 23 f Ga
Warren 3 m Ala
Walter 2 m "
Mary 2/12 f "

439 Farmer
SINGLETON, Eldred 24 m Ala
Theresa 20 f NC
Richard H.L. 1 m Ala
James (Laborer) 15 m "

983 Farmer
SINGLETON, Joseph 31 m SC
Mary A. 20 f "
Mary J. 9 f Ala
Mary S. 7 f "
Joseph 5 m "
Patty 3 f "
Martha 1/12 f "

SINGLETON, Reuben
(See Isaac Campbell).

883 Farmer ($200)
SINGLETON, Solomon 28 m Ala
Angeline 31 f "
Polly 7 f "
William 3 m "
Martha 1 f "

1334 Merchant
SINQUEFIELD, Asa 55 m Ga
Linny 43 f "
Mary 18 f "
Thena 15 f "
Susan 9 f "

351 Farmer
SKANES, Newton 37 m SC
Elizabeth 37 f "

SKANES, William
(See Philip A. McDaniel).

5-5 Farmer ($80)
SKIPPER, Everitt 24 m NC
Mary A. 23 f Ga

SKIPPER, John
(See Needham Lee, Jr.)

685 Farmer($300)
SKIPPER, John W. 41 m NC
Demaris 38 f "
John W. 20 m "
Nathaniel G. 14 m "
(Cont.)

(# 685 SKIPPER cont.)
Seddy Ann 13 f NC
Jacob A. 11 m "
Thomas 9 m "
Mary J. 7 f Ga
Anna 6 f "
George D. 6/12 m Ala

507 Farmer ($800)
SKIPPER, Nathaniel A. 58 m NC
Elizabeth 38 f Ga
Robert G. 17 m "
Harriet 12 f "
Sarah 10 f "
Jacob L. 15 m "
Wellington 4 m Ala

1240 Overseer
SLACK, Jesse 26 m Ga

2176 Farmer ($1,000)
SLACK, John 43 m Ga
Mary 38 f "
James (Farmer) 17 m "
Jesse " 16 m "
Ann 14 f "
Frances 12 f "
John 1 m Ala

1041 Farmer
SLAUGHTER, Daniel 70 m Va
Isabella 63 f SC
Oliver (Farmer) 22 m Ala
George 19 m "
Elias (Farmer) 16 m "

1044 Farmer ($800)
SLAUGHTER, James D. 38 m Ga
Elizabeth 21 f "
Elizabeth 7 f "
Henry 3 m Ala
Frances 8/12 f "

1040 Farmer ($2,500)
SLAUGHTER, Samuel 39 m Ga
Jane 22
(Married within the year).

2028 Farmer ($800).
SLOAN, David 41 m NC
Margaret 36 f Ga
Eliza 17 f "
Milton 13 m Ala
Emily 11 f "
Mahala 9 f "
William 7 m "
(Cont.)

(# 2028 SLOAN cont.)
Henry 5 m Ala
Dixon 3 m "
Andrew 3/12 m "

687 Farmer ($2,500)
SLOAN, John, Sr. 66 m Ire
Mary 47 f Ga
John, Jr. (Farmer) 25 m "
McDOWELL, Eliza 23 f "
(John Sr. & Mary married within the year).

1617 Overseer
SMART, Thomas 25 m NC
Clio 1 f Ala
George 2/12 m "
DAVIS, Mary 72 f NC

628 Farmer ($250)
SMILEY, A. H. 39 m Ga
Adeline 24 f "
Henry C. 4 m Ala
Daniel W. 2 m "
James M. 2/12 m "
John M. (Teacher) 21 m Ga

1375 Mail contractor ($1600)
SMITH, A. G. 35 m Va
Mary 29 f Ga
Louisianna 4 f Ala
Henrietta 1 f "
SIMONS, Peter 30 m Ga
(Stage Driver).

1382 Laborer
SMITH, Alexander 40 m SC
Margaret 30 f "

75-78 Farmer
SMITH, Allen 30 m Ga
Martha J. 28 f "
Louisa 10 f "
Francis 8 m Ala
Nathan W. 6 m "
Isey C. 3 f "
GARNER, James 37 m Ga
(Laborer)

SMITH, Amanda
Mary
(See Charles McAllister)

280 Farmer ($300)
SMITH, Caleb 58 m Ga
Saletha 40 f "
William (Farmer) 29 m "
Hezekiah " 22 m "
(Cont.)

(# 280 SMITH cont.)
Henry (Farmer) 21 m Ga
Ambrose " 16 m "
Caleb 10 m "

845 Farmer ($5,000)
SMITH, Cincinnatus 45 m Ga

1296 Laborer
SMITH, Colby 42 m Ga
Martha 38 f SC
Thomas 14 m Ga
Caneth 12 m "
Allathe 9 f "
Mitchell 7 m "
Martha 3 f "

221 Farmer ($100)
SMITH, David 27 m SC
Jane 35 f "
Daniel 7 m Ala
Martha 4 f "
Matthew 5 m "
Mary 2 f "
David 5/12 m "

1385 (Property: $200)
SMITH, Delilah 55 f SC
REEVES, Martha 30 f "
Lugenia 6 m Ga

1457 Farmer
SMITH, Edwin C. 43 m NC
Julia 33 f Ga
Mary 15 f "
James 13 m "
Harriet 12 f "
Amanda 10 f "
Milledge 8 m "
Bryant 6 m "
Martha 3 f "
Sarah 1/12 f Ala

1963
SMITH, Elizabeth 30 f Ga
Martha 10 f Ala
Nancy 8 f "
Henry 6 m "
Catherine 4 f "
Sally 2 f "
John 3/12 m "

SMITH, Ellen
(See James R. Hill).

171 Farmer ($225)
SMITH, Green 30 m Ga
Mary 27 f NC
(Cont.)

(# 171 SMITH cont.)
Frances 7 f Ala
John 5 m "
Axim 3 m "
Timothy 2 m "
HATCHER, Rebecca 16 f NC
Priscilla 24 f "

162 Farmer ($400)
SMITH, Isaiah 54 m SC
Elizabeth 47 f NC
Henry (Farmer) 17 m Ga
Elizabeth 15 f "
Moses 14 m "
Jonathan 12 m "
Lidia 10 f "
Joshua L. 8 m Ala
Josiah (?) 6 m "

747 Farmer ($2,000)
SMITH, James B. 42 m Ga
Lucinda 28 f "
Thomas (Farmer) 17 m "
Septimus 12 m "
Seaborn 5 m Ala
Nancy 8 f "
Roxanna 6 f "
Martha 2 f "

97 Farmer ($2,500)
SMITH, James B. R. 42 m Ga
Barbary 41 f "
John 21 m "
Margaret 20 f "
Sarah 19 f "
Martha 18 f "
Nathan 16 m "
Mary 14 f "
Prudence 12 f "
Susan 10 f Ala
Nancy 8 f "
William 6 m "
Acton 4 m "
James 2 m "

1018 Farmer ($400)
SMITH, James H. 35 m Ga
Mary 28 f SC
Elizabeth 14 f Ala
Milly 12 f "
Serena 10 f "
John 6 m "
Charity 1/12 f "

172 Laborer
SMITH, John 25 m Ga
(Cont.)

(# 172 SMITH cont.)
Julia 18 f Ga
Hilliard 1 m Ala

SMITH, John T.
(See William R. Smith).

250 Laborer ($250)
SMITH, Jordan J. 26 m Ga
Mary 20 f "
Mary A. 3 f Ala
Thomas 1 m "

846 Farmer
SMITH, Lovett S. 32 m Ga
Sarah 26 f "
Jane 3 f Ala
Nathan A. 6/12 m "
WHITTEMORE, Munro 21 m NC
(Overseer)

SMITH, Mary
(See Sampson Worsley).

SMITH, Mary
(See Robert Campbell).

SMITH, Milton
(See Jared Barber).

74-76 Farmer
SMITH, Needham 49 m NC
Louisa 47 f Ga
SEARCY, Harriet 31 f "
Louisa S. 13 f "
Margaret 11 f "
Martha 9 f "
Alcey 7 f "

2278 Farmer
Smith, Nicholas 26 m NC
Nancy 21 f "
William 4 m Ala
James 2 m "

559 Farmer ($2,000)
SMITH, Samuel J. 44 m Ga
Mary 41 f NC
Simon (?) (Farmer) 21 m Ala
(Property: $1,500)
Sion (Farmer) 18 m "
George " 16 m "
Thomas 15 m "

2288 Farmer ($200)
Smith, Sidney A. 50 m SC
Rebecca 42 f Ga
Benjamin 8 m "

383 Laborer
SMITH, Solomon 20 m Ala
Nancy 18 f "
(Married within year).
Jasper 1/12 m "

1973 Farmer
SMITH, Solomon, Sr. 53 m Ga
Sarah 48 f "
Martha 21 f "
Sarah 19 f Ala
Stephen (Farmer 17 m "
James " 15 m "
Jesse 12 m "
Nancy 10 f "
Margaret 8 f "
Mary 6 f "
Jethro 4 m "

SMITH, Thomas
(See George H. Sporman).

SMITH, William
(See Silas Frasier).

SMITH, William
(See Wesley H. Bodeford).

SMITH, William
(See Noel W. Turner).

577 Farmer
SMITH, Willian 28 m Ga
Arminta 23 f "
Lucinda 5 f "
Louisa 3 f "
BULLOCK, Polly 34 f "
William 8 m "

10-11 Farmer ($150)
SMITH, William R. 22 m SC
Eliza 18 f Ga
(Married within the year)
SMITH, John T. 21 m Ala

1942 Blacksmith
SMITH, Williamson 35 m Ga
Jane 30 f "
Jane 14 f Ala
Sarah 13 f "
Amanda 9 f "
William 7 m "
Elizabeth 3 f "

1740 Farmer ($3,500)
SMITH, Young 42 m NC
Sarah 43 f "
(Cont.)

1740 SMITH cont.)
William 17 m Ga
Ellena 16 f "
Allen 14 m "
Green 13 m "
Miles T. 10 m "
Sarah 9 f "
Henry 8 m "
Ann 7 f Ala
Isham 6 m "
SMITH, John G. 14 m Ga
William J. (Farmer) 15 m "
Young H. 8 m Miss

1395
SNIPES, E. 50 f SC
KING, Sheppard 12 m Ga
Marshall 9 m "

1603 (Property: $10,000)
SNIPES, Maria A, 47 f SC
Charles (Student) 20 m "
Henry (Farmer) 18 m "
Harriet 15 f "
John 11 m "
Marion 8 f Ala

554 (Property $1,000)
SNIPES, Martha 47 f SC
KING, Sheppard 13 m Ga
Marshall 9 m "
BROWN, Mary 14 f SC

1272 Dentist ($1,200)
SNOW, Charles W. 35 m Me
Emily 25 f Ga
Charles 3 m Ala
Jane 1 f "

427 Laborer
SNOW, James M. 36 m Ala
Edna 40 f NC
Elizabeth A. 17 f Ga
Harriet 15 f "
Catherine 13 f "
Bary 11 m "
Leroy 9 m "
Syre 7 f Ala
Stricklin 3 m "
Elizabeth 25 f Ga

1571 Coachmaker ($500)
SOMMERCAMP. F. S. C. 39 m Md
Mary 21 f Ga
Ferdinand 12 m Ala
Eugene 2/12 m "

1286 Shoemaker
SPEARS, Bennet 25 m NC
Luriney 21 f "
Elizabeth 2 f Ala

SPEARS, Henry G.
Willis
(See Sipra W. Martin)

1019 Farmer ($400)
SPENCE, Aaron T. 40 m Ga
Feriby 38 f NC
Lewis 13 m Ga
Nancy 11 f Ala
Kilby 10 m "
James 9 m "
John 7 m "
Julia 4 f "
DAVIS, William E. 44 m Ky
(Shoemaker)
Mildred 40 f NC

SPENCE, Louisa M.
(See J. B. Douglass).

1383 Grocer ($1,000)
SPORMAN, George H. 38 m Ger.
Louisa 42 f "
George 6 m Ala
Charles 2 m "
SMITH, Thomas 14 m Ga

738 Farmer
SPROUL, James J. 42 m NC
Catherine 24 f Ga
James 3 m Ala
William 2 m "
Harriet 1/12 f "

1076 Farmer
SPURLOCK, Daniel 18 m Ala
Mary 16 f Ga
(Married within the year).

SPURLOCK, Green
(See Dennis Nolen).

83 Overseer
SPURLOCK, James M. 28 m Ga

1815 Farmer
SPURLOCK, Meredith 18 m Ala
Mary 18 f Ga
(Married within the year).

SPURLOCK, Sela
(See Samuel Wallace).

6-6 Farmer ($700)
SPURLOCK, Solomon 52 m Ga
(Cont.)

(# 6-6 SPURLOCK cont.)
Maria 40 f SC
Mary 14 f Ga
Patience 13 f "
George W. 9 m "
Obedience 7 f "
Calvin 5 m Ala
John S. (Overseer) 22 m Ga
FRY, Edward 20 m "
(Farmer)

226
SPURLOCK, William 58 m --
Sarah 13 f Ga
(Above two married within the year).
BYRD, Daniel 52 m Ga
Nicey 49 f "

2190
STACEY, Mary E. 29 f Ga
Alabama 8 f "
Mary 4 f "
Alice 3 f Ala

STAFFORD, Judith L.
(See Lewis Rouse).

STAFFORD, Moses
(See Edward McPhail).

710 Physician
STANLEY, James G. 33 m Ga
Frances W. 23 f "
Chester 2 m Ala

2164 Overseer
STANLEY, J. D. 33 m SC
Mary 23 f "
James 2 m Ala
Sarah 6/12 f "

#906 Farmer ($2,500)
STANLEY, Lewis 58 m Ga
Elizabeth 45 f "
John 11 m "
Permenas 8 m "
Sarah 6 f Ala

333 Carpenter
STANLEY, Wiley 37 m NC
Mary 25 f Ga
Hamilton 7 m Ala
Mary 6 f "
Elizabeth 3 f "

1590 Farmer ($4,000)
STARKE, A. B. 35 m SC
Belton 5 m Ala
(Cont.)

(# 1590 STARKE cont.)
Oscar 3 m Ala
McCAY, Flora 21 f SC
CLARK, George 18 m Ga
(Overseer)
STARKE, Samuel 74 m SC
Frances 27 f Ga

1145 Farmer ($4,000)
STARKE, E. W. 23 m SC
Frances 16 f
(Married within the year).
J. T. Farmer 33 m SC

1591 Farmer ($800)
STARKE, John M. 27 m SC

STEARNS, Harris
Elizabeth
(See John H. Miller).

STEED, John
(See William G. Ford).

1285 Shoemaker
STEEDHAM, Thomas 36 m NC
Rosanna 25 f Ga
Nancy 12 f Ala
Mary 11 f "
INGLET, Georgia 4 f "

STEMBRIDGE, John
Sarah E.
(See Jacob B. Nelson).

421 Farmer ($400)
STEPHENS, D. D. 37 m SC
Nancy 36 f NC
Nelson 9 m SC
William 7 m "
Franklin 6 m "
Robert 2 m NC
Thomas 2 m NC

1594 Farmer ($150)
STEPHENS, Hanson B. 51 m NC
Mary 28 f "
Eliza 3 f Ala
Caroline 1 f "
BRADY, Elijah 10 m "
William 8 m "

1972 Farmer
STEPHENS, James 38 m Ga
Nancy 32 f "
William 9 m Ala
Martha 7 f "
(Cont.)

(# 1972 STEPHENS cont.)
James 5 m Ala
John 3 m "
Mary 1 f "

900 Farmer
STEPHENS, John 40 m SC
Seville 35 f Ga
Nancy 15 f "
Sarah 12 f "
Joseph 9 m "
Duncan 7 m "
Willoby 5 m Ala
Alexander 3 m "
Narcissa 1 f "

1971 Farmer
STEPHENS, Nelson 35 m Ga
Tabitha 40 f "
Thomas (Farmer) 17 m Ala
Wiley " 15 m "
William 13 m "
James 11 m "
Alsey 9 f "
Susan 7 f "
Sarah 5 f "
John 3 m "
Mary 1 f "

STEPHENS, Scarboro
(See Peter Stewart).

STEPHENS, Wesley
(See David B. Purviss).

2244 Shoemaker
SREPHENS, William 70 m NC
Luke (Laborer) 25 m "

1414 Farmer ($500)
STEPHENS, William 28 m SC
Elizabeth 28 f "
Daniel 6 m Ala
John 4 m "
Eugenia 1 f "

766 Farmer ($1,000).
STEPHENS, William H. 35 m NC
Martha 21 f Ala
Mary 6 f "
James 4 m "
Jane 2 f "
Lewis E. 6/12 m "

1198 Farmer ($150)
STEPHENS, William H.40 or 49 m. NC
Mary 38 f Ga
(Cont.)

(# 1198 STEPHENS cont.)

Elizabeth	18	f	Ala
Jane	14	f	"
Mahala	12	f	"
Mary	10	f	"
Malinda	8	f	"
Lucinda	8	f	"
George W.	4	m	"
Miranda	2	f	"

1762 Farmer

STEPHENSON, C.	46	m	NC
Jackyann	39	f	"
Mary	18	f	Ga
Susan	16	f	"
William (Farmer)	15	m	"
John	12	m	"
Sarah	10	f	"
Lavisey	9	f	"
Dicey	7	f	"
Frances	6	f	"
Queen Ann	5	f	"
Peter	3	m	"
ROGERS, Jas. (Farmer)	26	m	"
STEPHENSON, Council	4/12	m	Ala

1105 Farmer

STEPHENSON, Hardy	27	m	NC
Sarah	24	f	Ga
Elizabeth	4	f	Ala
Amanda	2	f	"
Silas	1	m	"

2175 Farmer ($500)

STEPHENSON, Kindred	36	m	Ga
Mary	31	f	"
William (Farmer)	16	m	"
Louisa	13	f	"
Elizabeth	11	f	"
Mary	10	f	"
James	8	m	Ala
Carey	6	m	"
Kindred	2	m	"

1104 Farmer ($2,000)

STEPHENSON, Silas	76	m	NC
Mary	60	f	"

1073 Teacher ($200)

STEWART, A. C.	31	m	NC
Martha	28	f	SC
John	2/12	m	Ala

314 Farmer ($200)

STEWART, Alexr.	52	m	NC

(Cont.)

(# 314 STEWART cont.)

Ann	44	f	NC
Ann E.	13	f	Ala
Alexr.	10	m	"
Margaret	6	f	"
Adeline	5	f	"

2230 Farmer

STEWART, Allen	70	m	Scot
Catherine	54	f	"
ROACH, Wm. G. B.	14	m	Fla

1438 Cabinet Maker

STEWART, Archibald	42	m	Scot
Jane	40	f	Eng

STEWART, Elizabeth
Charles
James
Sarah
Eli
(See Samuel Anderson).

574 Farmer

STEWART, James	53	m	Ga
Sarah	54	f	"
Mary	27	f	"
Lucinda	24	f	"
Sarah	22	f	Fla
James L. (Farmer) (Property: $300)	21	m	Fla
Candice	17	f	Ala

575 Farmer

STEWART, James L.	21	m	Fla
Lovey	23	f	Ala

(Married within the year).

2217 Farmer ($2,500)

STEWART, John	80	m	Scot
Nancy	73	f	NC
Daniel (Farmer)	36	m	"
PERRY, Elizabeth	29	f	Ga

318 Farmer ($800)

STEWART, John L.	50	m	NC
Christian	40	f	"
Catherine	16	f	"
James (Farmer)	15	m	Ala
Ann	12	f	"
Ceely	7	f	"
John	6	m	"
Marion	3	f	"

313 Farmer ($500)

STEWART, Norman	42	m	NC
Jane	25	f	SC

(Cont.)

(# 313 STEWART cont.)

Mary	18	f	SC
James (Farmer)	17	m	"
Seley	16	f	"
Charles (Farmer)	15	m	"
Caroline	14	f	"
John	13	m	"
William	11	m	"
Jane	10	f	"
Alexr.	9	m	"
Daniel	8	m	"
Archibald	4	m	"

STEWART, Peter
(See Arch'd. Carmichael).

834 Teacher ($350)

STEWART, Peter	52	m	Scot
Penina(?)	42	f	SC
James R.	22	m	"
Mary	18	f	"
William	14	m	"
Daniel	12	m	"
Charles	7	m	"
Janet	4	f	Ala
John	1	m	"
BAREFIELD, James (Laborer)	25	m	SC
STEPHENS, Scarboro	62	f	NC

520 Farmer ($200)

STEWART, Thomas	60	m	NC
Jane	46	f	SC
Delilah	27	f	Ga
Thomas	9	m	Ala
Serepta A.	5	f	"

1946 Farmer ($100)

STEWART, Thomas	50	m	--
Jane	48	f	Ga
Thomas	8	m	Ala

1993 Farmer ($2,500)

STINSON, George	54	m	Va
Matilda	50	f	Ga
Alexr. (Farmer)	20	m	"
Carey "	19	m	"
James "	17	m	"

STINSON, Sarah
(See Mary Codey).

1291 Shoemaker

STOCKWELL, Richard	32	m	Eng

STOKES, David F.
(See William Stuckey).

502 Farmer ($1,000)

STOKES, Henry	40	m	SC
Martha	36	f	Ga
Savannah A.	10	f	Ala
Susan	8	f	"
Mary	6	f	"
Melinda	4	f	"
Dolly	2	f	"

417 Farmer ($500)

STOKES, Irvin J.	45	m	SC
Matilda	43	f	"
Robert	21	m	Ala
Joel	19	m	"
William	17	m	"
Jefferson	15	m	"
Kenneth	12	m	"
Mary A.	13	f	"
Jackson	9	m	"
Henry	14	m	"
Washington	8	m	"
John	6	m	"
Matilda	5/12	f	"

STOKES, Salissa J.
(See Thomas M. Grant).

179 Farmer

STOKES, William R.	46	m	SC
Mary	38	f	Ga
Kinchen (Farmer)	17	m	Ala
Columbus "	15	m	"
NORRIS, H. K. (Farmer).	34	m	Ga

STONAKER, Eliza
(See James Brock).

STONE, John
(See John Bass).

1256 Boatman ($700)

STOW, Anthony	36	m	Conn
Adeline	27	f	Ga
Edward	10	m	Ala
Eugenia	7	f	"
James	1	m	"

1336 Merchant

STOW, L. F.	35	m	NY
Caroline	30	f	Mass
HENDRIX, Reuben (Clerk).	16	m	SC

70 Farmer

STRANGE, Samuel W.	26	m	SC
Polly	20	f	NC

(Cont.)

(# 70 STRANGE cont.).

William N.	4	m	Ala
Mitchell	1	m	"
HUGGINS, Robert (Laborer)	24	m	SC

1112 Farmer

STRANGE, William B.	40	m	SC
Mary	37	f	Ga
Susan	8	f	Ala
Mary	4	f	"
John	1	m	"

1598 Farmer ($2,200)

STREETER, Milton H.	32	m	NC

2149 Farmer ($3,600)

STRETER, Reddic	56	m	NC
Margaret	46	f	"
Mary	31	f	"
Elizabeth	29	f	"
Edna	27	f	"
Sarah	25	f	"
Henry (Idiot)	19	m	"
William (Farmer)	18	m	"
Thomas "	16	m	"
John H.	10	m	Ala
Emeline	6	f	"

820 Farmer ($2,000)

STREETER, Redic	56	m	Va
Margaret	45	f	NC
Mary	31	f	"
Elizabeth	27	f	"
Edna	25	f	"
Sarah	22	f	"
Richard (Farmer)	20	m	"
William "	18	m	"
Thomas	15	m	"
John	9	m	Ala
Emeline	6	f	"

1655 Farmer ($4,000)

STREETER, Sheppard M.	63	m	Va
Mary	45	f	NC
Benjamin (Farmer)	25	m	"
Christenberry "	23	m	"
Cornelia	19	f	"
Godwin (f?)(Farmer)	17	f	"
Caroline	14	f	"
Massalinia	12	f	"
LONG, Benjamin	7	m	Ala

2127 Farmer

STREETMAN, Walter	44	m	Ga
Rachel	41	f	"

(Cont.)

(# 2127 STREETMAN cont.)

Frances	16	f	Ga
Thornton	12	m	"
Lewis	6	m	Ala
Elizabeth	4	f	"
Sarah	1	f	"

14-15 Farmer

STRICKLAND, Blackmon	42	m	NC
Flora	35	f	"
Henry	16	m	"
Zilpha A.	13	f	"
Seaborn	11	m	Ga
John	9	m	"
Blackmon	4	m	Ala
Isaac	2	m	"

970

STRICKLIN, Elizabeth	50	f	SC
Nolin (Farmer)	20	m	Ala

1720 Farmer

STRICKLAND, Harmon	28	m	NC
Feriby	21	f	"
William	5	m	"
Daniel	3	m	"
Nancy	1	f	"
Eveline	9	f	"

1631 Farmer

STRICKLAND, Harmon	30	m	NC
Feriby	22	f	"
William	6	m	"
Daniel	4	m	"
Elizabeth	2	f	"
Emeline	12	f	"

1498 Farmer

STRICKLAND, Isaac	23	m	NC
Narissa	18	f	Ga

971 Farmer

STRICKLIN, John W.	31	m	SC
Elizabeth	30	f	NC
Sion	13	m	Ala
Lucinda	11	f	"
Mary	8	f	"
Thomas	6	m	"

1630 Farmer ($250)

STRICKLAND, Matthew	43	m	NC
Elizabeth	45	f	"
William (Farmer)	24	m	"
Matthew "	17	m	"
Mary	14	f	"
Elizabeth	12	f	"

(Cont.)

(# 1630 STRICKLAND cont.)
Martha 10 f NC
Jesse 8 m "
John 6 m "
Lewis 4 m "

STRICKLIN, Rufus E.
(See Edward McPhail).

969 Farmer
STRICKLIN, Thomas 28 m SC
Rebecca 39 f Ga
Louisa 2 f Ala

653 Blacksmith
STRICKLEN, Wiley 55 m NC
Mary 52 f SC
Jesse(Farmer, $300) 33 m NC
Celia 26 f "
Lott (Blksmith) 25 m "
Benj. E. (Student) 23 m "
Lucy A. 21 f Tenn
Mary J. 18 f NC
Eliza 13 f Ala
Mahala 10 f "

1187 Farmer ($6,000)
STRINGER, James A. 39 m Ga
Sarah 27 f "
Emma L. 3 f Ala
Lilly 1 f "
JUSTICE, John J. 38 m Ga
(Overseer)

2102 Farmer
STRIPLAND, Aaron 52 m SC
Susan 50 f Ga
Benjamin (Teacher) 25 m Ala
Mary 12 f "

STRIPLING, Benjamin
(See Jacob Parmer).

762 Farmer
STRIPLIN, Elisha 23 m Ga
Rebecca 18 f "
Thomas 1 m Ala

STRIPLIN, Francis M.
(See John Alley).

82 Farmer ($1,400)
STRIPLIN, James 41 m Ga
Frances 44 f "
Sarah J. 13 f "
James 9 m Ala

STUBBS, Albany
(See William W. Williams).

563 Farmer
STUCKEY, Henry E. 27 m SC
Elizabeth 28 f Ga
William 5 m "
Sarah 3 f "
John 2 m Ala
John B. (Farmer) 31 m SC

261 Farmer ($ 500)
STUCKEY, William 51 m NC
Rose 51 f Ga
STOKES, David F. 14 m "
FRY, Adeline 14 f "

SULLIVAN, Elizabeth
(See Thomas Fail).

1808 Farmer
SUMMERLIN, Henry 38 m Ga
Elizabeth 36 f "
Mary 17 f "
James (Farmer) 15 m "
John 13 m "
Henry 11 m "
Catherine 9 f "
Cinthia 6 f Ala
William 4 m "
Susan 2 f "

1582 Farmer ($300)
SUMMERLIN, J. B. 32 m SC
Rhody 23 f Ga
Angeline 4 f Ala
Eugenia 2 f "
Josephine 9/12 f "

SUMMERSET, Joseph
(See William Hinson)

1719 Farmer ($400)
SUTHERLAND, Jeremiah 44 m NC
Elizabeth 44 f "
Eliza 16 f Ga
Frances 14 f "
Susan 8 f "

1436 Farmer ($300)
SUTTON, Charles 63 m SC
Charity 50 f Ga
Benjanin (Farmer) 26 m Ala
Susan 20 f "
Mahala 19 f "
Francis 12 m "
Jackson 7 m "
BRYANT, Mary 96 f Va

415 Farmer
SUTTON, Jesse 57 m SC
Elizabeth 54 f Ga
Huldy 19 f Ala
Dizah 16 f "
Matilda 12 f "
Benjamin 9 m "
PHILLIPS, Caroline S. 25 f Ga
Nancy E. 6 f Ala
MOORELAND, James 22 m Ga
(Laborer)

2025 Laborer
SUTTON, Joshua 23 m Ala
Elizabeth 23 f Ga
John 1 m Ala

635 Farmer ($350)
SUTTON, N. B. 29 m Ga
Amanda 22 f Ala
Elizabeth 2 f "
William 2 m "

SWAN, John
(See Henry M. Tompkins).

419 Farmer
SWANNER, Thomas 40 m NC
Lydia 40 f "
Martha 17 f "
James 15 m "
Sarah 13 f "
Ann 10 f "
Ellen 8 f "
Liddy 6 f "
Zack 2 m "
Scott 1 m Ala

2220 Farmer
SYKES, J. W. 46 m NC
Susan 28 f Ala
Washington 12 m "
Robert 9 m "
Mary 7 f "
Harriet 5 f "
Eliza 3 f "
Jesse 2 m "

534 Physician
SYKES, John W. 47 m NC
Susan 26 f Ala
George W. 11 m "
Wilson I.(?) 8 m "
Mary 7 f "
Harriet 5 f "
Eliza 4 f Ga
(Cont.)

(# 534 SYKES cont.)
Seaborn 2 m Ga
Mahala 76 f NC

358 Farmer
SYKES, M. B. 23 m Ala
Elizabeth 26 f SC
Mary 4 f Ala
Thomas 2 m "

216 Farmer ($200)
SYKES, Solomon 57 m Ga
Nancy 41 f "
James (Farmer) 19 m Ala
Solomon " 17 m "
Martha 8 f "
William B. 2 m "

740 Farmer ($1,500)
SYLVESTER, D. (Demarcus) 47 m SC
Mary A. (Ann) * 46 f "
Mary A. 19 f "
Sarah A. J. ** 12 f Ga
Frances 10 f Ala
Camilla 8 f "
JORDAN, Hardy A. 19 m Ga
(Student)
HENDRIX, Benjamin 19 m SC
(Student).

SYLVESTER, Joseph A. (Asbury)***
(See L. J. Leaird).

1003 Farmer ($1,200)
SYLVESTER, T. R. **** 29 m SC
Alethia (Beckham) 27 f SC
Martha 7 f Ala
James E. (Edgar) 5 m "
William (Oscar) 3 m "
Leonidas (Taylor) 1 m "
BECKHAM, Amanda J. 28 f SC
HOLLEY, John 23 m Ga
BECKHAM, Green C. 17 m SC
(Brother to Alethia).

TABER, John W.
(See Ezekiel Martin).

* Mary Ann Rembert
** Sarah Ann Jordan Sylvester
*** Joseph Asbury Sylvester was the son of Demarcus and Mary Ann Rembert Sylvester
**** Son of Demarcus & Mary Ann Sylvester.

126 Carpenter ($75)
TALBOT, James 40 m Ga
Phoebe 36 f "
Lucretia 13 f "
Cadwallader 12 m "
Emily 7 f Ala
RAINES, John G. 41 m Ga
PARHAM, Jno. (Laborer) 24 m "
RAINES, Lucretia 65 f "

920 Farmer
TATE, Robert T. 26 m Ga
Eliza 23 f Ala
Margaret 3 f "
Jane 1 f "
Sarah 20 f Ga
APPLING, Sarah 11 f Ala

TATE, Henry D.
Rebecca
(See R. R. W. Richburgh).

1703 Farmer ($400)
TATE, V. H. 25 m Ga
Emily 25 f Ala
Julia 1 f "
HALL, Goodwin(Farmer) 65 m SC
DUBOSE, Jasper 9 m Ala
TATE, Nancy 40 f Ga

1704 Farmer
TATE, Zach 29 m Ga
Cinthia 29 f "
John 5 m Ala
William 3 m "
Aggy 3/12 f "
Elizabeth 29 f Ga

TAYLOR, General
Margaret E.
(See Needham G. Lee).

TAYLOR, George
(See Robert F. Hightower)

2245 Overseer
TAYLOR, Joshua 43 m NC
Sarah 37 f "
James (Student) 19 m "
Mary 16 f "
Elizabeth 13 f Ala
Buge 10 f "
William 6/12 m "

2197 Farmer
TAYLOR, Joshua 30 m SC
Elizabeth 23 f Ga
(Cont.)

(# 2197 TAYLOR cont.)
Mary 6 f Ala
Thomas 4 m "
John 2 m "

TAYLOR, Mary
(See Reuben E. Brown).

1733 Farmer ($300)
TAYLOR, Reddin 39 m NC
Martha 43 f SC
Epsey 19 f "
Mary 17 f Ga
Sarah 14 f Ala
Evaline 11 f "
Samantha 9 f "
Thomas 13 m "
William 4 m "

832 Farmer ($600)
TAYLOR, Robert P. 38 m Va
Sarah 28 f Ala
John 14 m Ga
James W. 12 m "
William 11 m "
Sarah 7 f Ala
Mary 6 f "
Elizabeth 4 f "
Susan 4 f "
Major W. 2 m "
General W. 1/12 m "

2152 Farmer
TAYLOR, Thomas 31 m SC
James 6 m Ga
Sarah 4 f "
Thomas 3 m "
Martha 6/12 f "

394 Farmer ($300)
TAYLOR, Washington 37 m Ga
Frances 37 f SC
Caroline 17 f Ga
Jacob 10 m "
Eliza 9 f "
Nancy 7 f Ala
Gillian 5 f "
Mary 3 f "
Emeline 1 f "
HURD, William 12 m Ga

2133 Laborer
TAYLOR, William 24 m Ga
Cinthia 18 f "

487 Farmer ($1,000)
TEAL, Allen 50 m NC
(Cont.)

(# 487 TEAL cont.)
Mary 19 f SC
(Allen & Mary married within the year).
Nancy 26 f NC
Margaret 22 f "
Laney 18 f "
William 5 m "
Isabella 4 f "
Jacob 2 m Ala
Sarah 1 f "

691 Farmer
TEAL, Daniel 25 m NC
Sarah 17 f Ga

677 Farmer ($800)
TEAL, William 51 m NC
Elizabeth 46 f "
Daniel 26 m "
Christopher 15 m "
Alexander 13 m "
Sarah 10 f "
Allen 7 m "
Margaret 2 f Ala

220 Farmer ($200)
TEEL, Robert 59 m Tenn
Hetty 55 f Ga
Joel (Farmer) 21 m Ala
Rachel 19 f "

219 Farmer ($100)
TEEL, William 26 m Ala
Keziah 19 f Ga
Amanda 3 f Ala

2194 Property: $200.
TEMPLES, Mary 48 f Ga
John (Farmer) 22 m "
William " 17 m "
Jane 12 f "
Thomas 9 m "

207
TERVEVILLE, Tarpley 45 m SC
Henrietta 36 f "
David B. 14 m "
Sarah A. 11 f "
John D. 8 m Ala
George W. 2 m "
William F. 6/12 m "

TERRY, John T.
(See Needham Lee, Sr.)

2005 Farmer ($200)
TEW, Allen 40 m NC
Mary 38 f "
James 14 m "
Elizabeth 12 f Ala
Sarah 9 f "
John 7 m "
William 5 m "
Mary 2 f "

440 Farmer
TEW, Jonathan 43 m NC
Nancy 36 f Ala
Henry 14 m "
Daniel 13 m "
John W. 11 m "
Janet 10 f "
Osborn 8 m "
Lucinda 7 f "
Nancy J. 6 f "
Jonathan 5 m "
Barbara 3 f "
Almeda 5/12 f "

388 Farmer
TEW, Peter 34 m NC
Rebecca 35 f "
Patience 11 f Ala
John 9 m "
Joel 8 m "
Rebecca 7 f "
Mary C. 6 f "
Nancy 4 f "
Peter 1 m "
Wallace M. 1/12 m "
BASS, Martin 16 m Ga
Meedy 23 f NC
Rebecca 74 f Va

390 Farmer ($200)
TEW, Wallace 46 m NC
Martha 35 f Ga
John (Farmer) 20 m Ala
Nathan W. " 16 m "
Hezekiah 14 m "
Alexander 12 m "
Zachariah 11 m "
Samuel 9 m "
Mary A. 6 f "
Martha P. 6/12 f "
Asbury 3 m "

2006 Farmer ($300)
TEW, William 43 m NC
Catherine 39 f "
(Cont.)

(# 2006 TEW cont.)

Thomas (Farmer)	18	m	NC
Sarah	15	f	Ala
Nancy	12	f	"
William	9	m	"
John	7	m	"
Thomas	4	m	"

THARP, Chilly
(See Samuel Nixon).

644 Farmer

THARP, Vincent	28	m	Ga
Martha	20	f	Fla
Nancy	2	f	Ala
Eliza	21	f	Ga

2246 Shoemaker ($1,000)

THARPE, W. A.	33	m	Ga
Elizabeth	31	f	SC
Jeremiah (Laborer)	15	m	Ga
William "	15	m	"
Benjamin	13	m	Ala
Elizabeth	10	f	"
Nancy	8	f	"
James	5	m	"
BAKER, Patience	70	f	SC

1853 Farmer

THARP, William A.	40	m	Ga
Ella	27	f	"
John	10	m	Ala
Henry	8	m	"
Reddin	4	m	"

THARPE, Windham A.
(See James Mabry).

1103 Farmer ($2,150)

THIGPEN, Joseph	50	m	NC
Clara	55	f	"
Brythel	19	m	Ala
Joseph	17	m	"
Joanna	14	f	"
Stephen E. (Farmer)	24	m	NC

(Property: $350).

THOMAS, Aaron
(See E. C. Joyce).

1996 Overseer

THOMAS, Alexr. H.	22	m	Ga

586 Farmer

THOMAS, Alfred	38	m	Ga
Belinda	28	f	"

(Cont.)

(# 586 THOMAS cont.)

Jasper	12	m	Ga
Benjamin F.	10	m	"
Letitia	8	f	"
LaFayette	3	m	Ala
Caledonia	1	f	"

1975 Farmer

THOMAS, Eli	26	m	Ala
Catherine	20	f	"
Mary	6	f	"
George	5	m	"
Zach. T.	2	m	"

THOMAS, Elisha
Nancy
(See Robert H. Rogers).

1068 Farmer ($3,000)

THOMAS, Elliot	61	m	Va
Isabella	30	f	SC
Charity	20	f	Ala
Elliot	17	m	"
BOYLESTON, Caroline	9	f	"

437 Farmer

THOMAS, Emanuel	39	m	NC
Martha	39	f	SC
Jason	5	m	Ala
Jonathan	2	m	"

403 Farmer

THOMAS, Hezekiah	37	m	NC
Elizabeth	36	f	Ga
Willemina (?)	14	m	Ala
William J.	13	m	"
James	12	m	"
Joseph	11	m	"
John	10	m	"
Sarah	9	f	"
Mary	8	f	"
Elizabeth	7	f	"
Jefferson	6	m	"

THOMAS, James
(See James Wood)

1976 Farmer Deaf & Dumb ($50)

THOMAS, James	29	m	Ga
Dorcas	32	f	NC
Ann	8	f	Ala
Josephine	2	f	"

583 Farmer ($500)

THOMAS, Jonathan	35	m	Ga
Maria J.	31	f	"

(Cont.)

(# 583 THOMAS cont.)

Zachariah (Farmer) 15 m Ala
Sarah J. 13 f "
Elliot J. 11 m "
Hamilton 9 m "
Crowell 7 m "
Carter 5 m "
David 3 m "

1860 Farmer
THOMAS, John 55 m NC
Mary 45 f "
Elizabeth 23 f "
Mary 19 f "
John (Farmer) 17 m "

128 Shoemaker
THOMAS, John D. 63 m NC
Nancy 45 f "
Emeline 20 f Ala
Elliot 18 m "
Henry A. 13 m "
John C. 8 m "
Nancy 7 f "
Christianna 5 f "

438 Farmer
THOMAS, John W. 81 m NC
Jeptha 19 m Ala
Mary A. 23 f "
Rebecca 18 f "

THOMAS, LaFayette
(See Hansford D. Price).

1083 Farmer
THOMAS, Leroy 55 m Ga
Polly 45 f "
Leroy 18 m Ala
Tabitha 17 f "
Mary 9 f "
John 11 m "
Lucy 1 f "

407 Farmer ($800)
THOMAS, Morton 51 m NC
Jackson (Farmer) 23 m "
Charles " 16 m Ala
Hiram 14 m "
Andrew 8 m "
Telitha 11 f "
Margaret 7 f "
Amanda 6 f "
Mary 13 f "

399 Farmer ($400)
THOMAS, Moses 58 m NC
(Cont.)

(# 399 THOMAS cont.)

Catherine 58 f NC
Adam (Farmer, $200) 25 m "
Jeptha 20 m "
Nancy 16 f "

400 Farmer
THOMAS, Moses, Jr. 23 m NC
Mary 18 f "
(Married within the year).

THOMAS, Orlando
(See Jacob Lampley).

871 Farmer
THOMAS, T. H. 34 m SC
Mary 32 f Ala
George 11 m "
Narcissa 8 f "
Martha 5 f "
Joseph 1 m "

1699 Farmer
THOMAS, William 47 m Ga
Sarah 42 f "
Eliza 21 f "
Elizabeth 18 f "

213 Farmer ($200)
THOMAS, William B. 34 m Ga
Catherine 35 f NC
Eliza J. 15 f Ala
Nancy C. 13 f "
Sarah E. 11 f "
William M. 9 m "
James D. 6 m "
Lewis B. 3 m "
Mary A. 5/12 f "

702 Farmer
THOMAS, William T. 25 m Ga
Elizabeth 25 f "
James M. 4 m Ala
William F. 2 m "
Francis M. 1 m "

8-9 Farmer
THOMPSON, A. G. 31 m NC
Mary A. E. 29 f Ga
Martha A. 7 f "
William D. C. 5 m "
James G. T. 3 m "

642 Farmer ($400)
THOMPSON, Aladdin 32 m SC
Susan 25 f Ga
Henry 9 m Ala
(Cont.)

(# 642 THOMPSON cont.)
Jesse 5 m Ala
Robert 8/12 m "

THOMPSON, George W.
(See Osborn T. Rogers).

2166 Farmer ($1,800)
THOMPSON, Henry B. 25 m Ga
Antoinette V. 20 f "

2035 Farmer
THOMPSON, J. A. 24 m Ga

208 Farmer
THOMPSON, James E. 53 m Pa
Haney 57 f SC
Edward 7 m Ala

423 Farmer
THOMPSON, John 21 m SC
Martha 20 f Ga
(Married within the year).

16 Farmer
THOMPSON, John T. 69 m Va
Delilah 50 f NC

THOMPSON, Louisa
(See William N. Richardson).

1347 Farmer ($500)
THOMPSON, Shadrach 32 m NC
Martha 23 f Ga
Georgia 1 f Ala
Elva 63 f NC

1016 Farmer ($300)
THOMPSON, William O. 39 m NC
Eliza 38 f Ga
John 17 m "
Elva R. 15 f "
Benjamin 12 m "
James 10 m "
Georgia A. 8 f "
Samuel 6 m "
John 2 m Ala

412 Farmer
THORN, John 25 m SC
Martha 20 f Ga
James E. 5/12 m Ala

THORN, Joseph
(See W. J. Grubbs).

411 Farmer ($225)
THORN, Nicholas 60 m SC
Martha 48 f "
Matilda 28 f "
(Cont.)

(# 411 THORN cont.)
Sarah 22 f SC
Pressley 14 m Ga

THORNTON, Hester
(See Ferney Westbrook).

1439 Physician ($650)
THORNTON, William H. 32 m Ga
Mary B. 22 f "
Mary R. 4 f Ala
Emily 1 f "
Edward Q. (Student) 19 m Ga
Joseph 13 m "

2074 Laborer
THREATT, Levi M. 31 m Ga
Sarah 20 f "
(Married within the year).

1888 Farmer
TILLMAN, Robert 50 m Ga
Nancy 50 f NC
Alfred (Farmer) 21 m Ga
John " 25 m "
Linsey 12 m Ala

TILLMAN, Stephen
(See James Young).

914 Farmer ($2,600)
TINDALL, John 52 m SC
Mary 44 f Ga
Seaborn (Farmer) 18 m Ala
Ann 15 f "
Cullin 11 m "
Henry 6 m "
Elizabeth 3 f "

1867 Laborer
TINNAN, David 45 m Ga
Caroline 16 f "
William 8 m "

715 Physician ($1,400)
TINSLEY, C. C. 36 m Ga
Albena 36 f "
Sarah 16 f "
Lucy 11 f "
Julia 9 f "
Frances 9 f "
James 7 m "
Charles 5 m Ala
Albert 6/16 m "
Margaret 16 f Ga

TISON, Henry C.
(See David Hall).

1664 Farmer ($3,000)
TISON, James G. 30 m SC
Adrianna 26 f "
Virginia 8 f Ala
Alice 6 f "
James 4 m "
Sarah 2 f "

402 Farmer ($400)
TOMLIN, Carson 37 m NC
Mary 37 f "
Wilson 16 m "
Calvin 13 m "
Jane 11 f "
David 8 m Ala
Emeline 4 f "
Mary 6 f "
Alexander 6/12 m "

2243 Farmer
TOMLIN, Jacob 27 m Ga
Mary 20 f Ala
Elizabeth 5 f "
John 3 m "
Mary 1 f "

2263 Farmer
TOMLIN, Pharo 50 m Ga
Lucy 45 f "
Frances 21 f "
William (Farmer) 18 m "
Joseph " 17 m "
Amanda 12 f Ala
John 10 m "
David 7 m "
Jesse 5 m "

2233 Lawyer ($2,000)
TOMPKINS, Henry M. 40 m SC
Henrietta 27 f Ga
Henry B. 6 m Ala
SWAN, John (Teacher) 60 m Va
WILLIAMS, James 40 m NC
(Saddler).
FARRER, Geo.(Saddler) 22 m Ga
PATTERSON, Newton 21 m "
(Laborer)
FOSTER, James (Laborer) 35 m Eng
EVANS, T. (Saddler) 30 m Ga
GRAVES, William 25 m SC
(Clerk)

TORRANCE, John
(See Green Malone).

1250 Boat & Shoemaker ($300)
TORTAT, Henry 40 m Fr
(Cont.)

(# 1250 TORTAT cont.)
Nancy 34 f Me
Henry 11 m SC
Amelia 8 f "
Caroline 4 f Ala
John 1 m "

2145 Farmer
TRAMMELL, Daniel M. 25 m Ga
Mary 19 f Ala
Nancy 2 f "
James 4/12 m "

245 Farmer
TRAYWICK, A. T. 26 m Ga
Margaret 30 f NC

775 Farmer ($2,500)
TRAYWICK, James 46 m Ga
Nancy 39 f "
LEWIS, William 10 m Ala

2088 Farmer
TRAYWICK, Osborn 23 m Ga
Mary 18 f Ala
(Married within the year).

2010 Farmer ($5,000)
TREADWELL, B. F. 42 m SC
Mary M. 33 f "

1353 Brickmason
TREADWELL, Henry 20 m Ga
Martha 20 f "

TREADWELL, James
(See John Black).

1435 Farmer
TREADWELL, Samuel 72 m NC
Mary 73 f NJ

392 Farmer
TRUET, William 46 m SC
Ailsey 40 f "
Martha 18 f Ala
John (Farmer) 16 m "
Charity 14 f "
Winney 12 f "
Nancy 10 f "
George 8 m "
BOWERS, Joseph 21 m SC
(Farmer)
McBRYDE, Robert 9 m --

1569 (Property: $800)
TRUETLEN, Ann 45 f SC
Mary 19 f "
(Cont.)

(# 1569 TRUETLEN cont.)
Caroline 15 f SC
Sarah 10 f Ala
Cornelia 8 f "
Julia 6 f "

TULLIS, Thomas E.
(See Green Beauchamp).

TURK, George
Lillis
(See Pulaski Hodges).

TURMAN, George J.
William
J. M.
(See William A. Barham).

1668 Farmer ($300)
TURNAGE, Kerney 45 m NC
Eliza 35 f "
Martha 18 f "
William (Farmer) 15 m "
Nancy 12 f "
Philip 10 m Ala
Louisa 4 f "
Wiley 2 m "

1222 Overseer
TURNER, Austin 25 m Ga
Sarah 19 f "
Jonathan 2 m Ala

85 Farmer ($1,000)
TURNER, George 58 m Md
Nancy 50 f Ga

TURNER, Henry S.
(See Edwin T. Sherman).

648 Farmer ($300)
TURNER, James K. 40 m Ga
Sarah 44 f "
SHANKS, Mary A. 17 f "
Jeremiah (Farmer) 23 m SC

2136 Laborer
TURNER, John D. 28 m Ga
Frances 30 f "
NELMS, John W. 10 m "
TURNER, Laura J. 4 f "
Zach T. 2 m Ala

1586 Overseer
TURNER, John M. 30 m SC
Eliza 23 f "
Mary 2 f Ala
Sarah 3/12 f "

1188 Farmer ($325)
TURNER, Noel W. 48 m SC
Margaret 45 f NC
John 10 m Ala
Caroline 8 f "
Sarah 94 f SC
SMITH, William 23 m Ga

2295 Farmer
TURNER, Robert H. 26 m Ala
Elizabeth 21 f "
Nancy 3 f "
Martha 1 f "

1009 Farmer ($325)
TURNER, Robert W. 22 m Ala
Mary 25 f "
John A. 1/12 m "

1034 Merchant
TURNER, Wingate M. 49 m Ga
Laura C. 42 f NC
Charles A. 11 m Ga
HOLT, Jane M. 15 f "

1065 Overseer
TYE, John 34 m SC
Mary 37 f NC
Shelineth 14 f Ga
Artemsia 13 f "
William 12 m "
Levinia 10 f "
Henry 8 m "
Amaziah 7 m Ala
Frances 5 f "
Wesley 2 m "

TYE, John
(See Elias G. Hodges).

TYE, Sarah
(See E. E. DuBose).

1049 Overseer
TYE, Thomas 46 m SC
Elizabeth 25 f Ga
John 19 m "
Mary 13 f "
William 12 m "
Francis 6 m "
Sarah 3 f Ala
Jane 2/12 f "

902 Blind (In the Poorhouse).
TYLER, James 34 m SC

1560 Tailor ($75)
UNDERWOOD, Thomas 45 m Eng
(Cont.)

(# 1560 UNDERWOOD cont.)
Ann 38 f Eng
Joshua 6 m Ga

2163 Farmer ($7,500)
UPSHAW, James R. 32 m Ga
Maria G. 24 f "
Eugenia 4/12 f Ala
PETTIGREE, James 26 m Ga
(Overseer)

2161 Farmer ($5,600)
UPSHAW, Leroy 27 m Ga

2162 Farmer ($7,500)
UPSHAW, William T. 29 m Ga
Mary E. 26 f "
Jack 6 m Ala
Susan P. 4 f "
Louisa 3 f "
Sarah 2 f "
HOLSEY, Antionette 21 f Ga
BOWEN, Elijah 25 m Ga
(Overseer)

1714 Farmer
URCEY, William 25 m Ga
Mary 23 f "

77-80 Farmer
URQUHART, Daniel 33 m Ga
Sarah 41 f "
Josiah 14 m "
Mary 14 f "
Elizabeth 9 f "
Martha 7 f "
James 5 m Ala
Daniel 2 m "
Neill 70 m NC

2012 Farmer ($350)
URQUHART, Henry 30 m Ga
Adeline 25 f "
James 6 m Ala
William 4 m "
Mary 2 f "
MOODY, John 27 m SC
(Laborer)

982 Farmer ($1,000)
UTSEY, A. F. 30 m SC
Mary 20 f Ala
Jacob 6 m "
John F. 4 m "
Thomas E. 1 m "

1953 Farmer ($300)
UTSEY, J. J. 24 m Ala
Martha 21 f "
Mary 2 f "

1952 Farmer ($1,000)
UTSEY, Jacob 60 m SC
Mary 50 f "
Goran(?) (Farmer) 21 m Ala
LaFayette " 19 m "
Catherine 16 f "
Mary 14 f "
R. V. 12 f "

1139 Farmer
VALENTINE, Matthew 52 m NC
Catherine 45 f "
William (Farmer) 21 m "
Effy 20 f "
Rebecca 18 f "
Christian 16 f "
Mary 14 f "
Isaac 12 m Ala
John 10 m "
Sarah 7 f "

1573 Dentist
VANN, James W. 34 m Va
Eliza 21 f Ga
Virginia 1 f "
SAWYER, Wilson 24 m "
(Dentist).

VANN, John
(See Jesse F. Johnson).

1352 Blacksmith
VAUGHN, John 30 m Ga
Rebecca 29 f "
Cinthia 7 f "
Gillam 4 m "
James 1 m Ala

1447 Teacher
VAUN, Edward 34 m SC
Sarah 60 f "
COLLINS, Elizabeth 22 f "
John H. 5 m SC
VAUN, Joseph 16 m "
(Student).
(Note: The Vaun family household almost illegible - five in the family.)

890 Farmer ($500)
VENTRESS, James 31 m Ga
(Cont).

(# 890 VENTRESS cont.)

Mary	22	f	Ala
Sarah	3	f	"
Ella	2	f	"
Wallace	3/12	m	"

VENTRESS, Nancy
(See Jesse B. Coleman).

876 Farmer ($400)

VENTRESS, Thomas	37	m	Ga
Mary	32	f	"
William	13	m	Ala
Stephen	7	m	"
Martha	5	f	"
Thomas	3	m	"
James	10	m	"
Cornelia	1	f	"

1141 Farmer ($1,000)

VICKERS, J. R.	37	m	Ga
Nancy	67	f	Va

1098 Overseer

VICKERS, James M.	22	m	Fla

VICKERS, Joseph W.
(See Elias Lewis).

1028 Farmer ($325)

VICKERS, Michael	25	m	Ga
Sarah	24	f	"
Joseph	4	m	Ala
Marthelia	2	f	"

2522 Farmer ($300)

VICKERS, Michael P.	34	m	Ga
Sarah	24	f	"
John	4	m	Ala
Martha	2	f	"
James	2/12	m	"

1157 Farmer ($1,000)

VICKERS, Thomas T. B.	43	m	Ga
Mary	34	f	"
Nancy	10	f	Ala
Thomas	9	m	"
Michael	7	m	"
Mary	4	f	"
Andrew	2	m	"

VINING, Eliza J.
Anna
(See John McBryde).

1456 Carpenter

VINING, Samuel	53	m	Ga

VINING, Washington
William
George
(See John P. Glover).

1458 Farmer ($3,500)

VINSON, Wesley	54	m	Ga
Sarah	40	f	NC
John A.	22	m	Ga
Charles	20	m	"
Mary	16	f	"
Martha	14	f	"
Matilda	9	f	Ala
Wesley	7	m	"
Sarah	5	f	"
Zachary T.	2	m	"

1516 Farmer

VISAGE, Pleasant B.	30	m	Ala
Sarah	25	f	"
Sarah L.	4	f	Ga
James	2	m	"
Narcissa	8/12	f	"
Artemisia	8/12	f	"

1159 Farmer

VORHEES, Cornelius	34	m	Pa
Elizabeth	25	f	Ga
Jemima	6	f	Fla
John	4	m	"
Elizabeth	2	f	"

1807 Overseer

WADE, H. L.	35	m	Ga
Mary	25	f	"
William	11	m	"
James	9	m	"

WAINWRIGHT, Charlotte
Zach T.
(See Wiley Oliver).

291 Occupation - none

WALDEN, Samuel	35	m	Ga

430

WALKER, Christina	80	f	SC
CARROL, Martha	20	f	"

194 Farmer ($200)

WALKER, George	28	m	SC
Mary	24	f	Ga
Lucy	3	f	Ala
Sarah	3/12	f	"

195 Farmer

WALKER, George, Sr.	63	m	SC
Sarah	65	f	NC

125 Laborer
WALKER, Hiram 52 m SC
Priscilla 40 f "
Mary C. 18 f Ga
Elizabeth 13 f Ala

WALKER, John
Joseph
(See Levi Mothershead).

WALKER, John
(See Lewis Ward).

WALKER, John
(See H. C. Ward).

304 Farmer ($800)
WALKER, Lewis 58 m NC
Nancy 40 f "
Masey 17 f Ala
Nancy 14 f "
Mary 11 f "
John 9 m "
Amanda 7 f "
David 3 m "
James 1 m "

429 Farmer ($200)
WALKER, Nathan 40 m SC
Elizabeth 38 f NC
Sarah 10 f Ala
Darling 8 m "
Mary 6 f "
Irena 4 f "
Christina 2 f "
Elizabeth 16 f "

1066 Farmer (300)
WALKER, Philip 42 m SC
Barbara 40 f "
Elizabeth 13 f "
John 12 m "
James 10 m "
Barzalia 9 m Ala
Philip 6 m "
Vicey 7 f "
Andrew J. 4 m "
Jason J. 1/12 m "

WALKER, Sarah
(See Daniel M. Western).

1313 Merchant ($5,000)
WALKLEY, S. S. 42 m Conn
COTTON, George W. 25 m "
(Merchant)
OLIVER, M. D. 22 m Ga
(Clerk)

249 Wheelwright
WALLACE, Samuel 29 m Ga
Margaret 22 f "
SPURLOCK, Selah 20 f "

1043 Farmer
WALLER, Benjamin H. 32 m NC
Rhody 27 f SC
Ethemore 2 m Ala
Delilah 1 f "

902 Insane. (Lived in Poorhouse).
WALLER, Elizabeth 35 f SC

790 Farmer ($400)
WALLER, Lewis(?) 42 m NC
Elizabeth 36 f "
Nathan (Farmer) 16 m Ga
Ichabod 14 m "
Martha 12 f "
Joseph 9 m Ala
Elizabeth 7 f "
William 5 m "
Lewis(?) 2 m "

53 Farmer ($1,000)
WALTERMAN, N. N. 46 m Va
Catherine 28 f Ga
Mary A. 8 f Ala
Isabella F. 6 f "
Nathaniel 3 m "
William S. 9/12 m "
BRASWELL, Green 23 m "
(Laborer).

1387 Harness Maker ($300)
WALTTES(?), William 30 m NJ
Sarah 28 f Tenn
Mary 6 f Ala
Ebenezer 4 m "
Zach. T. 1 m "

1361 Farmer
WALTON, James 35 m NC
Elizabeth 33 f Ga
John 11 m "
Mary 8 f "
Daniel 7 m "
Sarah 4 f "
James 2 m "

WALTON, Wilson
(See Samuel McBryde).

1344 Laborer ($500)
WAMBLE, Andrew 40 m NC

986 Farmer ($500)
(Cont.)

(# 986 cont.)
WARD, H. C. 20 m Ala
WALKER, John 22 m NC
(Farmer)
WARD, Lewis D. 22 m Ala
(Farmer)

734 Farmer ($200)
WARD, Lewis 23 m Ala
Henry (Farmer, $200) 20 m "
WALKER, John 21 m SC

WARD, Mary
(See N. G. Holmes & Nathaniel G. Holmes).

1855 Farmer
WARD, William 30 m Ga
Hetty 28 f Ala
May 6 f "
Sarah 5 f "
Catherine 3 f "
James 2 m "

WARE, Edward
(See William L. Cowen).

WARING, Jane M.
(See Martha A. Bludworth).

1566 Carpenter
WARLICK, A. H. 52 m NC
Ruth 42 f SC
Elizabeth 26 f "
William (Carpenter) 24 m "
(Property: $800).
James (Carpenter) 21 m "
Robert " 19 m "
Jane 16 f "
Joseph 13 m Ala
Munroe 10 m "

2267 Farmer ($1,800)
Warner, Benjamin 36 m Ga
Elizabeth 33 f "
Elmira 15 f "
Almira 13 f "
James 10 m "
John 7 m "
Franklin 4 m "
Jeremiah 7/12 m Ala
LOGUE, Sarah 55 f Ga
JOHNSTON, Turner 21 m "
(Farmer)

678 Farmer ($360)
WARR, E. S. 28 m SC
(Cont.)

(# 678 WARR cont.)
Pairsaday 24 f Ala
Sarah I. 6 f "
Martha A. 2 f "
Mary 1/12 f "
John 20 m SC

375 Farmer ($500)
WARR, John 53 m SC
Nancy 54 f "
Thomas 14 m "
Margaret 12 f Ga
Emily 10 f "

522 Farmer ($150)
WARREN, E. A. 38 m SC
Caroline 36 f Ga
James C. (Farmer) 16 m Fla
Burris A. 11 m Ala
Jane 14 f "
Rachel 6 f "
Columbus 3 m "

850 Farmer ($1,500)
WARREN, Jeremiah 40 m Ga
Mary 38 f "
William 13 m Ala
Thomas A. 11 m "
James 7 m "
HERRING, Mary 1 f "

1185 Farmer ($1,400)
WARREN, Joel D. 24 m Ala
Rebecca 60 f NC
James (Farmer) 23 m Ala
LEWIS, Martha 35 f NC
EAFORD *, Thomas 20 m Ala
(Farmer)
Gillis (Farmer) 18 m "
McSWAIN, James 85 m Scot
(Occupation - none).

1037 Property: $4,675
WARREN, Lucinda 39 f SC
Daniel (Farmer) 20 m Ala
Joanna 16 f "
Monroe 13 m "
Burris 11 m "
Georgianna 10 f "
Bates 8 m "

2239 Property: $2,500.
WARREN, Nancy 42 f SC
Thomas E. 20 m "
Julia Ann 18 f Ala
(Cont.)

* Eaford - should be EFURD.

(# 2239 WARREN cont.)

America	16	f	Ala
Frances	15	f	"
Jackson	13	m	"
Sarah	11	f	"
Adeline	9	f	"
Lancina *	7	f	"
Edmond	4	m	"
William	1	m	"

1186

WARREN, Nancy	75	f	SC
ROBINSON, Elizabeth	30	f	---
Sarah	6/12	f	Ala
WARREN, Thomas J. (Farmer)	40	m	SC

WARREN, Rebecca
Susan
Thomas
James
Joseph
(See Michael Lightner)

931 Farmer

WARREN, Thomas E.	20	m	Ala
Frances	15	f	"

(Married within the year).

985 Farmer ($200)

WATERER, Solomon	45	m	NC
Susan	40	f	"
Martha	18	f	"
Zilpha	16	f	"

2293 Farmer

WATERS, Benjamin	48	m	NC
Flora	37	f	"
William	16	m	"
John	14	m	"
Mary	11	f	"
Frances	9	f	"
Elizabeth	5	f	Ala
James	3	m	"

1989 Farmer

Watkins, James	26	m	Ala
Sarah	22	f	"
Robert	3	m	"
Martha	1	f	"

2094 Farmer

WATSON, D. G.	24	m	Ala

WATSON, David
Jincey
(See William J. Rollin).

* Lancina listed as Lucinda in O.R. BOOKS V & VI.

289 Farmer ($2,500)

WATSON, George	52	m	Pa
Sarah	55	f	Va
George (Farmer)	23	m	Ga
Marion "	21	m	"

6-7 Laborer

WATSON, Isaac	30	m	Ga
Ruth J.	25	f	"
James	5	m	Ala
Sarah	2	f	"

749 Farmer ($200)

WATSON, Jacob	24	m	Ga
Nancy	22	f	"

(Married within the year).

797 Farmer ($3,200)

WATSON, J. Z.	(?)28	m	Ala
Elizabeth	52	f	Ga
Rebecca	21	f	Ala
Nathan (Farmer)	20	m	"
John "	18	m	"
Francis "	16	m	"
Peter	14	m	"
BOND, James	24	m	Ga

290 Farmer

WATSON, John	24	m	Ga
Mary	17	f	Ala

(Married within the year).

731 Machinist ($900)

WATSON, O. H. P.	26	m	Ga
Harriet	21	f	"
Benjamin F. C.	4	m	"

1154

WATSON, Susan	35	f	Ala
William	1	m	"

732

WATSON, Susannah P.	49	f	Ga
Martha	15	f	"
Perkins H.	13	m	"
Benjamin J.	8	m	"

1781 Farmer ($900)

WEATHERS, Samuel	40	m	Ga
Jane	35	f	NC
Emeline	12	f	Ga

1752 Farmer ($1,000)

WEATHERS, William	60	m	Ga
Margaret A.	30	f	"
William (Farmer)	20	m	"
Thomas "	18	m	"

(Cont.)

(# 1752 WEATHERS cont.)
Sarah 16 f Ga
Elizabeth 14 f "
HOUSE, Jackson 14 m "
Irwin 12 m "
Emily 13 f "
Lewrana 8 f "

2132 Farmer ($2,500)
WEAVER, Absolom 45 m Ga
Mary 42 f "
Daniel (Farmer) 20 m "
Rebecca 15 f "
Louisa 11 f "
Minerva 10 f "
Larkin 8 m "
Jacob 6 m "
Ella 3 f Ala
Zachariah 1 m "

WEAVER, David
(See William Cobb).

WEAVER, F. J. (female)
(See Hansford Dowling).

254 Farmer
WEBB, John 27 m Ala
Talitha 25 f NC
Mary 5 f Ala
Angus 3 m "
Richmond 1 m "
PAGE, Samuel (Laborer) 65 m NC
Allen (Laborer) 35 m "

2219 Farmer ($350)
WEBBER, Richard 40 m Tenn
Emeline 38 f "
Nancy 14 f "
Richard 12 m "
William 10 m "
Mary 8 f Ala
James 4 m "
Elizabeth 1 f "

WEEKS, Martha
(See William Adkins).

2107 Farmer ($1,200)
WELDON, William A. 26 m Ga
Rebecca 25 f "
John 3 m Ala
Florida 1 f "

2108 Laborer
WELDEN, William H. 30 m Ga
Minna 45 f SC
Frances 10 f Ga

1335 Occupation - none
WELLBORN, J. C. 25 m Ga
Mary 19 f Fla
John 1 m Ala

19-20 Farmer ($3,000)
WELLBORN, Johnston 56 m Ga
Elizabeth 30 f "
Catherine S. 19 f "
Juan(?) F. (Farmer) 17 m "
Rollin S.A. " 16 m "
William R. 13 m "
Felix G. 5 m Ala
Genatus 3 f "
Victoria 3/12 f "

1301 Clerk
WELLBORN, L. S. 32 m Ga
Ann 28 f SC

1392 Lawyer ($4,000)
WELLBORN, M. B. 25 m Ga
Roxanna 49 f "
Julia 18 f "
Frances 16 f "
John 14 m "
William 11 m Ala

1236 Farmer
WELLBORN, Solon A. 30 m Ga
Frances W. 26 f "
Constantine 8 m Ala
Randolph 6 m "
Solon 3 m "
Ambrose 1/12 m "

247 Farmer ($125)
WELLS, Isaac 23 m Ga
Alley 22 f "

127 Farmer
WELLS, William 58 m Ga
Nancy 57 f Md
Marticia 19 f Ga
John L. 18 m Ala
Osborn 14 m "

27-28 Miller
WELLS, William T. 32 m Ga
Sarah A. 21 f "
Andrew 2 m Ala
Camilla 10/12 f "
RHODES, John 24 m Ga
(Boatman)

WENCH, William
James
(See Esther Phillips).

WESCOTT, Hampton
(See J. B. Heidle)

# 2038 Farmer ($10,000)			
WEST, Joseph	44	m	NC
Elizabeth	22	f	Ga
Sarah	17	f	"
Angeline	8	f	"
Hetty	6	f	"
David	3	m	Ala
John	3/12	m	"

# 2037 Farmer ($500)			
WEST, Samuel	33	m	NC
Susan	25	f	Ga
Sena	13	f	"
Ann	9	f	"
Frances	7	f	"
Harrison	5	m	"
Susan	4	f	"
Shelton	2	m	"
Ellen	1	f	"

# 704 Farmer ($350)			
WESTBROOK, Ferney	37	m	NC
Zilpha	33	f	"
Catherine	9	f	"
Clarissa	7	f	"
James	5	m	"
John C.	2	m	"
Zilpha	1	f	Ala
THORNTON, Hester	30	f	NC
ALBRITTON, William	12	m	Ala

# 1892 Farmer			
WESTBROOK, John M.	27	m	NC
Sarah	21	f	Ala
William	10/12	m	"

# 1891 (Property: $900)			
WESTBROOK, Zilpha	58	f	NC
Harriet	23	f	"
Henry (Farmer)	18	m	"
Zilpha	15	f	"
James	13	m	Ala

# 1577 Harness Maker ($150)			
WESTERN, Daniel M.	42	m	SC
Sarah	31	f	"
Sarah J.	14	f	"
Newton	10	m	"
Amanda	8	f	Ga
Elizabeth	6	f	Ala
James K.	4	m	"
Martha	1	f	"
WALKER, Sarah	65	f	Va

# 1576 Farmer			
WESTERN, William W.B.	43	m	SC
Martha	34	f	"
Samuel	14	m	"
William	12	m	"
Charles	10	m	"
Martha	17	f	"
George	8	m	Ala
Caroline	6	f	"
John	4	m	"
Lucy	6/12	f	"

# 1609 (Property: $1,000)			
WEYMAN, Mary R.	45	m	SC
Lidia C.	27	f	"
Mary R.	25	f	"
BUTT, Elizabeth	14	f	Ga

WEYMAN, Rebecca
(See Junius Jordan).

# 2055 Farmer			
WHEELER, James	31	m	Ga
Elizabeth	22	f	"
Pamelia	3	f	Ala
Seaborn	2	m	"

# 1031 Farmer ($8,000)			
WHEELER, Noah	67	m	NC
Luraney	50	f	SC
OLIVER, Augustus	25	m	Ga
Anna	17	f	Ala

# 1639 Farmer			
WHIGHAM, John M.	27	m	Ga
Susan	17	f	"
Chalmers	6/12	m	Ala

# 1637 Farmer ($2,100)			
WHIGHAM, Joseph	51	m	Ga
Elizabeth	51	f	"
Thomas (Farmer)	23	m	"
Sarah	17	f	"
Margaret	15	f	"
Nathan	13	m	"
Auraline	10	f	"
Amanda	9	f	"
Mary	15	f	"

# 1640 Farmer ($400)			
WHIGHAM, Joseph, Jr.	26	m	Ga
Jane	19	f	"
Augustus	3	m	Ala
John	6/12	m	"
HALL, Samuel (Farmer)	20	m	Ga

1638 Farmer ($2,100)
WHIGHAM, Thomas 55 m Ga
Margaret 51 f "
Auraline 23 f "
Joseph (Farmer) 18 m "
Nancy 20 f "
James (Farmer) 16 m "
Margaret 15 f "
Thomas 11 m "
Elizabeth 9 f "

572 Carpenter ($1,500)
WHIPPLE, George W. 33 m RI

1667 Teacher
WHITE, John 30 m Ga
Mary 25 f "
Thomas 5 m Ala
Emma 4 f "
George 2 m "

1047 Farmer ($4,000)
WHITE, R. T. 44 m Ga
Mary E. 40 f "
Ann 14 f Fla
James 12 m Ala
Florence 10 f "
Ellen 9 f "
William 7 m "
Walter 6 m "
Joseph 4 m "
Atlanta 2 f "
JONES, Elijah 48 m Ga
(Saddler)

2251 Carpenter
WHITE, Washington 26 m NC
Matilda 26 f Ga
William 1/12 m Ala

1871 Farmer
WHITE, Wiley 35 m NC
Celia 25 f "
Mary 3 f Ala
Jane 8/12 f "
Wiley 5 m "
Vincent (Farmer) 46 m NC

113 Carpenter
WHITE, Willis 48 m SC
Louisa 41 f "
Nancy L. 17 f "
Rebecca 15 f "
Georgia A. 13 f Ala
Mary J. 11 f "
Caroline 9 f "
(Cont.)

(# 113 WHITE cont.)
Willis L. 9 m Ala
Josephine 1 f "

186 Farmer
WHITE, Wilson 40 m SC
Jane 52 f "
Watson 10 m "

461 Farmer
WHITE, Wylie 36 m NC
Delilah 22 f "
Marion N. 6 m "
Margaret O. 4 f "
Vincent 51 m NC
(Occupation not given).

1746 Boatman
WHITEOAK, Andrew 47 m Eng
Margaret 43 f NJ
Jemima 11 f Fla
William 6 m Ga
Sarah 3 f Ala
Margaret 1 f "

WHITNEY, Francis
(See J. W. Johnston).

1060 Farmer ($450)
WHITSETT, Samuel 52 m NC
Elizabeth 51 f "
Thomas (Farmer) 26 m "
Ruth 19 f "
MILLS, Wm. (Farmer) 22 m Ga

308 Farmer ($450)
WHITSETT, Samuel 52 m NC
Elizabeth 51 f "
Thomas (Farmer) 27 m "
Ruth 18 f "
MILLS, Wm. (Laborer) 23 m Ala

WHITTAKER, Jackson
Matilda
Stephen
John
Frances
(See R. Sheffield).

1749 Machinist
WHITTEMORE, Clement J. 32 m NC
Munroe (Farmer) 22 m "

WHITTEMORE, Munro
(See Lovett S. Smith).

WHITTINGTON, Jacob
(See William Cobb).

1652 Farmer ($120)
WHITTLE, A. D. 23 m Ga
Mary 19 f NC
Daniel 1/12 m Ala
Kinchen (Farmer) 19 m Ga
McNAIR, Alexr. 28 m NC
Margaret 60 f NC
Sarah 55 f "
Deaf & Dumb).

938 Farmer ($800)
WHITTLE, Maston 34 m SC
Elizabeth 36 f "
Charity 17 f "
John 14 m Ala
Reuben 13 m "
Jincey 11 f "
Emeline 9 f "
Edna 7 f "
Sarah 6 f "
Lucinda 5 f "
Wade 4 m "
Julia 2 f "
Elizabeth 6/12 f "

206 Farmer
WHOOTEN, Jordan 47 m NC
Mary 50 f "
James D. (Farmer) 22 m "
Frances 18 f "
Jane 16 f "
Isaac 15 m "
William J. 12 m "
Mary M. 8 f Ala
Joseph S. 6 m "

131 Miller
WICKART, Henry 33 m Ga
Nancy 32 f SC
Martha 6 f Ala
Dilley 6 f "
Julia 5 f "
Albeno 3 f "
James 1 m "

1494 Farmer
WILCOX, Abijah 58 m SC
Mary 25 f Ga
Abijah J. 4 m Ala
Mary E. 1 f "

692 Farmer
WILDER, John 38 m Ga
Sarah 30 f "
Frances 13 f "
(Cont.)

(# 692 WILDER cont.)
Aletha 11 f Ga
Archibald 8 m Ala
John H. 6 m "
JACKSON, William 25 m Ga
(Laborer)
WILDER, Sarah 1 f Ala

669 Machinist ($500)
WILKES, Elias 68 m SC
Hannah 70 f "
James W. (Farmer) 20 m "
Jesse 22 m "

1143 Farmer
WILKES, James 60 m Ga
Susan 16 f "
Blaeston(?)(Farmer) 15 m "
Catherine 10 f Ala
Lidia 13 f Ga
LeJeffries 7 m Ala

WILKES, Sarah
(See J. T. Hood).

1894 Farmer ($1,000)
WIKLES, William N.(?) 37 m SC
Sarah 28 f Ga
William 4 m Ala
Laura 2 f "

1864 Laborer
WILKINS, Anderson 40 m Ga
Sarah 28 f Ala
John 13 m "
Elizabeth 9 f "
Sarah 6 f "
Mary 4 f "
Jane 2 f "

553
WILKINS, Elizabeth 66 f Ga
Elizabeth 31 f "
Williamson 5 m Ala
Martha 3 f "

284 Sawyer ($500)
WILKINS, Henry 29 m Ala
Matilda 25 f Ga
Matthew 7 m Ala
Emily 2 f "
Miles W. 2 m "
Henry 6/12 m "

1325 Laborer
WILKINS, James 37 m Ga
(Cont.)

(# 1325 WILKINS cont.)
Sarah 26 f SC
Milly (illegible) 1? f Ga
Abraham 10 m Ala
Nancy 8 f "
Eugenia 6 f "
Matilda 3 f "

551
WILKINS, Jane 37 f Ga
Elizabeth 17 f Ala
Giles 12 m "
James 6 m "

WILKINS, Jemima
(See Nancy Campbell).

282 Laborer
WILKINS, Jonathan 30 m Ala
Rebecca 21 f Ga
Elizabeth 6 f Ala
Nancy 3 f "

283 Laborer
WILKINS, Moses S. 26 m Ala
Obedience 26 f "
William 2 m "
Isaac 7/12 m "

101 Farmer
WILKINS, Weldon 24 m Ala
Catherine 26 f Ga
Vira 6 f Ala
Elizabeth 2 f "
Sarah 7/12 f "

286 Laborer
WILKINS, William 66 m SC
Kate 66 f Ga
Matthew (Laborer) 20 m Ala
DICKSON, Ann 13 f "

100 Laborer ($100)
WILKINS, William, Jr. 37 m Ga
Lucy 23 f "
Susan 4 f Ala
Alvilda 3 f "
Missouri 2 f "
William M. 3/12 m "

473 Saddler ($80)
WILKINSON, J. O. C. 30 m NC
Nancy 36 f SC
Elizabeth 7 f Ala
Mary 4 f "
Indianna 2 f "

614 Farmer ($1,000)
WILKINSON, Samuel 33 m SC
Elmira 35 f Ga
Sarah 13 f Ala
Jeremiah 11 m "
John B. 10 m "
Ailsey J. 7 f "
Green B. 5 m "
Samuel 4 m "
Harriet 2 f "
HICKS, Adam 19 m "

WILLARD, Emma P.
(See William S. Paullin).

317 Farmer
WILLIAMS, Alexr. D. 37 m Ga
Lucinda 37 f "
Mary 14 f Ala
Owen 11 m "
Elizabeth 9 f "
Cinthia 7 f "
Hester 4 f "
John C. 2 m "

1601 Carpenter
WILLIAMS, Allen 38 m Ga
Sarah 35 f SC
Mary 17 f Ala
Juliann 15 f "
Lively 12 f "
George 8 m "
Andrew 6 m "
Allen 3 m "

2173
WILLIAMS, Ann M. 45 f Ga
John L. (Farmer) 24 m "
(Property: $500)
Robert T. (Farmer) 22 m "
William " 20 m "
Anna 17 f "
Thomas (Farmer) 15 m "
Laura 13 f "
WILLIAMS, John L., Sr. 63 m "

711 Merchant ($6,000)
WILLIAMS, Austin 57 m Conn
Mary 44 f "
Mary 18 f Va
John (Student) 15 m Conn
IVES, Mary 22 f Va

1600 Farmer ($600)
WILLIAMS, Barley C. 69 m Ga
Mary 67 f Va

WILLIAMS, Braddock
(See Greenberry Bush).

720 Farmer ($1,700)
WILLIAMS, Buckner 55 m Ga
Rhody 39 f SC
George W. 19 m Ala
Louisa 16 f "
Ann L. 13 f "
Mary 12 f "
William H. 9 m "
Leonora 4 f "

WILLIAMS, Daniel
(See B. A. Rogers).

1744 Farmer
WILLIAMS, Edward 66 m NC
Sarah 62 f "
Cinthia 24 f Ga
Lucinda 22 f "
Sarah 19 f "

Williams, Effy
Ann
Mary
Eady
(See Michael McPhail).

1378
WILLIAMS, Elizabeth 46 f SC
Duncan (Laborer) 17 m Ala
John 12 m "
Thomas 3 m "

WILLIAMS, Ella
(See David Danforth).

1505 Farmer
WILLIAMS, G. D. 33 m Ga
Sarah 25 f Ala
Gazeline 5 f "
Mary 3 f "
Anderson 6/12 m "
HARRIS, Matilda 51 f Ga

WILLIAMS, George
(See R. S. Johnston).

WILLIAMS, George
(See B. H. Brantley).

323 Farmer ($600)
WILLIAMS, George W. 30 m Ga
Sarah 25 f "
Georgia Ann 8 f Ala
Risden 6 m "
William 4 m "
John 2 m "

80 Farmer
WILLIAMS, James 28 m NC
Mary 20 f Ga
Thomas 6 m "
Winney 5 f "
William 3 m Ala
Causey 6/12 m "

582 Farmer ($500)
WILLIAMS, John G. 29 m Ala
Christian 21 f "
Sarah 13 f "

WILLIAMS, John H.
(See R. Sheffield).

1061 Farmer ($1,200)
Williams, John L. 44 m Ga
Sarah 37 f "
Amanda 14 f Ala
Josephine 13 f "
Jane 11 f "
John 10 m "
Sarah 8 m "
George 6 m "
Charles 5 m "
Susan 3 f "
Mary 9/12 f "
LEVERETT, Lively 55 f Ga

1962 Laborer
WILLIAMS, John T. 75 m NC
Nancy 58 f "
Mary 21 f Ala
Claiborne (Laborer) 15 m "

472 Farmer ($3,000)
WILLIAMS, Judge S. 46 m Ga
Euphenia 43 f NC
William H. (Farmer) 23 m Ala
John " 19 m "
Richard 11 m "
Emily 13 f "
Victoria 8 f "
GOUMILLION, Joseph 23 m SC
(Property: $100).

947 Blacksmith
WILLIAMS, L. L. 29 m NC
Martha 26 f "
James 7 m "
Samuel 5 m Ala
Frances 1 f "
Cornelia 9 f NC

1207 Farmer ($700)
WILLIAMS, M. D. 42 m NC
(Cont.)

(# 1207 WILLIAMS cont.)
Frances 41 f NC
Augustus 17 m Ga
William 13 m "
JONES, Adaline 16 f "

1937
WILLIAMS, Mary 35 f Ga
Eliza 15 f Ala
William 7 m "
James 6 m "
Samuel 4 m "
Jane 3 f "

196 (Property: $500)
WILLIAMS, Mary 46 f SC
Cornelius (Farmer) 22 m "
Nathan (Miller) 20 m "
Martha 17 f "
Elizabeth 15 f "
Wesley 13 m "
Mary 11 f Ala
Caleb 8 m "

727 Tavern Keeper ($2,500)
WILLIAMS, O. J. 51 m Ga
Sophia 40 f "
James 5 m Ala

1506 Physician ($30,000)
WILLIAMS, R. W. 44 m Ga
Zachariah (Physician) 38 m "

WILLIAMS, Stephen
(See Thomas S. Locke)

192 Farmer ($100)
WILLIAMS, Tobias 24 m SC
Sarah 21 f NC
Abagail 1 f Ala

1120 Carpenter ($400)
WILLIAMS, Turner 67 m NC
SAUNDERS, Elizabeth J. 30 f "
(Property: $400)
Mary 6 f Ala
WILLIAMS, Mary M. 28 f NC

948 Farmer ($400)
WILLIAMS, Wesley 49 m Ga
Charity 33 f "
George 10 m Ala
Elizabeth 7 f "
BRIDGES, Mary 10 f Ga
WILLIAMS, Mary 5 f Ala
Feriby 4 f "
Lucinda 1 f "

WILLIAMS, William
(See Matthew Fenn).

WILLIAMS, William
(See C. B. Anderson)

1599 Farmer ($600)
WILLIAMS, William 33 m Ga
Arincey 25 f Ala
Amanda 9 f "
Jane 7 f "
Columbianna 5 f "
Sarah 2 f "

886 Farmer ($300)
WILLIAMS, William W. 39 m NC
Ann 37 f "
Albaney 9 f Ga
Mary A. 7 f "
Nancy 4 f Ala
Columbus 7/12 m "
STUBBS, Albaney 50 f NC

237 Farmer ($1,700)
WILLIAMSON, Charles 51 m NC
Sarah 48 f "
John (Farmer) 19 m "
Susan 23 f "
Nancy 20 f "
Henry (Farmer) 17 m "
Sarah 15 f Ala
Thomas 14 m "
Uriah 9 m "
Alexander 5 m "

579 Farmer ($700)
WILLIAMSON, John 46 m NC

874 (Property: $100)
WILLIAMSON, Mary 52 f SC
Franklin (Farmer) 17 m Ala
Thomas 14 m "
Simeon 7 m "
Eli 6 m "
Mary 5 f "

580
WILLIAMSON, Mary 37 f SC
Charles (Farmer) 17 m Ga
Sarah 16 f Ala
Mary 12 f "
Andrew J. 10 m "
Caroline 8 f "
Munro 3 m "
Jane 1 f "

2045 Farmer ($500)
WILLIAMSON, Nathan 39 m SC
(Cont.)

(# 2045 WILLIAMSON cont.)

Sarah	30	f	SC
Ava Ann	5	f	"
Nancy	2	f	"
WILLIAMSON, Eve A.	84	f	"

1729 Farmer

WILLIAMSON, Shadrac	27	m	NC
Malinda	23	f	Ala
John	8	m	"
Sarah	10	f	"
Munroe	2	m	"
Andrew S. (Farmer)	23	m	NC

2044 Farmer ($3,000)

WILLIAMSON, William	47	m	SC
Naomi	40	f	"
Hardy (Farmer)	15	m	"
Josiah	13	m	"
Martha	12	f	"
Minerva	10	f	"
Sidney	8	m	"
Thomas	6	m	"
Susan	4	f	"
Ann	3	f	"

2052 Farmer

WILLIS, Asa	34	m	Ga
Seymore	27	f	Ala
Mary	11	f	"
Samantha	9	f	"
Sarah	7	f	"
Seymore	5	f	"
James	3	m	"
Robert	1	m	"

767 Farmer ($500)

WILLIS, Edmund G.	30	m	Ga
Missouri	21	f	"
Carey	2	m	Ala
Robert	9/12	m	"

2053 Farmer

WILLIS, Joel	63	m	NC
Elizabeth	52	f	Ga
Elizabeth	17	f	Ala
Sarah	10	f	"
James (Farmer)	20	m	"

774 Farmer

WILLIS, W. A.	26	m	Ala
Ann E.	20	f	"
Thomas	3	m	"
Epsy A.	1	f	"

1428 Farmer ($1.000)

WILSON, A. J.	35	m	SC

(Cont.)

(# 1428 WILSON cont.)

Hephizibah	30	f	SC
Emma	13	f	"
Caroline	8	f	Ala
Ann	6	f	"
Amanda	5	f	"
Joseph	4	m	"
George	2	m	"

1754 Farmer ($1,600)

WILSON, Corinden	49	m	NC
Eliza	35	f	"
Augustin	11	m	"
Jesse	10	m	"
Elizabeth	8	f	"

228

WILSON, David	45	m	NC
Nancy	37	f	SC
Charles	14	m	Ga
Elizabeth	12	f	Ala
Emeline	10	f	"
John	6	m	"
Nancy	5	f	"
David	4	m	"
William M.	8/12	m	"

182 Farmer

WILSON, George E.	37	m	SC
Effey	28	f	"
James R.	9	m	Ala
Nancy L.	7	f	"
Flora L.	5	f	"
George	2	m	"

2156 Farmer ($400)

WILSON, James	38	m	Ga
Mary	36	f	"
Amanda	14	f	"
James	12	m	"
Mary	10	f	"
Frances	8	f	"
Thomas	6	m	"
John	4	m	"
William	2	m	"
Elizabeth	4/12	f	Ala

54 Farmer ($800)

WILSON, Joseph	55	m	Va
James (Farmer)	19	m	Ga
Melinda	16	f	"
Andrew J.	14	m	"

1423 Farmer ($2,000)

WILSON, Levi R.	39	m	SC
Margaret	39	f	"
James (Student)	17	m	"

(cont.)

(# 1423 WILSON cont.)

John	15 m SC
Simpson	13 m "
Louisa	11 f "
Ella	9 f "
Martha	7 f "

321 Farmer

WINDHAM, Anthony	42 m SC
Epsey	33 f Ga
Edward	13 m Ala
Thomas	12 m "
William	10 m "
Rebecca	8 f "
Wright	6 m "
Julia	4 f "
Mary	2 f "
HOPE, Charlotte	63 f SC

697 Laborer

WINDHAM, Cary F.	19 m Ga
Sophia	19 f NC

(Married within the year).

WINDHAM, Elisha 50 m Va
(See Jefferson S. Bonds).

696 Farmer ($800)

WINDHAM, William	61 m SC
Abagail	51 f "
Emory	13 m Ala
Harmon	11 m "
Eliza A.	7 f "

2157 Farmer

WINGO, Allen	30 m Ga
Sarah	24 f "
Thomas	5 m "
James	3 m Ala

WINN, E. W.
(See Jared P. Barber).

1649 Farmer ($1,600)

WINSLETT, Joel	47 m Ga
Mary	36 f SC
John	14 m Ala
Sarah	12 f "
William N.	10 m "
Francis	8 m "
Mary	6 f "
Joel	5 m "
Alexander	3 m "
Nancy	1 f "
GILLIS, Neill	20 m SC

WINSLETT, Madison
(See Hansford Dowling).

1679 Laborer

WINSLETT, William	18 m Ala

WISE, Archibald
(See James Clark).

218 Farmer ($400)

WISE, Ephriam	50 m SC
Ann	35 f NC
Nancy	17 f Ala
William (Farmer)	16 m "
Martha	13 f "
Ezekiel	10 m "
John	5 m "
Maria	3 f "
infant	1/12 m "

299 Farmer ($1,600)

WISE, Ezekiel	53 m NC
Winneferd	45 f Ga
Elizabeth	18 f Ala
James (Farmer)	15 m "
Thomas	10 m "
Lemuel	14 m "
Mary	12 f "
Edward	7 m "
Amanda	3 f "
BULLOCK, Isabella	76 f Md
PRICE, Caswell (Laborer)	22 m Ga

1862 Farmer

WOOD, Ellis	48 m SC
Maria	46 f "
Charity	23 f "
Elizabeth	17 f Ala
George	11 m "
James	4 m "
John	2 m "

62 Farmer

WOOD, James	49 m NC
Nancy	49 f "
Abagail J.	19 f "
Furneyfold (Student)	15 m "
Zilpha C.	13 f Ala
Rosa A.	11 f "
Amanda	9 f "
Josephine	7 f "
James S.	5 m "
Leonora	3 f "
Richard R.	1 m "
Ollin M. P. (Farmer)	47 m NC
THOMAS, James (Laborer)	18 m Ga

WOOD, Jesse
(See William E. Price).

52 Miller ($300)
WOOD, McKinney 38 m NC
Frances 29 f Ga
Pauline A. 10 f Ala
America H. 9 f "
Frances S. 6 f "
James C. 4 m "
McKinney 3 m "
WOOD, William 50 m NC
(Farmer)

WOOD, Mildred
Benjamin
(See William F. Harper),

WOOD, Ruben J.
John
(See William Kennedy).

WOOD, William
(See John Condry).

WOOD, William
(See McKinney Wood).

1501 Farmer ($600).
WOOD, William 30 m Ga
Sarah 25 f "
John 2 m Ala
Mary 6/12 f "
John (Farmer) 56 m Ga
Jackson " 18 m "
BARNES, Milton 26 m "
(Laborer)

202 Farmer ($400)
WOOD, William R. 28 m NC
Hannah 25 f "
Ursula 8 f Ala
Ann C. 6 f "
Alif 5 f "
Catherine 4 f "
Amanda 1 f "
LEWIS, Stephen B. 14 m NC

174 Farmer ($1,500)
WOOD, Young 55 m NC
Rosanna 47 f "
John R. 22 m "
Green 20 m "
William D. 14 m Ala
REDDY, Stanmore 12 m SC

1259 Merchant
WOODS, C. R. 40 m SC
Harriet 40 f "
Charles (Clerk) 16 m "
Harriet 14 f Ala
(Cont.)

(# 1259 WOODS cont.)
Julia 12 f Ala
William 10 m "
Robert 8 m "
Clayton 6 m "
Mary 4 f "
Martha 2 f "

1431 Laborer
WOODMAN, Jesse 49 m Ga
Elizabeth 40 f "
Riney 12 f Ala

902 (Poorhouse)
WOODWARD, John 38 m SC
Sarah 35 f "
Stephen 14 m Ala
Mahala 11 f Ga
Elizabeth 8 f "
Jane 4 f "
Nancy 1 f "

902 (Poorhouse)
WOOTEN, Fereby 78 f NC
(Blind).

1169 Farmer ($200)
WORRELL, Elisha 50 m NC
Linsey 25 f Ga
Susan 4 f Ala
Ann 3 f "

WORRELL, Eliza
Julia
Ann
Charlotte
(See William Brantley).

1716 Physician
WORSLEY, Sampson 68 m NC
Albina 40 f "
Mary 23 f Ga
SMITH, Mary 10 f "

962 Farmer ($5,000)
WORTHINGTON, Robert 50 m NC
Hallen 48 f "
Robert (Farmer) 24 m "
Joseph " 21 m Ga
George " 19 m "
Moses " 17 m "
Aaron " 17 m "
Mallory 10 f Ala
GLOVER, E. E. 30 m Ga
(Teacher)
WORTHINGTON, Elizabeth 14 f "
Mary 12 f "
Martha 8 f Ala
(Cont.)

(# 962 WORTHINGTON, cont.)
Nancy 4 f Ala
CASSIDY, Crissey 58 f NC
(Insane).

1500 Overseer
WRIGHT, James A. 33 m Ga

844 Farmer ($1,200)
WRIGHT, R. S. 33 m Ga
Nancy 28 f SC
George 10 m Ga
Martha 8 f Ala
Henry C. 5 m "
John 3 m "
Daniel 1 m "

272 Farmer
WRIGHT, William 51 m NC
Pheribe 35 f "
Sinthey Ann 15 f Ga
Mary 13 f "
Prior 11 m "
John 8 m "
Eliza 7 f "
Elizabeth 4 f "
Charles 1 m Ala

300 Farmer
YONN(?), John 62 m SC
Sally 61 f
(Born in West Indies)
MIXON, Richard 22 Ga
(Laborer)
Sarah 16 f Ala
YONN(?), Amanda 18 f "

1774 Carpenter
YOUNG, Archibald 30 m Ga
Elizabeth 39 f "
Mary 15 f "
Elizabeth 13 f "
John 11 m "
William 9 m "
Jane 6 f Ala
Catherine 4 f "
Daniel 2 m "

1255 Merchant ($7,000)
YOUNG, E. B. 48 m NY
Ann 39 f Ga
James (Student) 16 m NY
Henry 14 m Ga
Anna 12 f Ala
Mary 9 f "
Ada 4 f "
(Cont.)

(# 1255 YOUNG cont.)
Helen 2 f Ala
Edward 10/12 m "
DANIEL, James 17 m "

1889 Farmer
YOUNG, James 32 m NC
Cinthia 30 f "
Louisa 12 f Ala
James 6 m "
TILLMAN, Stephen 23 m Ga
(Farmer)
CASEY, Louisa 10 f Ala

1898 Farmer ($1,000)
YOUNG, James B. 34 m NC
Cinthia C. 30 f Ga
Sarah 6 f Ala
Frances 4 f "
Daniel 3 m "
Mary 2 f "
James 6/12 m "
Mary 21 f NC

2266 Farmer
YOUNG, Reuben 38 m Ga
Dicey 30 f "
Matilda 16 f "
Calvin 14 m "
Feriby 12 f "
William 7 m Ala
Louisa 6 f "
Harriet 3 f "
James 4/12 m "

843 Farmer ($800)
YOUNG, William C. 35 m SC

593 Farmer ($1,200)
ZAWN (Zorn?), Nicholas 42 m SC
Sarah 42 f "
Mary 18 f Ala
Jane 16 f "
James D. 13 m "
Dennis 7 m "
George 4 m "
Zachary T. 1 m "

1676 Farmer
ZITEROUR, Charles T. 23 m Ga
Nathaniel 59 m "
(Farmer, $700)
Sarah 55 f "
Jane 14 f "
John 11 m "
Archibald 8 m "
George 6 m "
POWELL, Milton 14 m Ga

www.ingramcontent.com/pod-product-compliance
Lightning Source LLC
Chambersburg PA
CBHW031125020426
42333CB00012B/237

* 9 7 8 1 6 3 9 1 4 3 0 9 2 *